Documents in Modern History

British Communism

MANCHESTER
1824

Manchester University Press

DOCUMENTS IN MODERN HISTORY

Series editor:
Dr G. H. Bennett (University of Plymouth)

Series advisor:
Dr Kevin Jefferys (University of Plymouth)

The *Documents in Modern History* series offers collections of documents on the most widely debated and studied topics in modern British and international history. The volumes place fresh primary material alongside more familiar texts, and provide thought-provoking introductions to place the documents in their wider historical context.

All volumes in the series are comprehensive and broad-ranging. They provide the ideal course textbook for sixth-form students, first-year undergraduates and beyond.

Also available:

*Roosevelt's peacetime administrations, 1933–41:
a documentary history of the New Deal years*
Harry Bennett

The American civil rights movement
Robert P. Green, Jr. and Harold E. Cheatham

*The making of German democracy:
West Germany during the Adenauer era, 1945–65*
Armin Grünbacher

*From Beveridge to Blair: the first fifty years of Britain's welfare state
1948–98*
Margaret Jones and Rodney Lowe

*Women, politics and society in Britain, c.1770–1970:
a documentary history*
Fiona A. Montgomery

The impact of immigration in post-war Britain
Panikos Panayi

The Vietnam wars
Kevin Ruane

Britain in the Second World War: a social history
Harold L. Smith

Documents in Modern History

British Communism
A documentary history

John Callaghan
and Ben Harker

Manchester University Press
Manchester and New York
distributed in the United States exclusively by Palgrave Macmillan

Published by Manchester University Press
Oxford Road, Manchester M13 9NR, UK
and Room 400, 175 Fifth Avenue, New York, NY 10010, USA
www.manchesteruniversitypress.co.uk

Distributed in the United States exclusively by
Palgrave, 175 Fifth Avenue, New York,
NY 10010, USA

Distributed in Canada exclusively by
UBC Press, University of British Columbia, 2029 West Mall,
Vancouver, BC, Canada V6T 1Z2

British Library Cataloguing-in-Publication Data
A catalogue record for this book is available from the British Library

Library of Congress Cataloging-in-Publication Data applied for

ISBN 978 0 7190 8210 8 *hardback*
ISBN 978 0 7190 8211 5 *paperback*

First published 2011

Typeset in Sabon by
Koinonia, Manchester
Printed in Great Britain by
TJ International Ltd, Padstow

Contents

Abbreviations

AEU	Amalgamated Engineering Union
BWSF	British Workers' Sports Federation
CEMA	Council for the Encouragement of Music and Art
CND	Campaign for Nuclear Disarmament
CPGB	British Communist Party
CPI	Communist Party of India
CPSU	Communist Party of the Soviet Union
CUL	Communist University of London
DATA	Draughtsmen's and Allied Techncial workers' Association.
ETU	Electrical Trades Union
ILP	Independent Labour Party
KPD	Communist Party of Germany
NCC	National Cultural Committee
NUM	National Union of Mineworkers
PCF	Communist Party of France
PCI	Communist Party of Italy
TGWU	Transport and General Workers Union
TUC	Trades Union Congress
UCATT	Union of Construction, Allied Trades and Technicians
WMA	Workers' Music Association
WPP	Workers' and Peasants' Parties
WTM	Workers' Theatre Movement
YCL	Young Communist League

Introduction

Why do people study the British Communist Party, an organisation with never more than a feeble presence in parliament or local government, and one that was a massive failure by its own measures of success? Let us begin to answer this question by starting where it started in 1920. At this time the importance of the Communist Party was clear. In the calculations of the Communist movement Britain was important both because of its powerful trade union movement, most of which was affiliated to the Labour Party, and also because of the British Empire – the leader of global anti-Communism in the years before the Second World War, but also an immense field of potential anti-imperialist agitation.

Most Communist parties were established after the foundation of the Communist International (Comintern) in Moscow in March 1919. In many countries, including Britain, the inspiration of the founders was both the Bolshevik Revolution of October 1917 and the prospect of imminent revolutionary change in their own countries – expectations that Lenin shared and encouraged. In the British case the perception of political crisis predated the Great War as rapid growth in trade union membership after 1910, national strikes, constitutional crisis and civil disobedience gave the appearance of momentous change in the making. Total war brought about a further doubling of trade union membership and by 1918–20 there were signs of growing class tensions and a new spirit of rank and file militancy among the organised workers. Indeed, Lenin saw the real basis of a future British Communist Party in the shop stewards' movement of those years. The economic slump of 1921 and chronic unemployment in heavy industrial districts throughout the 1920s helped to undermine that forecast, but trade unionism remained formidably strong in Britain by international standards and the Communist International continued to regard the British Communist Party (CPGB) as an important section of the Communist movement primarily for this reason. After the disappointments of repeated insurrectionary failures in Germany up to the autumn of 1924, the Comintern's main hope for a breakthrough in Europe focused on the industrial conflicts in Britain that culminated in the General Strike of May 1926. Even after the defeat of the General Strike, expectations of mass radicalisation persisted. Though such projections were disappointed, by the 1930s the CPGB had established permanently strong roots in a variety of industries and unions. It remained prominent in both the national leaderships of the trade unions and their rank and file throughout the period from the Second World War up to the late 1970s.

Throughout these years the strength of the trade unions affiliated to the Labour Party presented the tantalising prospect to the Communists of radicalising 'social democracy' from within. All that the Communist Party had to do was affiliate to the Labour Party itself. When this became impossible, after a Labour Party rule change in 1946, the Communists simply focused on obtaining powerful positions within the Labour-affiliated trade union leaderships, as well as building its strength among the rank and file, from which vantage points they might wield influence within Labour's annual conference and at meetings of its National Executive Committee. In short, influencing the powerful trade unions affiliated to the Labour Party remained a major factor in the calculations of the CPGB until the 1980s. The importance attached to the CPGB by the Comintern rested to a large extent on the same basis.

However, the Comintern was also deeply committed to the overthrow of British imperialism and this was another reason why the CPGB was important. After the Bolsheviks seized power in Russia in October 1917 they made efforts to enlist the support of the many nationalities of the economically backward territories of the Caucasus and Central Asia in their attempts to consolidate the Bolshevik state and undermine the hostile imperialist powers surrounding it, particularly the British Empire. The Bolsheviks demanded self-determination both for the subaltern nationalities of the former Tsarist Empire and for the colonies of the European powers. They promoted October 1917 as an anti-imperialist revolution as well as an anti-capitalist revolution. The colonies, they maintained, were 'the Achilles heel of British imperialism' and, by extension, of every other imperialism.[1] The British Communists were charged with responsibility not merely for linking Moscow and the colonies but also for actually promoting Communist influence throughout the Empire. Communist agents were repeatedly sent to establish revolutionary and trade union organisations in India in particular. British Communists such as Ben Bradley and Philip Spratt were eventually successful in these aims, while Rajani Palme Dutt continued to supply advice to the Communist Party of India (CPI) (and link it to Moscow and the Comintern) from the leadership of the CPGB, until the late 1940s. From the beginning of these efforts the CPGB had to reckon with the problem that there were very few Marxists of any persuasion in most territories of the British Empire. Nationalists were more plentiful, though alliances with them had to be managed carefully and were not always possible or even desirable. Complicating and dominating everything was the priority that had to be accorded to the interests of the Soviet Union to which all Communists had given their 'unconditional support' as a condition of joining the Comintern. The 2nd Congress of the Comintern expressed this complication thus:

> all events in world politics are necessarily concentrated on one central point, the struggle of the world bourgeoisie against the Russian Soviet Republic, which is rallying round itself both the soviet movements among the advanced workers in all countries and all the national liberation movements in the colonies and among oppressed peoples [...] our policy must be to bring into being a close alliance of all national and colonial liberation movements with Soviet Russia; the forms taken by this alliance will be determined by the stage of development reached by the communist movement among the proletariat of each country or by the revolutionary liberation movement in the underdeveloped countries and among backward nationalities.[2]

Though Lenin in 1920 was insistent that proletarian internationalism demanded that the Soviet state shall 'make the greatest national sacrifices in order to overthrow international capitalism', the opposite was also true;[3] proletarian internationalism demanded 'subordination of the proletarian struggle in one country to the interests of the struggle on a world scale'.[4] Since Lenin himself had characterised world politics as being concentrated on the central point of struggle between the world bourgeoisie and the Soviet Republic, it was an easy matter to convince Communists to support policies that the Russians demanded – on the grounds that these represented the central 'contradiction' of the world struggle – even if they were of dubious value to national 'sections' of the Comintern such as the British, or actually destructive of local political opportunities, as they were in the so-called Third Period.

Nevertheless it was a settled Communist conviction that an imperialist epoch characterised by wars, civil wars and revolutions had begun some time in the late nineteenth/early twentieth century. The general crisis of capitalism, as Communists called it, involved a crisis of empires. Anti-imperialist struggles culminating in colonial independence would deepen that crisis because the standard of living in countries such as Britain depended on colonial exploitation. This was conventional wisdom among Communists until the 1960s when theories of neo-colonialism tried to explain why decolonisation had not led to the predicted outcomes.

If Britain's imperial position and the strength of its labour movement explain much of the early interest that Moscow showed in the CPGB, what is it that makes the study of British Communism of interest today? One answer is that the CPGB played a role in the intellectual life of the left that was out of all proportion to its size – especially in the 1930s and 1940s. Even as recently as the 1980s Communists, now changed out of all recognition, led much of the left in coming to terms with Thatcherism. Then, as earlier, Communists played a significant role in the ideological world of socialism in Britain. For many decades this owed a great deal to the authority of the Soviet Union as a pioneer of socialist economics. During the years 1930–60, for example, Soviet models of planning in a state-owned economy fascinated the broader socialist left because they were widely believed to be successful. But Communist political influence could also rest on the party's ability to shape an alternative programme or platform to those that dominated the Labour Party and the Trades Union Congress (TUC), as they did in the construction of the Alternative Economic Strategy in the 1960s and 1970s.

Communists were not simply a significant force in many of the organisations of the British labour movement. They helped to set broader political, cultural and intellectual agendas. In the 1930s, for example, Communists were central to the Left Book Club, which attracted 57,000 members at its height, and functioned as a key institution of the Popular Front period (1935–39).[5] Communists

4

also dominated the cultural journal *Left Review* (1934–38), a significant publication in a decade when many prominent writers – including Edgell Rickword, Cecil Day Lewis, Stephen Spender and Hugh MacDiarmid – joined the party.[6] In the middle third of the twentieth century Communist ways of seeing also made their presence felt across a wide range of other cultural forms and media, from the radically accented music of composer Alan Bush or folk-singer and songwriter Ewan MacColl, to the artwork of Barbara Niven or Paul Hogarth, the art history of John Berger, and the politically driven drama of Theatre Workshop and Unity Theatre.[7] Perhaps most significant of all was the Communist Party Historians' Group, whose intellectual authority influenced the historiography of the sixteenth and seventeenth centuries for several decades after 1945. Two of the original major debates within this group, on absolutism and ideology, produced international agenda-setting research that overturned existing paradigms and structured discussions of the meaning of the English Civil War for years to come. The group responsible for this was never concerned with abstract theory or historical methods per se but was composed of people who actually conducted their own historical research and engaged in the writing of histories. Nevertheless it was a group that was more theoretically sophisticated than most of the non-Marxists historians of the period and most of its members – people such as Christopher Hill and Victor Kiernan – rejected economic determinism (as found in the work of non-Marxists such as R. H. Tawney, Hugh Trevor-Roper and Lawrence Stone) and gave serious attention to the religious, constitutional and other ideological and institutional expressions of sixteenth- and seventeenth-century politics and society.

Recent research on the Communist Party has been stimulated by the opening of archives and the greater preparedness of Communists to talk and write about their political commitment and experiences since the collapse of the Soviet Union in 1991. One of the main themes of recent publications on Communism in Britain is the matter of its relationships to the Soviet Union and the British labour movement. An argument about the degree of the CPGB's dependence on Moscow and the extent of its role as an expression of Soviet state interests has developed, which echoes similar arguments found in other countries today.[8] Of course this argument reaches back to the very formation of the Comintern in 1919 and had already divided opinion from the earliest days of international Bolshevism.[9] The debate drew significant contributions from former Communists such as Franz Borkenau, Fernando Claudin, Ante Ciliga, Milovan Djilas, Isaac Deutscher, Louis Fischer and Leon Trotsky himself – but it was inevitable that new sources, such as the Moscow archives, would attract researchers and that new evidence would be found to support competing interpretations.[10] Recent research has also paid attention to the national, regional and local supports of Communist politics. What it meant to be a Communist varied in important respects according to a multiplicity of factors, including the politics of the moment and the place where one was active. There was a world of difference between a relatively stable parliamentary democracy like Britain and the conditions of extreme repression in which Communists were active in South Africa or Nazi Germany. But there were also significant differences within British Communism between trade union activists and student members, men and women, those active in the 1920s and those who joined in the 1960s – to take only a few instances. Even the most subservient of Communist parties could only pursue the Moscow-approved tactics – in the days when the Comintern tried to micro-manage such things – in the conditions peculiar to particular countries and this often involved innovations and particular adaptations in accordance with calculations made locally. One can also find evidence of local motivations for the acceptance of a 'general line' imposed by the Comintern and Moscow leadership. Such is the case, for example, even in a moment of major miscalculation, as when the Comintern ruled that socialists and social democrats were simply enemies of the working class, to be shunned completely, as it insisted between 1928 and 1934.[11] Some British Communists had their own reasons for wanting a 'left' turn in 1926 and after, just as some of their German counterparts did in 1928.[12]

Another common strand in the current literature on Communism is an interest in biography. The end of the Soviet Union, the opening of party archives and the preparedness of individuals to openly discuss their Communist commitment has made this sort of work possible, not only in Britain. During the Comintern period the CPGB amassed around 500 short biographies of its members and many more were added in 1941–42. The practice was common to all Communist parties. In France the biographies compiled by the Communist Party of France (PCF) have been described as instruments of 'an almost perfect system of surveillance'.[13] In the British case they were usually generated by attendance at party schools or in applications for party jobs, rather than for disciplinary purposes.

Academic interest in the individual activist is not new. Historians have always been interested in the mentality of an age or society and concern with the mentality of Communists has a long history of its own, giving rise to some of the earliest studies of the 'psychopathology' of inter-war political 'extremism' in Europe and the rise of what are often called 'political religions'. Cold War propaganda made productive use of such studies of the 'true believers', but the question of beliefs, values and attitudes was always of wider interest. The impact of the Communist parties on the mentality of Western workers – through, for example, the formation of political sub-cultures – was thought to be highly significant as recently as the 1970s.[14] Communists themselves, as well as former Communists, often talked as if there was a special Communist personality, and the party was obviously credited with the capacity to shape the beliefs of those it came into contact with. Eric Hobsbawm once referred to the peculiar 'temper' of Communists, at least in the Comintern years, while Annie Kriegel identified a Communist mentality.[15] Raphael Samuel's affectionate portrait of the *Lost World of British Communism* (originally published in *New Left Review*) likewise aimed to 'reconstitute a political mentality'. Samuel also showed the broader cultural significance of this lost world. By comparison with the present day, he argued, political formations generally aspired to monolithicity. They demanded exclusive loyalties and fervent supporters, suitably deferential to party leaders. But to be a Communist, he claimed, 'was to have a complete social identity, one which transcended the limits of class, gender and nationality'. 'We lived', according to Samuel, 'in a private world of our own ... a tight ... self-referential group', though 'we had far more in common with the national culture than we realized at the time'. Such commonalities included a shared patriarchal system of authority; conformism to rules; a mania for 'collective responsibility'; tolerance for bans, proscriptions and censorship; and the 'will to unity', which treated dissent as tantamount to treachery.[16] The study of the CPGB, if one accepts this argument or variants of it, opens a line of analysis of the broader socialist milieu, its values and assumptions, and offers a way in to an understanding of political activism, collective identities, the understanding of ideology, organisational cultures and so on.

For Samuel the Communist Party supplied philosophical certainty, belief in progress, selflessness, courage and consciousness of a world struggle centred on the fortunes of the Soviet Union. The military metaphor was insistent, the experience of being a Communist often made it real. The motivation – 'to judge by some stray but suggestive evidence' – was sometimes 'a way of making *amends* for the hardships and indignities suffered by parents, a retrospective act of justice on behalf, or in the name, of those who had been less able to take up the fight'.[17] The party was conceived as an instrument of class struggle and revolution. Its decisions were binding, 'irrespective of the means by which they had been arrived at'. There was no antagonism between centralism and democracy. There was no conceptual space even for private judgement. The point was to achieve disciplined efficiency in the prosecution of the struggle in order to drive the whole working class movement in the desired direction. All this was in sharp contrast to the CPGB of a later period. By the 1980s the world of Communism Samuel remembered from his youth in the 1940s was lost and in its place stood an organisation he hardly recognised as Communist at all.

In its early years the CPGB had almost a 'cradle to the grave' ambition for its membership and the 'Communist life cycle' began with mothercraft and childrearing and could end with perorations at the graveside of those of its stalwarts who had been 'killed by capitalism'. This is a 'complete party identity' with a vengeance and the offspring of Communist parents remember it with every emotion from fond gratitude to deep resentment.[18] Thomas Linehan sees it as a type of political religion and draws on the experiences, recollections and commentaries of long-serving members to reconstruct the party's social and cultural history in the inter-war years.[19] The model of the Soviet Union is everywhere, 'beginning' with practical advice on childrearing and mothercraft, leading to visions of both the home and family of the future. Its influence was channelled through Comintern-inspired structures such as the children's organisations launched in 1924 and their monthly publication *The Young Comrade*. The Young Communist League (YCL) took responsibility for the children's sections (ages 10–14) which became known as the Young Pioneers' League in 1925 (renamed Young Comrades' League in 1926), charged with the task of building nuclei in the schools. In February 1927 the CPGB launched *The Workers' Child* to dispense advice on childrearing. In December 1931 the *Red Book*

Corner was published to rival the standard Christmas children's annual. Other forays into children's publishing included *Our Lenin* and *Martin's Annual,* not to forget the work of Geoffrey Trease in such re-worked classics as *Bows Against the Barons* (1934), his socialist Robin Hood.

The YCL itself was originally conceived as a serious alternative to the youth organisations of the Independent Labour Party (ILP) which, according to YCL leaders, catered only for 'cultural faddists and intellectual idlers'. The YCL, by contrast, was supposed to fight for the rights of young workers in the factories. Linehan quotes one of its members, Margaret McCarthy, recalling 'the love and spiritual sympathy of comrade for comrade' and how the same young people in the late 1920s were 'dedicated to hatred, destruction of the old capitalist regime, sanguinary class war and apocalyptic revolution'.[20] But even at this moment of revolutionary purity the party changed its tune on the functions of the YCL. From 1927 a new emphasis on cultural pursuits – rambling, music, theatre – entered its profile, though the Third Period had nearly killed the organisation by the time it was 'liquidated' in 1930. It was re-started within months, however, and reached as many as 20,000 through the sales of its journal *Challenge* by 1938.

The Communist Party was 'saturated with married couples' and other family connections.[21] It made enormous demands of its members and endured an equally enormous turnover rate. Those who were married to non-members were encouraged to convert their spouse; those who couldn't often faced severe marital strains. The party recognised some of these stresses of membership and encouraged physical fitness and healthy diet. It infiltrated the British Workers' Sports Federation and was virtually running it from 1927. Again there was a Soviet inspiration – the Red Sport International founded by the Comintern in 1921. Lenin, it was said, swam, did daily gymnastics, enjoyed cycling and hiking and followed a strict dietary regime. The fact that he died prematurely, just fifty-three years old, was not allowed to interfere with his status as a model in these matters at a time when Communist iconography supplied the abiding image of Soviet man as muscular, athletic and indomitable. Lenin set the standard intellectually too and as a paragon of clean living, respectability, personal asceticism and moral propriety in the manner of all the dangerously 'pure' revolutionaries since Robespierre. The student of Communism has the opportunity to study 'the true believer'; the nature of political commitment and political beliefs; the personal satisfactions, motivations and frustrations of activism; the remarkable history of an ideal that turned foul; the illusion of an epoch, the deceptions and self-deceptions that sustained it.

However, the idea of Communism as a political religion is not as clear-cut as it is often made to seem. The 'closed world' idea of the CPGB can also be misleading. Even Samuel acknowledged the shared aspects of the political culture of Communists and British society and it is easy to see parallels between the Communist mentality and those to be found in the broader Labour movement, with their mutual insistence on solidarity, militancy, organisation, unity, leadership, self-sacrifice and so on. Even Annie Kriegel and Harvey Klehr distinguished between an inner elite and ordinary members, who were something less than real Leninists, something short of the ideal.[22] The Communist parties recruited different people at different phases of their history. The motivation for joining was not necessarily the same in say 1936, as it was in 1966 or 1926. The demands of membership were not fixed and unalterable. And of course the variations between countries, in terms of what it meant to be a Communist, could be vast. The CPGB was always small and legal, without the extensive, self-contained sub-cultures and organisations of the PCF and the PCI (Communist Party of Italy), deprived of the great power resources that might have sustained the Comintern's early ambitions for it. The CPGB members came from labour movement backgrounds and felt at home in this milieu, though by the mid-1950s up to a third of recruits came from party families.[23] The numbers joining the CPGB were so small that whatever the social group one looks at, exceptional factors have to be invoked to explain recruitment. Prosopographical analysis can arguably isolate such factors. The typical member of the party was socialised in the older cultures of the left but combined that experience 'with a process of dissociation that was as likely to be social or geographical in character as political'.[24] Founding members of CPGB branches, for example, were disproportionately migrants with a history of labour movement activism in another part of the country. But '[w]hatever the differences in policy and ideology, compared with the larger body of people who never became active in politics, the CPGB in its social aspects was far closer to established models of labour movement activism than either the party or its detractors ever quite understood'.[25] In any comparative typology of Communist parties the British party represents 'a relatively high level of interaction with a variety of radical and labour movement milieux'.[26]

Perhaps even more than the milieu of that broader labour movement, the culture of Communism in Britain bore the imprint of a strong autodidactic tradition; for CPGB bibliographer Dave Cope, the party's 'belief in the written word was immeasurable'. 'The CP', he adds, 'produced far more material than any other political organisation': in such material much of the party's history is archived.[27] There was material generated through day-to-day political operations – the minutes, reports and resolutions proliferated by the institutional apparatus of branch meetings, district meetings, committees, sub-committees and party congresses. A well-organised CP branch would also have a designated 'literature secretary' tasked with supplying members, fellow travellers and possible recruits with appropriate reading material (also sold through the more public-facing Communist-run bookshops in Britain's major cities). And there was plenty for Communists to buy, sell and read. In the course of its history the CPGB would operate a number of publishing houses, including Martin Lawrence (whose initials members took as code for the 'Marx and Lenin' who dominated the company's list), Lawrence & Wishart (formed in 1936 when Martin Lawrence merged with liberal publishers, Wishart Books) and Modern Books, established in 1929 to circulate material from the Communist International.[28] Books published included the Marxist canon, monographs by party intellectuals on the Soviet Union and a wide range of other political and historical matters; in the case of Lawrence & Wishart, it also included fiction written by Communists or considered of interest to them. There were also pamphlets, some of which were centrally written, others produced by branches and districts to reflect local campaigns. There were factory papers – agitational publications sharply attuned to exploitative conditions and any openings for resistance in a specific workplace. There was the wide network of journals, organs of Communist thought – from the densely theoretical to the more directly instructive – conceived as both an authoritative source of the party line and an approved, official channel for debate (all journals set up by party members required approval from the Executive Committee).[29] From 1930 the CP also ran its own newspaper, the *Daily Worker*, a mouthpiece of the party concerned with projecting a Communist voice beyond party membership into the broader working-class and labour movement constituencies. As such, the paper's fluctuating fortunes provide a rough barometer of the party's profile, integration or isolation in relation to those communities. Circulation briefly touched 200,000 during the Popular Front years of the late 1930s, remained a healthy 120,000 in 1948 (CP membership had peaked at 56,000 in 1942), but was down to 63,000 by the end of 1956.[30] Rebranded as the *Morning Star* in 1966, the plummeting circulation in the 1980s cruelly measured the party's decline. By 1990 a paper launched sixty years earlier as 'the voice of the entire working class' was controlled by a faction of the splintering party, and was selling just 12,000 copies, and half of these to the rapidly disintegrating Soviet Union.[31]

British Communism: A Documentary History is a book which seeks to reconstruct the trajectory, concerns and contradictions of the CPGB by retrieving and restoring to view a selection of the voluminous and scattered printed material in which its history is inscribed. As such it is intended to complement CP historiography – such as Willie Thompson's *The Good Old Cause: British Communism 1920–91* (1992) – and the more recent work, mentioned above, which explores the motivations, experiences and structures of feeling of the party membership.[32] It is not a book about how the Communist Party was perceived in broader society and culture; we have not therefore included MI5 surveillance of Communists from the National Archives KV2 files, which frequently reveal more about the watchers than the watched.[33] Instead, in the mould of Albert Fried's *Communism in America: A History on Documents* (1997) it is an institutional history, a record of the party's seventy-one years assembled from its textual traces. It is an internal history, in that the documents sampled are written by Communists themselves (active and occasionally lapsed), and in some cases by non-members close to the party, observing its disciplines and advancing its cause.[34] The book attempts to allow the Communist Party 'to speak for itself', although the story it tells is inevitably mediated by our editorial decisions. One of which was to focus on the Communist Party as it operated at the time, and largely to exclude the rich genre of Communist retrospective memoir and autobiography in favour of documents generated from history's midst.[35] In almost all cases the documents included were either circulated within the party circles or published at the time (if they were not, our editorial annotations explain why); in this respect each item forms at least one small detail in the shifting kaleidoscope of the party's culture.

The documents sifted and chosen run the spectrum across that culture, including selections from daily, weekly, fortnightly and monthly party publications; pamphlets, manifestos and published correspondence; books and book reviews; congress and committee reports and resolutions; party statements and press releases. The challenge throughout has been to do justice to the complexity of the party's long history and the breadth of its concerns within the space of a single volume (it would be possible, for example, to fill a book of this length with illuminating Communist documents concerned with cultural matters alone). As Albert Fried notes in the introduction to his book, 'every addition requires a deletion', and we have tried to reflect the broad contours of the party's history, its most significant moments and patterns.[36] Some of the documents suggested themselves for their striking historical and political insight and prescience, especially into the structures and operations of capitalism and colonialism. Others were chosen precisely because they are guardedly unrevealing or flatly dishonest about historical realities but, in their obfuscations, repressions and prevarications, prove deeply revealing about the defensive or self-deluding mindset which would find a resonant theatre in the inner-party conflicts of 1956.

In cases where party discipline was rocked by dissent – in and around 1956 and during the party's long decline – we have attempted to re-stage the central debates by including material to represent the different perspectives. The book covers the party's entire history but privileges documents from the years when it mattered most; the process of fragmentation and disintegration is covered, but not chronicled blow-by-blow. In order to bring into view as many documents as possible, texts have been editorially trimmed, and all our elisions are marked [...]. In some cases we give just a few lines of text that get to the nub of a wider argument; in the case of the CPGB's talismanic 'programmes', whose purpose was precisely to detail the party's long-term vision and strategy, we have included extracts of much greater length.

The book is divided into twelve chapters. Over half form a broadly chronological narrative of the advances and reversals in the party's fortunes. Framed by introductions which contextualise and map CPGB policy, these chapters track the party's emergence (chapter 1), the adoption of New Lines and the shifts in policy and strategy that these lines shaped in the national context (chapters 5, 6, 7 and 8), moments of damaging crisis and political isolation (chapter 9), and the widening faultlines that eventually led to the party's dissolution (chapters 11 and 12). Where necessary we include the Comintern and Soviet documents that drove agendas, such as those that called for reorientation in the lines of national parties. Running through this overarching narrative are more thematic chapters providing magnified coverage of key and abiding concerns: the relationship between the CPGB and the Soviet Union (chapter 2); between the CPGB, the Labour Party and the trade unions (chapters 3 and 10); and the party's critique of imperialism and engagement with anti-colonial struggles (chapter 4). There are inevitably significant intersections between the thematic chapters and more narrative-based chapters; in these cases the former embellish the latter, providing broader contexts and extra layers of detail.

A number of documents have been sourced from the Communist Party Archive; here full catalogue references are given. The editors would like to thank staff there, and at Manchester Central Library, the British Library, the Marx Memorial Library and Salford's Working Class Movement Library for all their help. We would like to thank Lawrence & Wishart for permission to quote from their publications listed in the bibliography. We would also like to thank those who gave permission for copyrighted material to be reproduced. Every effort has been made to trace copyright owners. To those we have been unable to track down, should they come forward, the editors will make amends, not least by ensuring acknowledgement in subsequent editions.

Notes

1 'Theses on the National and Colonial Question', 28 July 1920, second congress of the Comintern, J. Degras (ed.), *The Communist International 1919–43; Volume One 1919–22* (London: Frank Cass, 1971), pp. 138–9.
2 Ibid., p. 141.
3 Ibid., p. 143.
4 Ibid., p. 143.
5 See John Lewis, *The Left Book Club: An Historical Record* (London: Victor Gollancz, 1970).
6 See David Margolies (ed.), *Writing the Revolution: Cultural Criticism*

from Left Review (London and Chicago: Pluto, 1998).

7 Nancy Bush, *Alan Bush: Music, Politics and Life* (London: Thames, 2000); Ben Harker, *Class Act: The Cultural and Political Life of Ewan MacColl* (London: Pluto, 2007); Paul Hogarth, *Drawing on Life* [1997] (London: Royal Academy of Arts, 2002); Colin Chambers, *The Story of Unity Theatre* (London: Lawrence & Wishart, 1989). For an overview see Andy Croft (ed.), *A Weapon in the Struggle: The Cultural History of the Communist Party* (London: Pluto, 1998).

8 For example, in the USA there is M. Isserman, *Which Side Were You On? The American Communist Party During the Second World War* (Middleton: Wesleyan University Press, 1982); M. Naison, *Communists in Harlem During the Depression* (Urbana: University of Illinois Press, 1983); and H. Klehr, *The Heyday of American Communism: The Depression Decade* (New York: Basic Books, 1984).

9 For example in B. Russell, *The Theory and Practice of Bolshevism* (London: Allen and Unwin, 1920).

10 See A. Thorpe, 'Comintern "control" of the Communist Party of Great Britain, 1920–43', *English Historical Review*, 113 (June 1998), pp. 637–62; M. Worley, 'The Communist International, the Communist Party of Great Britain and the Third Period, 1928–32', *European History Quarterly*, 30 (April 2000), pp. 353–78; J. McIlroy and A. Campbell, 'For a Revolutionary Workers' Government: The Communist International, the Communist Party of Great Britain and Revisionist Interpretations of the Third Period, 1927–35', *European History Quarterly* , 32 (2002), pp. 535–69; K. Morgan, 'Labour with Knobs On: The Recent Historiography of the British Communist Party', in S. Berger (ed.), 'Labour and Social History in Great Britain: Historiographical Reviews and Agendas', *Mitteilungsblatt des Instituts fur soziale Bewegungen* , 27 (2002); G. Cohen and K. Morgan, 'Stalin's Sausage Machine: British Students at the International Lenin School, 1926–1937', *Twentieth Century British History*, 13 (2002), pp. 327–55; J. McIlroy and A. Campbell, 'Histories of the British Communist Party: A User's Guide', *Labour History Review*, 68, 1 (2003), pp. 33–59; J. McIlroy, B. McLoughlin, A. Campbell and J. Halstead, 'Forging the Faithful: The British at the International Lenin School', *Labour History Review*, 68 (2003), pp. 99–128; N. Fishman, 'CPGB History at the Centre of Contemporary British History', *Labour History Review*, 69, 3, 2004, pp. 381–3; A. Campbell, B. McLoughlin and J. Halstead, 'The International Lenin School: A Response to Cohen and Morgan', *Twentieth Century British History*, 15, 2004, pp. 51–76.

11 Nicholas N. Kozlov and Eric D. Weitz, 'Reflections on the Origin of the Third Period', *Journal of Contemporary History*, 24, 3 (July 1989), pp. 387–410. See also Weitz's *Creating German Communism, 1890–1990* (Princeton: Princeton University Press, 1997).

12 See Matthew Worley, *Class Against Class: The Communist Party in Britain Between the Wars* (London and New York: I. B. Tauris, 2002).

13 Kevin Morgan, Gidon Cohen and Andrew Flinn, *Communists and British Society, 1920–1991* (London: Rivers Oram Press, 2007), p. ix.

14 M. Mann, *Consciousness and Action Among the Western Working Class* (London: Macmillan, 1973), especially chapter 4.

15 A. Kriegel, *The French Communists: Profile of a People* (Chicago: University of Chicago, 1972); E. Hobsbawm, 'Problems of Communist History' in his *Revolutionaries* (London: Weidenfeld and Nicolson, 1973), pp. 3–11.

16 Raphael Samuel, *The Lost World of British Communism* (London: Verso, 2006)

17 Ibid., p. 57.

18 P. Cohen (ed.), *Children of the Revolution* (London: Lawrence & Wishart, 1997).

19 Thomas Linehan, *Communism in Britain, 1920–39: From the Cradle to the Grave* (Manchester: Manchester University Press, 2007).

20 Ibid., p. 61.

21 Ibid., p. 75.

22 H. Klehr, *Communist Cadre: The Social Background of the American Communist Party Elite* (Stanford CA: Hoover Institution Press, 1976).

23 Morgan, Cohen and Flinn, *Communists and British Society*, p. 21.

24 Ibid., p. 29.

25 Ibid., p. 55.

26 Ibid., p. 273.

27 Dave Cope, Introduction to online version of the CPGB Bibliography, www.amielandmelburn.org.uk/cpgb-biblio/maintextt.htm (accessed 11 February 2010).

28 For Martin Lawrence and the merger with Wishart, see Christopher Hilliard, 'Producers by Hand and Brain: Working-Class Writers and Left-Wing Publishers in 1930s Britain', *Journal of Modern History*, 78 (March 2006), p. 45.

29 There were also broader-based journals dominated by individual Communists but not run by the party; these often enjoyed a wider circulation than in-house publications. While the party's weekly *World News and Views* would sell around 14,000 copies per issue in the early 1950s, for instance, *Our Time*, an inclusive cultural journal run by party intellectuals would sell 18,000 at the height of its popularity.

30 John Callaghan, *Cold War, Crisis and Conflict: The CPGB 1951–68* (London: Lawrence & Wishart, 2003), p. 28.

31 'Daily Worker: Your Paper', *Daily Worker* (1 January 1930); Alison Macleod, *The Death of Uncle Joe* (London: Merlin, 1997), p. 243.

32 Linehan, *Communism in Britain*; Morgan, Cohen and Flinn, *Communists and British Society*.

33 Officers monitoring Jimmie Miller/Ewan MacColl in the late 1930s noted, for example, that his accomplishes 'have the appearance of Communist Jews', National Archives KV2/2175/28. For the state's surveillance of the party from the 1920s, see C. Andrew, *Defence of the Realm: The Authorized History of MI5* (London: Allen Lane, 2009).

34 Examples here include John Strachey (document 6.2) and Jack Lindsay (6.8).

35 Such as Doris Lessing, *Walking in the Shade* (London: Harper Collins, 1997). One exception here is extract 4.3 from Philip Spratt's book, *Blowing-Up India: Reminiscences and Reflections of a Former Comintern Emissary* (Calcutta: Prachi Prakashan, 1955). This atmospheric retrospective account details Spratt's underground work in India, activity by its nature 'undocumented' as it occurred.

36 Albert Fried, Introduction to *Communism in America: A History in Documents* (New York: Columbia University Press, 1997), p. xv.

1

Defining Bolshevism

Support for the overthrow of the Tsar and the formation of a provisional government in March 1917 was universal among Liberal and Labour politicians in Britain and accompanied by hopes that the new regime in Petrograd would stiffen the Eastern Front. When the Bolsheviks seized power in November these hopes were dashed. The new government was committed to a separate peace, 'without annexations and indemnities'. The Bolsheviks had opposed the war from the beginning as an inter-imperialist conflict. The Labour Party leadership, having supported the British war effort since August 1914, had no reason to trust Lenin who openly denounced them as enemies of socialism. But elements within the party that had opposed the war, such as the ILP, and larger numbers that were growing tired of it, were pleased that self-proclaimed socialists had acquired power in what had been regarded as the most reactionary state in Europe. They looked on this new government with hope that the war might soon end and socialist reconstruction begin. But only small numbers of British socialists wanted to copy the Bolsheviks' revolutionary methods.

The most enthusiastic supporters of the Bolsheviks in Britain belonged to small socialist groups such as the Socialist Labour Party, the British Socialist Party, the Workers' Socialist Federation and groups and individuals within the ILP. When the time came to form a Communist Party in Britain in July–August 1920 (a process not completed until the following January) it was largely drawn from these groups. The fact that membership of the party amounted to only 2000 members or so was indicative of the weakness in Britain of the revolutionary standpoint that the Bolsheviks represented. But within these small circles the prestige of the Bolsheviks derived from the fact that they had led a successful revolution, acquired state power and put themselves at the head of a new Communist

International formed in 1919. For these people the revolutionary road had worked in most of the Tsarist Empire and promised to do so in the rest of Europe – Bolshevik-style revolts having occurred also in parts of Germany and Hungary. But what was Bolshevism, why had it succeeded and what was the nature of the new Bolshevik state? The revolutionaries drawn to the Comintern were keen to find answers to these questions. Some of them did not like what they discovered and withdrew. Ellen Wilkinson, the future Labour MP, decided in December 1919, after making her first contact with the Bolsheviks in Geneva at an international students' conference, that 'this is the most ghastly, callous, inhuman machine that I have ever witnessed'. Others, such as Raymond Postgate and Frank Horrabin, dropped out soon after the party's foundation. Rajani Palme Dutt concluded from the same experience that repelled Wilkinson that he had finally 'found what I had been looking for; socialists who mean business'.[1] Those who took Dutt's view became enthusiastic students of Bolshevism. They recognised its novelty as a theory of party organisation, a science of tactics, a conception of the imperialist epoch and a workers' state. They strove to turn themselves into Bolsheviks and accepted the authority of Lenin and his colleagues to guide them on their way. This meant turning their backs not only on the varieties of socialism that had made their mark in Britain – such as Fabianism, Guild Socialism and ethical socialism – but also all rival varieties of Marxism, whether they were thought of as revolutionary or not. The Communists had to renounce earlier forms of revolutionary purism. Leninism required its converts to contest local and parliamentary elections and to affiliate to the Labour Party – two sticking points for many of the radicals drawn to Communism in Britain. They had to comply more broadly with Lenin's version of Marxism and in July 1920 the 2nd Congress of the Comintern – convened in Moscow just before the CPGB was founded – adopted 'twenty-one conditions' of membership intended to block the polluting influence of rival Marxisms and generalise the Leninist experience. Once a Communist Party was founded – and in Britain Silvia Pankhurst's Workers' Socialist Federation was not reconciled to all of this until January 1921, at a second Unity Convention – it was then 'Bolshevised' more thoroughly on an ongoing basis.

1.1 Communism

Rajani Palme Dutt, who became a leading full-time theorist of Communism, was precocious in understanding the essentials of the Leninist position at a time when other members of the party were still finding their way.

[...] The First manifesto of the new Communist International describes the modern communist outlook. It sees in the ruin of the world war and the peace that succeeded it the fulfilment of the Marxian prediction of the catastrophic destiny of capitalism ... 'This is the epoch of the decomposition and break-up of the world capitalist system, which will mean the break-up of European culture in general if capitalism with its irreconcilable antagonisms is not destroyed ... The catastrophe of imperialist war has with one swoop swept away all the gains of experts and of Parliamentary struggles'. Not only the populations of Europe, but the colonial populations of Asia and Africa, have been dragged into the vortex ... In the midst of this upheaval there is the need of a strong revolutionary power that can alone form the coherent force to carry through the necessary change and establish the new system ... it is the object of the Communists to end those conditions by giving conscious direction to the instinctive forces of revolt, instead of vainly seeking to stem them. No error in fact could be greater than to suppose that the Communists are out to 'make' a revolution in order to impose their system upon mankind. 'The Communist Parties, far from conjuring up civil war artificially, rather seek to shorten its duration'.

[...] The Communists do not reject the current conceptions of democracy because they believe in the superiority of the few ... The divorce between the realities of power and the theory ... is inherent in the nature of capitalist democracy ... because of the fundamental helplessness of the propertyless mass: the Parliamentary forces only serve to veil the reality of the 'bourgeois dictatorship' by the appearance of popular consent ... and even this veil is cast aside in moments of any stress by the open assumption of emergency dictatorial powers ...

On the other hand ... the glorification of the minority and of the coup d'etat really belongs to the Blanquist school, which was always vigorously opposed by Marxism. Marxism taught that the liberation of the workers could only be the act of the workers themselves ... Communists differ from other believers in the ultimate victory of the working class in that they do not believe that victory will be achieved until after a very much more severe struggle than is ordinarily contemplated ...

[...] The fully organised Communist Party ... must be based on the strictest internal discipline ... but this internal strictness of theory and discipline must be accompanied by an external policy of revolutionary opportunism which is in contrast with the usual 'purism' of the revolutionary sect ... This discipline is ultimately international in character, because the struggle is regarded as international. To the Communist the International ... is the union of different divisions in a single army, each with its own tactical problems, but all with a single directing centre. For this reason an absolute ultimate authority is vested in the International executive ... not only for the immediate struggle, but as the nucleus of future international authority in the World Soviet Republic'.

Rajani Palme Dutt, 'Communism', extract from entry in the 12th edition of the *Encyclopaedia Britannica*, 1922, pp. 732–3.

1.2 The Soviet

Communism attracted advocates of direct democracy such as Guild Socialists and proponents of rank-and-file power within the unions. The idea that Bolshevik power was built upon the soviets was one of the reasons for this attraction. But what were the soviets? On this there was considerable confusion initially among Bolshevik sympathisers in Britain. The twenty-one conditions of membership of the Comintern, however, included the requirement that Communists establish a network of soviets within factories and mines as a necessary means of seizing power. After the revolution these soviets would constitute the new socialist state, the dictatorship of the proletariat. Here the new doctrine is explained, including the monopoly role of the Communists within the soviets.

[...] When all the processes of production are brought to a standstill simultaneously – in a general strike – all functions of the State are stopped abruptly ... the workers ... have necessarily to hand over all *their* interests to a hastily-constructed organisation, which assumes all the public functions previously carried out by the State that they are now fighting.
    The workers have thus produced their *own* organ of government.
    [...] it is obvious that it is not at such a moment ... that the workers' main concern would be with elections ... frittering away of precious time on elections ... destroyed the Paris Commune – the first attempt of the workers to control their own affairs.
    This applies no less to the first Russian Soviets ... In neither case did they

contain representatives of the provinces. And yet the Petrograd Soviet of 1905 for a time was the real master of Russia ... And the Petrograd Soviet itself was not by any means formally representative of *all* the workers in the city [...]

'But would not that qualification make the Communist Party itself eligible for the post of dictator?' one can hear some enquirer asking. Precisely; that is what actually happened, and there is nothing for us to be ashamed of or for the masses to fear ... it is the Communist Party ... with its strict party discipline, that is bound actually to wield power, through its organised groups in the Soviets, so long as the Soviet regime is in danger (1917–1920 in Russia).

In general terms ... we have arrived at an answer to our question: 'What are the Soviets?' ... the central fighting organisations of the struggling proletariat during the period of revolution ... finally emerging from the struggle as the State organisation of the victorious proletariat during the period of Communist reconstruction.

W. E. Harding, 'What Are the Soviets?', *Communist Review* (May 1921), pp. 10–12.

1.3 State power

In this review of *The Decay of Capitalist Civilisation* by the Fabian socialists Sidney and Beatrice Webb, the Cambridge economist Maurice Dobb takes issue with their argument about state ownership of industry. In doing so he defends the socialist credentials of the Bolshevik state, which under Lenin's New Economic Policy (NEP) since 1921 had retreated from physical controls over the economy, to permit the resurgence of market forces. Non-Communist Marxists such as those within the Pleb's League attracted the scorn of the Communists and were constantly corrected by them. Plebs lecturers had identified NEP as a return to capitalism. But the Communists reasoned that as long as the Bolsheviks held state power, the working class controlled the state and policy ultimately favoured its interests, however much appearances – and even the harshest techniques of capitalist exploitation – suggested otherwise.

[...] We chant the slogan 'economic power dominates political power' ... But to interpret events in this way is to neglect the dominant part which *control of the State* plays in imperialist capitalism ... Where does political 'sovereignty' actually and in fact rest? ... Herein lies the difference between the Fabian school and the Marxian school of thought. The Fabian emphasises the issue of social *v.* private enterprise in industry. The Marxist emphasises the issue of *class in relation to the State.*

[...] the Webbs' proposals, in fact, amount merely to control of industry by the capitalist-controlled State – State Capitalism ... But even supposing the existing State took over the control of Vickers – would this make any *serious* difference to the balance of political power, and hence to the essential problems of Imperialism and the Class Struggle? ... It would be State Capitalism; it would be the Servile State, which Belloc saw over ten years ago as the logical outcome of Fabianism; it would not be socialism [...]

The essential problems of to-day are political struggles of rival national states and the class struggle for control of the State. 'The decay of civilisation' can only be arrested ... by the passing of sovereign power in society ... from the capitalist class to the working class.

This question of where ultimate power resides is the important thing, and not the mere superficial *forms* of industrial administration. However far in response to economic expediency the forms of industrial administration in Russia may be modified to a superficial resemblance to capitalist forms (e.g. scientific management, bonus wage-payments, credit and currency system, etc.), Russia will remain separated by a great gulf from the capitalist world, *so long as supreme power rests with the working class.*

The duty of the real workers' party must be ... to convert every sectional workers' struggle ... into a *political struggle* – a struggle to get power ...

To do this a workers' revolutionary party must be composed of ... the active members of the working class, who are alive to this struggle ... It must be an organisation, under efficient central control and *direction* ...

Maurice Dobb, 'The Webbs, the State, and the Workers', *Plebs*, 15, 4, 1923, pp. 167–71.

1.4 Class consciousness

The Communists imagined themselves to be the vanguard of the working class. Communists often spoke of their party as synonymous with the most class-conscious workers and presented it as the custodian of working-class interests. Leninism was understood to be

Marxism updated for an imperialist epoch of wars, civil wars and revolutions. Leninism was thus the science of tactics appropriate for this imperialist epoch. The next three documents illustrate various aspects of that conviction.

The workers only gain their strength when they become conscious of themselves as a class.

Millions of workers are held in subjection because they are still sleeping. They obey the will of their masters – without other thought of their own; they do the work of their masters and fight one another to work harder and wear themselves out to pile up more profits for them; they vote for their masters; they read the press of their masters and find relief in the sports and shows provided by their masters; they go to war to fight the battles of their masters, and die in their service or return with broken bodies to be thrown on the streets as wasters or work under harder conditions. Thus, despite their many millions, they are slaves; they are not yet a class.

A class exists by will and consciousness of its members. The ruling class, the bourgeoisie, is a class with full consciousness. All their acts and words and writings, their institutions and customs, all the details of their system, are directed to maintaining their power, in the upholding of property and keeping down the lower orders, all the members of the bourgeoisie, the lawyers, the politicians, the professors, the financiers, the manufacturers, the shareholders, the landlords, the military and naval officers, the civil servants, are united in a common consciousness, whatever their other differences. This common consciousness makes them a class and a ruling class.

[…] The first need of the workers is of consciousness of their class. All that the workers have won they have won only by their common consciousness and action as a class. All that the workers suffer they suffer by their lack of class consciousness …

Class consciousness is the will of the working class to struggle and to conquer … It is to know the goal and to fight for it […]

The Communist Party is the Party of the class conscious workers all over the world. Its task is to make the rest of the workers class conscious, to arouse them to the struggle and victory of the working class.

'The Class Struggle: OUR PROGRAMME EXPLAINED', *Workers' Weekly*, 10 March 1923.

1.5 Leninism and the party

Communists in Britain, as elsewhere, believed, and were encouraged to believe by Comintern interventions, that the key to revolutionary transformation was the creation of a Leninist party. All parties affiliated to the Comintern were accordingly 'Bolshevised', a process that began even before the announcement of a formal campaign of Bolshevisation at the 5th Congress of the Comintern in 1924.

[...] A Communist Party is a party, embracing or aspiring to embrace all the advanced members of the working class. It incarnates the collective experience of the working class gained in the struggle against capitalism. Such a party must be closely linked up with the workers, understanding their problems, sensing their moods, and assisting, them in the every-day struggle. It is fatal for a workers' party to pursue a policy which does not take into consideration the state of mind of the masses.

It must be in contact not with the more active workers in the trade union branches and the Local Labour Parties, but must also be in contact with the masses of workers in the workshop. (Hence factory groups.)

A revolutionary party must, however, lead the workers. It must not allow itself to be dragged along by the masses, but must understand the development of events, give its lead to the workers in order that their struggle can be waged in the most effective and revolutionary fashion. *It must become the political leader of the working class.*

It is worth mentioning that Lenin had, in building the Bolshevik party, to combat a theory similar to one which has been widely spread in Marxist circles in Britain, though it has never been given a name. It was called by Lenin the theory of 'spontaneity' *and its essence is that it neglects or despises the role that a revolutionary party plays in the struggles of the workers.* We have all met its British protagonists.

[...] Leninism is the application of Marxism to the problems confronting the workers in the period of Imperialist capitalism, and to the problems of socialist reconstruction where the capitalists have been overthrown. It is not a final theory, but a theory capable of amplification in the light of knowledge gained in the struggle of the workers.

The Communist parties move in the light of Leninism. Unlike the parties of the Second International they are ideologically united.

A revolutionary party must also be organised itself. It must learn to move sharply in response to a Communist lead, and to move as a united body.

This necessitates an iron discipline and a capable centralized leadership
[...]

J. R. Campbell, 'Leninism and the Party', *Workers' Weekly*, 16 January 1925.

1.6 The Minority Movement

The Communist Party was dwarfed by both the Labour Party and the trade unions, the most important of which were affiliated to it. The CP applied for affiliation itself, but was rejected. An alternative was quickly found. In August 1924 the CP launched the Minority Movement within the unions and in 1925 established a National Left-Wing Movement working within the Labour Party.

[...] The crisis which the workers' movement has passed through for the last three years has openly betrayed the bankruptcy in ideas and leadership of the reformist elements directing the activities and struggles of the workers.

The existing organisations of the workers no longer respond to the new demands of the workers for united action to secure common demands. Hence the workers are forced into a struggle with the existing reformist leadership in order to realise their most immediate needs and demands. The growing opposition movements now springing up in the leading trade unions, industries, and the Labour Party, are the first expression of the concrete raising of the demands of the workers and of a definite challenge to the existing leadership.

The Communist Party welcomes these minority movements as the sign of the awakening of the workers. [...]

[...] The Communist Party, however, declares unhesitatingly to all the workers that the various minority movements cannot realise their full power so long as they remain sectional, separate and limited in their scope and character. The many streams of the rising forces of the workers must be gathered together in one powerful mass movement which will sweep away the old leadership and drive forward relentlessly to the struggle for power [...]

[...] in the actual fight to achieve their immediate demands the workers will be brought up against the whole organised power of capitalism – the State, and they will be forced further forward in the actual process of this struggle [...]

[...] Out of the struggles of the opposition movements of to-day will be forged the Communist Party of to-morrow [...]

Speeches and Documents of the Sixth (Manchester) Conference of the
Communist Party of Great Britain, May 17, 18, 19 1924 (London: CPGB,
1924), and Marxists Internet Archive.

1.7 The imperialist epoch

The central rationale for the Leninist party was Lenin's conception
of the imperialist epoch. If wars and civil wars were endemic to
modern times, the revolutionary party had to be able to survive
and give leadership in such conditions. The years 1914–45 provided
plenty of evidence to support Lenin's contention. Wars, civil wars,
economic crises and the threat of more upheavals to come supported
Lenin's vision and the sense that preparing for revolution was practical politics. This vision was far less obviously useful in Western
Europe by the 1950s when 'the actuality of the revolution' had
faded from view.

The centre of Lenin's teaching was to make conscious that the world revolution was no longer a dream of the future, but was the direct, urgent,
indispensable task of the present stage; that the objective conditions were
already fully present in this final stage of 'rotten-ripe' dying capitalism; that
it was urgently essential for the subjective factor of the world proletariat
to become conscious of the situation and act; and that the delay could only
mean ever increasing 'torment, hunger and brutalization', 'the destruction
of millions and millions of human beings'. The two decades since 1914
have abundantly shown the truth of this, as the imperialist world, through
delay of the revolution, advances through increasing crisis towards a new
world war.
  [...] All the contradictions of capitalism reach their highest point in the
conditions of imperialism: first, the struggle of the proletariat against the
bourgeoisie in the leading imperialist countries; second, the struggle of the
colonial peoples for liberation from the imperialist yoke; third, the conflict
of the imperialist powers among themselves; and fourth – in the post-war
stage – the conflict of imperialism against the new rising workers' power,
the Soviet Union. Through combined development of all these conflicts
the world revolution develops. 'Imperialism', said Lenin, 'is the eve of the
socialist revolution'.
  [...] Lenin was not anti-democratic, as his enemies and some ignorant bourgeois admirers allege ... he fought with such hatred the sham of

bourgeois democracy, and fought for proletarian democracy as a very much higher democratic form [...]

The dictatorship of the proletariat is a dictatorship of the immense majority against the minority of exploiters. It is the necessary weapon to carry through the class struggle to completion, to destroy the remains of the old order and build the new order.

R. Palme Dutt, 'The Chief Task Now', *New Masses*, 27 February 1934.

1.8 For Soviet Britain

Formally adopted at the 13th Congress in 1935, 'For Soviet Britain' would remain the party's programme for sixteen years. Though rooted in the insurrectionist mindset of the Third Period, its attention to the rising threat of fascism also anticipated the New Line adopted in 1935.

[...] Fascism is the weapon of the millionaires against the working class. Fascism is the dictatorship of the most ruthless, reactionary and jingo section of monopoly capitalism. The paymasters of Hitler and Goering are the biggest millionaire financiers and capitalists of Germany. The whole aim and object of the setting up of Fascist Governments, as can be proved in detail from the experience of Fascist Italy, Fascist Germany, and Fascist Austria, has been to reduce wages, lengthen hours of work, abolish social services, curtail education and cut unemployment pay. The object of the violence and barbarity used by the Fascists in crushing the workers' trade unions, political parties and co-operatives is to prevent any resistance to this policy. [...]

In Britain the capitalist preparations for a Fascist form of Government are not only Mosley's blackshirt gangs, financed and organised by rich capitalist groups. The 'National Government' is also preparing the ground, with its militarising of the police, putting in middle-class officers and mobilising middle-class 'specials'; it is swelling the numbers of its secret police, to spy upon working-class organisations; it is organising concentration camps for the unemployed, suppressing still further the workers' right of free speech, and abolishing many other existing rights through the Sedition Act, and taking additional measures to concentrate control in the hands of central officials instead of elected local bodies. This is exactly how the Governments in Germany and Austria prepared the way for open Fascism. [...]

The British workers must face with full and serious determination the situation as it is; face the fact that all capitalism has to offer them to-day is poverty, malnutrition, low wages, speeding-up and unemployment, Fascism, war and slavery; and that neither they nor their families have any hope or future under capitalism. [...]

How can the workers end Capitalism? Many workers still believe that all they need can be obtained by Parliamentary action. The Communist Party declares it is not possible to end capitalism and establish socialism in Britain by the election of a majority in the House of Commons. The capitalist class will never allow itself to be gradually expropriated by successive Acts of Parliament. [...]

But since capitalism cannot be overthrown through Parliament, how then is it that the workers can win power, and construct Socialism in Britain? [...]

The answer is that a workers' revolution can do it. But that revolution is not a single spontaneous act, coming like a bolt from the blue. It is a continuous process. It begins with victorious struggles of workers uniting to win their elementary demands: the struggle against wage cuts, the struggle against high rents, the struggle against speed-up and wholesale dismissals. The fight against hunger is the fight against the capitalist class. The fight against Fascism and War is the fight against the capitalist class. The struggle for colonial liberation is the fight against the capitalist class.

By every victory in that struggle on a united front against the capitalist class, the workers step by step develop unity, power and organisation. Bit by bit the workers become more and more conscious of what they have to do and how they can do it. Out of their own ranks there develops in the course of struggle a working-class party that can be the vanguard of the fight, that can lead the whole class in its day to day struggles and therefore in the final struggle for the overthrow of capitalism and the establishment of the workers' rule. This party is the Communist Party.

Not only is this the way by which the workers can and will win: *but there is no other way.* The choice put by capitalism to the working class to-day is not some imaginary alternative of socialism by parliament, or socialism by revolution, but the grim choice of 'starve or rebel.'

For in the end, the workers' refusal to submit to ever worsening conditions, their fight against quick-coming Fascism and War must either be crushed by the capitalists or must lead to the overthrow of capitalism. Nor has the Communist Party ever denied that this overthrow must be a forceful one; for the capitalists are certain to resist with all their might. It is because of this that the capitalists have accused it of 'advocating violence.' But what insolence and fraud is involved in that accusation! The capitalists, who are themselves already employing unceasing violence against the workers in every part of the world, and who are on the point of drowning the human race in the ocean of blood involved in modern war, accuse the Communist Party of 'advocating violence'! The revolutionary struggle which the resistance of the capitalists makes inevitable will be but a thousandth part of the growing violence which is already being used by the capitalists. Civil War is forced upon the working class. Moreover, the only effect of the perpetual violence of the capitalists is to destroy human civilisation. But the revolutionary struggle of the workers can, and will, open the way to a new epoch of human progress better than anything the world has yet experienced. [...]

For Soviet Britain: The Programme of the Communist Party adopted at the XIII Congress, February 2nd 1935 (London: CPGB, 1935).

1.9 The Socialist USSR

By 1936 Communists maintained, following Stalin, that socialism had been achieved in the Soviet Union. This underlined the importance of defending the Soviet state, giving priority to its interests and regarding its leadership as the leadership of world Communism. Page Arnot was writing at a time when British Communists, following Soviet diplomatic requirements, were refusing to support the war against Nazi Germany on the grounds that it was an inter-imperialist war of no interest to the workers – an argument that became instantly redundant once the Nazis invaded the Soviet Union on 22 June 1941.

For a generation mankind has been passing through the epoch of wars and revolutions. The forces of revolution are becoming stronger and stronger. Not only the working class in the home countries of Imperialism, but around them the mass of the people oppressed by monopoly-capitalism: not only the half of mankind, the masses of the colonial peoples struggling for liberation; but also, strongest of all, the victorious workers and peasants of the USSR, the builders of socialism in the fortress of World Revolution [...]
     In a draft programme of the Communist Party the role of the U.S.S.R. is set forth thus:–
     [...] The Socialist State has no economic crises; it has abolished poverty, illiteracy and unemployment; it has won security and abundance and a full cultural life for all; it has made it one of the foremost industrial countries; it has established powerful defence forces against attacks from the hostile capitalist world and to help forward the working-class struggle for world Socialism. On the basis of this achievement the new Constitution of the Socialist democracy has been established, which for the first time ensures real democracy for all.

All this the Socialist revolution has been able to accomplish in a few years in what was an extremely backward country. This has been an object lesson to the working people of all countries of the capacity of the workers to build Socialism and has spread the conviction of the need for the Socialist revolution.

The victory of Socialism in the Soviet Union represents not only the victory of Socialism in one country, but the most powerful pivot of advance of the world Socialist revolution.

The division of the world into a capitalist section and a Socialist section is the most important fact of the world situation; it is the greatest weakness of capitalism and governs and increases all the other contradictions of capitalism. The class struggle is now being conducted on a world scale. The international working class has its own State, which is able to act with increasing power and initiative in the world situation. Every increase of strength of the first Socialist State increases the strength of the working class in all countries, increases the balance of forces on the side of the working class and weakens Imperialism.

R. Page Arnot, *Twenty Years: The Policy of the Communist Party of Great Britain since its Foundation July 31st 1920* (London: Lawrence & Wishart, 1940), pp. 73–4.

1.10 Marxist science

Winston Churchill's speech at Fulton, Missouri on 5 March 1946 was an early indication of the rising tensions between the Soviet Union and the Western allies, which became known as the Cold War. Dutt's address, while conscious of this problem and its relationship to the perception of Communism as an 'organised conspiracy', was full of confidence that the rise of Communism was far from over. Like the article that follows it, it is chiefly remarkable for the naively positivist understanding of Marxist science that Dutt subscribed to.

[...] The address which I was to have given you this evening on The Power of Marxism has been forestalled and my subject stolen from me by that more distinguished orator who has made a much publicised speech at Fulton, Missouri, and devoted his address to his kind of inverted tribute to the power of Marxism in the world ... It is worth recalling the words he is alleged to have used at the time of his wars of intervention against the young Soviet Republic:

'It were better to smash the Bolshevik egg before it hatched than be compelled to chase Bolshevik chickens all over the world'.

[...] It is time to end the conspiracy mania in dealing with Communism ... it is time to end this claptrap and seek seriously to understand why millions place their confidence in Communism today. If the French people have given the first political position in their country to the Communist Party with 5 million votes ... If the Italian Communist Party at its last Congress reported 1,800,000 members; if the Czech Communist Party has 1 million members out of a population of 12 millions [and] ... this growth has gone forward against all obstacles and obstruction of the powers in possession ... it is only possible because it corresponds to the deep historical needs and aspirations of the people [...]

What, then, is the power of Communism? It is at once the power of an idea and of a movement [...]

Marxism is a scientific world theory, the first completely critical, completely scientific world theory, without dogma, not static, embodying the sum of human knowledge and living and growing with the growth of human knowledge [...]

Concretely applied to our epoch, Marxism laid bare the laws of the modern era, of capitalist society [...]

[...] Marxism is not only a scientific theory ... but a living movement of millions; a movement of the immense majority [...]

[...] The old ruling classes fear the advance of the people after liberation following the downfall of Fascism. It is therefore no matter for surprise that at this moment a campaign of hostility is let loose against the Soviet Union ... At the present moment it is opportune to recall those final speeches of Goebbels made only a year before the collapse ... He described how Europe and Germany would be divided between the Anglo-American victors and the Soviet Union, and how Eastern Europe would be organised behind an 'iron curtain' ... And it was on this basis he declared that Nazism would thrive [...]

It is here that arises the significance of Churchill's speech. Churchill is adopting the language and the slogans of the Anti-Comintern Pact and even the racial theory of Anglo-American domination [...]

R. Palme Dutt, 'The Power of Marxism' (Marx Anniversary Lecture 1946), *Modern Quarterly*, 1, 3 (Summer 1946), pp. 3–19.

1.11 The genius of Stalin

Dutt's certitude concerning Marxist science was always accompanied by great flexibility in its application, as his devotion to the twists and turns of Soviet policies attested. Here it takes the form of adulation of Stalin, the greatest master of Marxism in Dutt's estimation, who died on 5 March, just days before the publication of this piece.

'The teachings of Marxism are all-powerful because they are true'. Lenin [...]

Today Marxism ... leads one third of the world; and its close approaching victory throughout the world is universally foreseen, whether with hope or fear, by friend or foe ... It demonstrates that this first all-embracing world science, this unity of science and practice, which is Marxism ... is a new constructive force in the world today which can solve, and is in process of solving, all the old problems – of poverty, ignorance, war, racial conflict, social inequality, helplessness before nature – that have wracked humanity these thousands of years.

[...] Marxism, above all, precisely because it is fully objective science, because it understands the anatomy of human society, the role of classes and the struggle of classes, and therefore the role of the theoretical and political representatives and leaders of the classes in conflict, understands the role of the human being, the person, in the development of society ... Marxism is no textbook of ready-made formulas and recipes to be applied by fools. Marxism is a science ... and precisely because it is a science, and all the more because it represents the highest level of science, it requires mastery; and mastery implies a master. For this reason living Marxism finds its expression in the living person, and its highest expression in the 'greatest head' ... And it is testimony to the vitality of Marxism ... that this very moment of the seventieth anniversary of the death of Marx should have seen the birth of a new classic of creative Marxist genius in J. V. Stalin's *Economic Problems of Socialism in the USSR* [...]

R. Palme Dutt, 'Marxism After Seventy Years', *Labour Monthly*, March 1953, pp. 97–110.

1.12 Orwell and *Nineteen Eighty-Four*

In December 1954 the BBC broadcast a dramatised version of George Orwell's *Nineteen Eighty-Four* on television. By now the Soviet Union was widely regarded as a cruel totalitarian state, like the one depicted in Orwell's famous novel. The distressing scenes depicted in the televised version led to some public complaints that it was inappropriate viewing for a Sunday evening and provided the occasion for Harry Pollitt and R. Palme Dutt to make the following debating points in the controversy that followed.

You know the name. That of an author with a diseased mind who wrote diseased books. I remember this creature coming to my office with a letter of introduction from a famous author. It was to ask me to make arrangements for him to go to Spain during the civil war there. I asked him a few questions and it came out that he had been a sergeant with the Burma police. I showed him the door, and said, 'Nothing doing, copper'.

However, he got there, and landed where one would expect, with the Trotskyists of Barcelona.

He also wrote a book that was published by the Left Book Club called 'The Road to Wigan Pier'. It was a rotten book, full of insults to the working class, and I had the greatest pleasure in the world reviewing it, and I hope knocked the hell out of it.

Those who most praise his '1984' with its theme of terrible 'Big Brother', are precisely those who are licking the feet of their really terrible, ignorant, brutal and sadistic Big Brothers of the USA.

ORWELL, Harry Pollitt, in CP/IND/DUTT/ 08/16, and 17 December 1954 in *World News and Views*.

The most horrible tortures, exceeding anything in '1984', are going on at this moment in Iran and Guatemala. Not a word in the general press; not the hint of an echo by the BBC. Why suppress the facts of real tortures in order to expatiate on imaginary ones for an obvious political purpose?

[...] Authority has tried to force Orwell down the throats of the public, and the public has spewed him up. It is evident from the examples given that only a minority of the protests are consciously political. A few Labour party members have recognised in this travesty of socialism, drawn from an amalgam of war-time rationing and controls in Britain, big business racketeering in America, and the Nazi *fuhrerprinzip* and torture systems, the lowest essence of commonplace Tory anti-Socialist propaganda by an ex-Etonian former Colonial policeman ... the majority ... have merely found it filthy and disgusting.

CP/IND/DUTT/08/16, and *Manchester Guardian*, 22 December 1954, letter from R. Palme Dutt.

The philosophy of Orwell is that violence, lies, and torture can enslave humanity. This pessimistic thesis ... is not true, and it is a blasphemy against humanity ...

The ideas which Orwell depicts as dominating the world in 1984 reflect the ideas not of communism, of which he knew very little, but of present-day Western monopoly capitalism, whose outward manifestations he experienced with horror and loathing but without understanding either the cause or the cure.

CP/IND/DUTT/08/16, and *Manchester Guardian*, 5 January 1955, letter from R. Palme Dutt.

1.13 Democratic centralism

When Nikita Khrushchev's 'secret speech' to the 20th Congress of the Communist Party of the Soviet Union (CPSU) officially acknowledged what he called the 'crimes of Stalin' in 1956, the CPGB was thrown into a crisis which led to the loss of around one-third of its membership (see chapter 9). The organisation held firm to its founding principles, however, as revealed in the document below, which restates the doctrine of the Leninist party in much the same way as it was understood in the 1920s.

I. The Communist Party and the class struggle – why we need democratic centralism
The Communist Party exists to lead the working class and the working people in class struggle against capitalism [...]

The Communist Party is the vanguard of the working class. Its members are prepared to devote their political activity to the achievement of Socialism and Communism, and know that to do this it is necessary that political power should be in the hands of the working class and its allies.

To realise our aims it is necessary that they should become the will of the people. The people can be won for our policy only through the organised activity of the members of our Party. This activity determines the fate of our political decisions.

Because our policy expresses the class interests of the workers, it can only be realised through the struggle of the working class against the capitalist class.

Our Party has to be organised so as to be able to convince the workers that our policy expresses their interests, to help to bring them into action for their demands and to help them to victory.

The nature of this struggle necessarily imposes certain requirements upon the organisation of the Party.

The Communist Party has to be a unified political force, able to give leadership in all circumstances of the class struggle. Such unity and militancy are only possible if all members and organisations of the Party work together within the discipline of the Party.

The Communist Party needs a single leading centre, with an Executive Committee able to lead the whole Party and to influence the workers and the Labour movement.

The Communist Party needs strong and numerous cadres, responsible comrades continually growing in their experience of struggle and their understanding of Marxism-Leninism. Our cadres have to stand resolutely with the Party, and even in the most difficult situations, rally the whole membership for the struggle.

The Communist Party needs scores of thousands of members who are politically active and in close contact with the workers, knowing their views and needs, and able to explain our policy. Communists need to serve the working class in many ways and to win their confidence while at the same time clearly explaining the policy and aims of our Party.

A long and persistent struggle is necessary to build such a Party.

In this struggle has evolved the principle of democratic centralism, which combines democracy and centralism, both essential in our organisation [...]

Democratic centralism means: (i) That all members have the right to take part in the formation of policy and the duty to fight for the policy on which the Party decides. (ii) That all members have the right to elect and be elected to the leading committees of the Party, and to be represented at the National Party Congress, the sovereign authority of the Party. It decides policy, determines the Rules, and elects the Executive Committee, which between Congresses leads the Party. (iii) That all members have the right to contribute to the democratic life of the Party, and the duty to safeguard the unity of the Party. (iv) That the elected leading committees have the right to make decisions which are binding on the lower organisations. The duty of higher organisations is to consult to the maximum possible before making such decisions, and fully to explain the reasons for them. The duty of the lower organisations is to express their views before the decision is made by the higher body and to carry it out when it is made. (v) That all organisations and members abide by the Rules of the Party. That the obligations of membership and the discipline of the Party, voluntarily accepted on joining, apply to all members whatever their position. (vi) That decisions are reached by the majority vote, and the minority accepts the decision of the majority. (vii) That during discussion there is freedom of criticism and self-criticism, and that when a decision is taken it is the duty of all to carry it out. (viii) That higher organisations pay attention to the views and experiences of lower organisations and of the members, and give prompt help to solving their problems. (ix) That lower organisations report on their work to the higher organisations, present their problems and ask for guidance on matters requiring decision by the higher organisations. (x) That all Party organisations combine collective leadership and individual responsibility. (xi) That factional activity of any kind is not permitted because it destroys the unity of the Party. Some people suggest that Britain is different – here things are done in a peaceful and democratic way. Parliament decides, there is a strong organised Labour movement, so that the working class does not require an ideologically united revolutionary party organised on the principle of democratic centralism.

But the necessity for ideological unity and for democratic centralism arises from the character of the class struggle and does not depend upon whether there is peace or violence, or whether capitalist power is maintained by open dictatorship or screened by democracy. To defend its interests, the capitalist class has developed a centralised state power over which the working class has no control.

John Mahon, 'Report on Inner-Party Democracy' (extract from 25th Congress Report, CPGB, 1957), pp. 43–56.

Note

1 Wilkinson and Dutt both quoted in J. Callaghan, *Rajani Palme Dutt: A Study in British Stalinism* (London: Lawrence & Wishart, 1993), p. 34.

2

Defending the Soviets

The international authority of the Bolsheviks among Communists rested on the success of the Bolshevik Revolution and the intellectual and political leadership of Lenin. The Bolsheviks commanded a state – the only one in the world committed to socialism. Lenin's death in 1924 opened a power struggle within the party leadership that lead to Stalin's eventual dominance by 1928. Stalin's victory in this struggle indicated the strength of his support within the Communist Party of the Soviet Union (Bolsheviks), as well as the success of his ruthless methods in exercising control over the Soviet party-state. Foreign Communists, dedicated as they were to the defence of that state as disciples of the Bolshevik party, mostly rallied to Stalin. Those that did not were treated as enemies of socialism. First among these 'renegades', in the Communist view, were the followers of Leon Trotsky, who insisted on calling themselves the authentic heirs of Lenin, to the evident discomfort of CPGB loyalists. Trotskyists were persecuted inside the Soviet Union as Stalin consolidated his grip on the CPSU. But even after their complete removal from all positions within the party and state, Stalin embarked upon the physical elimination of his rivals – Trotskyists and anti-Trotskyists alike – in a series of show trials, which opened in Moscow in 1936. Former Communist leaders and colleagues of Lenin confessed to charges of conspiracy to overthrow the Bolshevik state in the service of foreign and fascist powers. By 1939 the Bolshevik Old Guard had been exterminated. Trotsky himself – exiled abroad since 1925 – was murdered in Mexico by a Stalinist agent in 1940.

These convulsions caused no great debate within the CPGB, much less a damaging split in the organisation. The British Communists remained unswerving apologists for the Soviet state and supported the ruthless measures taken against Stalin's opponents. As Stalin himself was increasingly promoted as a genius of socialism, British

Communists joined in the cult of his personality. In explaining this loyalty it is relevant to mention the financial support that the CPGB, in common with other Communist parties, received from the Soviet state. But it is also necessary to acknowledge the conviction prevalent among Communists that in the global struggle against capitalism and imperialism the Soviet Union was the only socialist redoubt and the only sure friend. Between the world wars democracy was in retreat and authoritarian regimes of the right were in the ascendancy throughout Europe. First among these forces of anti-socialism were fascist movements bent on the elimination of the left. World economic crisis after 1929 added to the sense of foreboding and capitalist decay. Stalin, who personally charmed Western visitors – even leaders such as President Roosevelt and Winston Churchill – as well as the foreign Communists who testified to his modest ways and sound judgement, was powerfully associated with the construction of socialism after 1928, in the age of the Five-Year Plans. His popularity inside the Soviet Union with wide sections of the population was real and foreign observers might easily imagine – as John Foster Dulles and Harry Truman did during the Second World War – that there must be much that was constructive about the Soviet state under Stalin for this to be the case. Communists were certainly predisposed to think so.

The fact that the Soviet state could be ruthless did not present Communists with a problem. Advocates of the revolutionary road had to be ready for violence and Communists had always been prepared to justify the measures taken by the Bolsheviks to hold on to state power, as during the civil war of 1917–21. But reports of mass terror in the construction of socialism, such as accompanied collectivisation of agriculture and the consolidation of Stalin's personal dictatorship, were dismissed as the fantasies of its enemies. When, in 1956, Nikita Khrushchev admitted to some of the truth about the levels of irrational violence and cruelty in the Soviet Union under Stalin it came as such a shock to many foreign Communists that their parties were thrown into crisis. Thousands left the Communist parties in the course of this crisis and some of them never recovered from it. Yet in Britain most Communists remained members and though loyalty to the Soviet Union was never again so unquestioning as it had been, open criticism remained a rarity. Years after Khrushchev many stalwarts of the movement could not or would not comprehend the scale of the Stalinist disaster and continued to regard the Soviet Union as an advanced civilisation compared to capitalism.

2.1 Basic faith

Harry Pollitt was one of the founders of the Hands Off Russia Campaign and its national organiser in 1919. He was general secretary of the CPGB between 1929 and 1956, with a brief interruption during the Second World War. Although the passage below is from a work of 1947, it reminds us that unconditional support for the Bolshevik Revolution and the state that it founded was at the core of Communist convictions.

[...] The thing that mattered to me was that lads like me had whacked the bosses and landlords ... These were the lads and lasses I must support through thick and thin ... for me these people could never do nor can do any wrong against the working class ... you cannot be a real Socialist and enemy of reaction and at the same time assist in any way to carry on a struggle against the Soviet Union ... however cunningly you try to pretend that it is 'only the tactics of certain Soviet leaders' that you are protesting against [...]

Harry Pollitt, *Looking Ahead* (London: Lawrence & Wishart, 1947), pp. 41–3.

2.2 First contact

In this autobiographical note Rajani Palme Dutt recounts his first contact with the Communist International and the reasons for his attraction to Bolshevism. Ellen Wilkinson was a founder member of the Communist Party but resigned from it in 1924; later that year she was elected Labour MP for Middlesbrough East.

[...] My first contact with the then newly founded Communist International was in December 1919 in Geneva. An International Socialist Students'

Conference had been called to resume the links from the old Socialist International which had been interrupted by the war. The invitation was addressed on behalf of the Swiss to our University Socialist Federation in very broad terms in the spirit of internationalism and unity [...] Accordingly it was decided to send a delegation of four, with a strict mandate of neutrality between Second and Third [Internationals]; I was appointed Chairman; Ellen Wilkinson was a member [...] the real purpose behind the smoothly broad terms of the original invitation was to establish an international Communist students' organisation associated with the CI [...] I had to explain our position that, while I was personally entirely for the CI, we in Britain had found it most useful to organise students on this unitary basis [...] as so often in international conferences there arose an 'English problem': in this case, whether to accept us in the proposed International organisation of socialist students or not. Accordingly that night a fraction meeting was called of the communist representatives at the conference to decide what to do with the English; we were allowed to be present as silent spectators [...] The pros and cons were weighed; our organisation and line was analysed relentlessly like a body being dissected on a mortuary slab; at the end the decision went against us. As we came away in the cold air of that December night (it was Christmas), Ellen Wilkinson said to me (and she had plenty of experience of trade union, Fabian, and Labour in-fighting): 'This is the most ghastly, callous, inhuman machine I have ever witnessed'. I said to her: 'At last I have found what I have been looking for: socialists who mean business'. Through all the return journey I pursued the argument with her on the principles of the dictatorship of the proletariat; we reached Paris at the réveillon or New Year's Eve, and all that night of the réveillon on the hotel balcony we continued the argument while the crowd danced below in the square; and by the morning she had promised to join the future Communist Party when it would be formed in Britain [...]

'Rough Draft of Some Experiences of the Communist International and the Period of Stalin's Leading Role', CP/IND/DUTT/01/01.

2.3 Trotsky's apostasy

Trotsky's rebellion was the biggest challenge to the leadership of world Communism from within the Communist Party of the Soviet Union. It was successfully contained, however, and – after prompting from the Comintern[1] – 'loyalist' responses were drawn from the CPGB, illustrating the extent to which the doctrine of unity and infallibility of 'the Party' had been accepted within the CPGB, just over four years since its foundation.

Why has Trotsky resigned his post in the Soviet government?

[...] For eighteen months Trotsky has been conducting a violent discussion with the leaders of the Party. The overwhelming majority of the Party has been against Trotsky, but right up to this day he refuses to acknowledge that he was wrong.

To-day, however, he sees that he has no supporters in the Party, and that he stands absolutely alone: in other words, that he has lost the Party's confidence. Therefore, he has offered his resignation as chairman of the Revolutionary Military Council, and his resignation has been accepted by the Central Committee of the Party.

What were the points of difference between Trotsky and the party leaders?

Nominally, the differences have been very many and various. In reality, they all reduce themselves to one. In the discussion of 1923, Trotsky advocated freedom to form fractions within the Party; the Central Committee said the Party must be single-minded, once it has thoroughly discussed its problems.

Trotsky said the Party must look upon its youth as its political barometer; the Central Committee said the Party, on the contrary, must give its youth a more thorough Marxist and Leninist training.

Trotsky set the 'rank and file' of the Party against the officials; the Central Committee tried to bring the officials and the membership at large closer together.

Trotsky demanded the adoption of an 'economic plan,' to guide the steps of the Party towards Socialist reconstruction for a period of years: the Central Committee declared that such a plan, in the changing and still unfathomed economic conditions of to-day, would either have to be scrapped in a few months, or must prove disastrous to real reconstruction.

Trotsky's supporters defended the Right Wing of the German Communist Party, who failed to take advantage of the revolutionary situation in Germany in October, 1923, and Trotsky did not open his mouth to disavow them; the Central Committee condemned the Right wing, and approved their removal from the German Party executive.

Finally, he has written a book this year purporting to be a history of 1917, but in reality devoted to belittling the part played by the Party as compared with Lenin (indirectly with Trotsky himself), and particularly to throwing mud at the present Party leaders. The Central Committee takes the view that this is a renewal of the attack upon the Party made last year, in defiance of the decisions of the thirteenth Party Congress and the fifth World Congress. On all these points the Central Committee has been upheld by the vast majority of Party members. But the Central Committee has pointed out that all these points reduce themselves to one, namely, an anti-Party, anti-Bolshevik outlook on Trotsky's part, which is no new event, and which springs from a petty-bourgeois intellectual psychology.

Why is Trotsky's present attitude no new event?

From 1903, when Trotsky helped to organise the first Menshevik fraction within the old Social-Democratic Party, until July, 1917, when he joined the Bolshevik Party, Trotsky was one of the bitterest enemies of the Bolshevik Policy and of Leninism [...]

Did Trotsky change his policy after 1917?

Trotsky entered the Party in July, 1917, and went through the November Revolution side by side with Lenin. During the next three years he made a great name for himself in history, and did splendid service to the Revolution, as organiser and inspirer of the Red Army. But even before 1923, already referred to, Trotsky deviated sharply, from the Party on two occasions of the highest importance.

One was in January, 1918, on the question of the Brest-Litovsk Peace ...

The second was in 1921, just on the eve of the new economic policy, when trade unions with the maximum of independence and mass support were required, and when Trotsky advocated the transformation of the Unions practically into State bodies [...]

What has been wrong with Trotsky all these years?

[...] Always and everywhere he has tried to play, some unique, extraordinary and entirely individual part, and he has always and everywhere shown the maximum impatience of collective discipline and control, the maximum unwillingness to admit his mistakes.

All these characteristics point to one source – the outlook of the petty bourgeois intellectual [...]

Why did our Central Committee condemn Trotsky's attitude?

[...] Those few comrades in our party who think that our Executive Committee should not have adopted any decision until it (or even until the whole Party membership) had become acquainted with the full text of Trotsky's book (instead of a summary as was actually the case) only show that they have a terrible deal to learn yet before they become real Communists, *i.e.*, class-conscious members of the revolutionary *political* Party of the proletariat ... But our Party will repel the attacks as our Russian comrades have done and are doing: and *it is to be hoped that any comrades who have made such mistakes will realise the anti-Communist, anti-Party, and anti-revolutionary path they have been treading, before it is too late,*

and before they have irretrievably reached the point at which it leads out of
the Party and out of the Communist International.

C. M. Roebuck (Andrew Rothstein), 'The Resignation of Trotsky', *Workers'*
Weekly, 25 January 1925.

2.4 Supremacy of the party

Another of the party's leaders, its Colonial Secretary Arthur Mac-
Manus, laments Trotsky's indiscipline and asserts the supremacy of
'the party'.

[...] The book is teeming with defects; not only does it fail to give an accurate impression of Lenin, but even as a piece of literary work it completely
lacks the usual brilliance of Trotsky, and is quite his weakest piece of work.
Hesitant, uncertain, undecided – one gets an uneasy impression of intense
nervousness in the compilation of the book. The outstanding failure of the
book, however, is the entire omission throughout of the Party. To present a
picture of Lenin and to ignore the Party, is to fail completely biographically.
The Russian Communist Party, more than anything else, constitutes Lenin's
real greatness. The Communist International is the enduring monument to
this greatness. More than anyone in the annals of our movement, Lenin was
the embodiment of the revolutionary party of the workers. More than any
other, Lenin appreciated and understood the role of the party. His genius
lay in appreciating the impossibility of a successful working class revolution
without an iron disciplined political party as its leader. His greatness lay not
only in perceiving this, but in his capacity to subordinate everything, himself
included, to the creation of that party. The real history of Lenin during the
period covered by this book of Trotsky, 1902–1917, is the history of the
building of the Russian Communist Party. Hence, therefore, I say that if the
purpose of the book was to give a portrait of Lenin in his genius, the book
is a complete failure. Lenin without the party is Lenin without his genius –
Lenin as he now is, in the Mausoleum in the Red Square [...]

Arthur MacManus, book review of *Lenin* by Trotsky, *Workers' Weekly*, 24
April 1925.

2.5 Napoleon-Trotsky

Trotsky is identified as a potential Napoleon, which for the Communists – great students of the French Revolution that they were – meant grave-digger of the revolution. The author – W. N. Ewer – was both a party member and foreign correspondent of the *Daily Herald*. Ewer was regarded as a Soviet spy by British intelligence but by the end of the 1920s he had turned against the party and the Soviet Union and became actively anti-Communist.[2]

[...] Postgate and Horrabin are displeased with me ... because in the *Labour Monthly* and in the *Daily Herald* I spoke my mind about that tragically bad book of Trotsky's on Lenin.

[...] Why is it that Postgate and Horrabin are ... so blindly devoted to Trotsky that any criticism of their idol has brought them out with bell, book, and candle against the critic? ... It is not because they have studied carefully the controversies in the Russian Communist Party and have come to the considered conclusion that Trotsky was right ... No. Their enthusiasm for Trotsky is based simply on the fact that they conceive him to be in revolt against the Russian Communist Party. And, having themselves resigned in pique from the British Party, they are thrilled to find Trotsky – as they fondly imagine – playing the same role in Russia.

They are furious that Trotsky should have been forced to resign his office. They demand apparently that he should have been allowed to continue, while a member of the Government, to launch attack after attack on his colleagues ... no executive organ can function if its members are carrying on open polemics against each other. It is not anything to do with 'Communist discipline'. It's just common sense ...

Trotsky disagreed with his colleagues, fought for his point of view, was beaten, and proceeded to campaign against them publicly. It was an intolerable situation that had to be ended.

[...] Postgate and Horrabin ... at once became 'Trotskyists', hoping, under the banner of his great renown, to damage the Communist Party [like] their analogues in Russia ... Disgruntled Bolsheviks, Mensheviks, S.-R's, even monarchists [who] began to look to him as the leader who would break the Party [...]

Trotsky was ... not aiming at becoming a Napoleon ... But events are apt to be too strong for men. Suppose that Trotsky ... had won. His triumph would have been a personal one. His power would have been a personal power ... And what in the world is that if not Napoleonism?

There, for those with eyes to see, was the tremendous danger ... Either

Trotsky must, at any cost, be disciplined; or he might, by reason of his very greatness, destroy the Revolution [...]

W. N. Ewer, 'Trotsky and his "Friends"', *Labour Monthly*, 7, 6 (June 1925), p. 373.

2.6 Soviet Communism

By 1930 the coincidence of world economic crisis and the beginning of rapid economic growth in the Soviet Union generated enormous interest in economic planning and collective ownership of industry and agriculture. The extracts below illustrate that pro-Soviet enthusiasm and the conviction that Western supporters of the socialist experiment were well informed and impartial. Sidney and Beatrice Webb, leading members of the Fabian Society, had enormous reputations as objective analysts and no record of uncritical admiration for the USSR, until the advent of the Five-Year Plans and the collapse of the second minority Labour government in 1931 converted them to a pro-Soviet outlook.

Soviet Communism, by Sidney and Beatrice Webb, review by R. Bishop
'Although Russia has become respectable and joined the League of Nations, exchanging its Ambassadors with all the major Powers of the world, it remains a land of mystery of which the outside world still knows remarkably little of a really tangible character'. So ran the editorial of a Lancashire newspaper [...]
    It is amazing how old legends linger on. To-day there is no country in the world of which more is known than the USSR [...]
    [...] 'Soviet Communism' ... is in the true sense of the word a masterpiece [...]
    The Webbs – the father and mother of Fabianism – are the last people in the world to be swept into unthinking praise of revolution ... Yet in this book they become positively lyrical about the fruits of the great revolution of October 1917. Not that they are uncritical – far from it. But with all their criticism, which there is no space to combat here, they arrive at the conclusion that Soviet democracy is true democracy, that Soviet progress is of a kind that the world has never witnessed before, and that it has only been possible because of the organised socialist planning on which it is based [...]

Left Review 2, 8 (May 1936), pp. 395–9.

2.7 Soviet science

J. G. Crowther was the Manchester *Guardian*'s first science correspondent, appointed by its great editor C. P. Scott. He was an
immensely industrious populariser of science who subscribed to the
argument that science would only properly flourish in a planned
socialist society – an argument associated with leading scientists of
the 1930s (and Communists) such as J. D. Bernal and J. B. S. Haldane.
Tom Wintringham achieved distinction as a military expert, both in
his writings for the CPGB and as an expert on street fighting and
guerrilla warfare.

Soviet Science, by J. G. Crowther, review by T. H. Wintringham
Mr. Crowther's book on Soviet science covers the organisation of scientific
work, and an outline of the work being done in physics, chemistry, applied
science, biology, and the history of science.
   [...] The account of the work of Soviet scientists shows that their conditions of work are becoming enviable, their achievements remarkable.
   [...] From [the] far edges of knowledge the book travels to the application
of science to industry, medicine, agriculture and heredity. It is impressive not
only in the amount of scientific work and scientific eagerness described, but
also in its clear picture of the influence of the Communists among scientists,
and the influence of science on the framing of the Five-Year Plans.'

Left Review, 2, 9 (June 1936), p. 470.

2.8 Soviet democracy

Once again a book acquires authority because it is reviewed favour-
ably by someone regarded as an expert, rather than a committed
Communist.

Soviet Democracy, by Pat Sloan, review by Sidney Webb
[...] Mr Sloan has done more than visit the USSR ... He has lived there for
six years on end, earning his living in a succession of salaried jobs ... he
describes how the Soviet worker lives and talks and works and plays. He
gives us the 'feeling' of Moscow's inhabitants, in crowds and as members of

families, as trade unionists and as co-operators, in factory meetings and at elections. I have read no book better fitted to make the reader understand what it all amounts to ... He knows, too, how to be quietly and effectively critical, both of some of the shortcomings of the Soviet Union, and of some of the animadversions expressed in works of greater pretension. This emphatically [is] a book to be read.

Left Review, 3, 6 (July 1937), p. 356.

2.9 Soviet culture

Lehmann was a poet and the founder of the immensely influential literary journal *New Writing* (1936–40), which served as an outlet for W. H. Auden, Stephen Spender and Christopher Isherwood, among others.

Prometheus and the Bolsheviks, by John Lehmann, review by Gore Graham
[...] Lehmann's informal investigations into the cultural life of the Georgian people provide some interesting examples of the application of the Leninist national policy in daily practice. Impressed by the vitality of the Georgian theatre, he declares that he was confirmed in his opinions – derived from a study of modern Georgian poetry and novels – that 'the Revolution had been the climax of a national as well as a class struggle, a fact which must have had a great deal to do with bringing the intellectuals over to the Bolshevik side and keeping the Georgian artistic tradition unbroken'.

Left Review, 3, 8 (September 1937), p. 495.

2.10 Trotskyist lies

Dissenting voices were dismissed as enemies of socialism, sometimes renegades from socialism as in the case of the Trotskyists. C. L. R. James was a Trinidadian Marxist resident in Britain in the 1930s and one of Trotsky's most gifted sympathisers.

World Revolution, 1917–1936: The Rise and Fall of the Communist International, by C. L. R. James, review by R. F. Andrews
[...] Mr. James is particularly eloquent, not so much about the errors of Lenin or the wickedness of Stalin, as about the political incompetence, ignorance, irresponsibility, imbecility and criminal disruption which distinguishes the dupes of Trotsky.

[...] It would be insulting the reader's intelligence, and the numerous testimonies as to conditions in the USSR, to deal with the grotesque picture he draws of life and conditions there – a picture which one would have to go to the *Daily Mail* to parallel. 'Starving' Soviet workmen, contact between the Red Army and the people 'abolished', the Young Communist League 'forbidden to take part in politics', the 'restoration of private property in the countryside' ... they are all there, all the old friends and phantoms, seeking to justify the Trotskyist policy of counter-revolution and apologising for its agents.

Left Review, 3, 5 (June 1937), pp. 291–300.

2.11 Moscow Trials

Again, it was useful that non-Communist observers could be invoked to support the Communist standpoint. Here T. A. Jackson, by reputation an independent-minded member of the CPGB, is able to invoke Walter Duranty, the American journalist resident in Moscow between 1921 and 1934, who was one of those non-Communists, now regarded as an apologist for Stalinism, whose views on Soviet Russia were taken to be objective in the inter-war period. The same could be said of Dudley Collard QC, a British lawyer who never belonged to the party but is now thought of as one its fellow-travellers.

Report of Court Proceedings in the Case of the Anti-Soviet Trotskyite Centre, Verbatim Report, review by T. A. Jackson
From the purely juridical standpoint little difference is made by the fuller details given in this verbatim report. It explains thoroughly why every trained observer of repute present at the trial – lawyers like Dudley Collard, journalists like Walter Duranty – was unhesitatingly and unreservedly convinced of the scrupulous fairness of the trial, and the unquestionable and entire guiltiness of the accused.

From the political, moral and aesthetic angles the extra details make a profound difference [...]

Politically, the extent to which the Trotskyite conspiracy was working upon a definite concrete programme is made clear beyond dispute. As is also the extent to which the conspiracy had become consciously as well as objectively allied with the vanguard of the counter-revolutionary bourgeoisie, and its instruments – Hitlerite fascism and Japanese Militarism.

[...] the war upon the soil of the USSR in the form of wrecking, disorganisation, conspiracy to murder, and preparations to ensure military defeat when circumstances made it possible to enter upon the stage of open military operations.

[...] All the romantic nonsense elaborated on the score of bogus confessions extorted by drugs or torture is annihilated by this report ... They confessed because they saw it was the only rational thing left for them to do.

[...] It all began in lack of faith: lack of faith in the ability of the Soviet Government to carry through its programme of Socialist construction ...

[...] [Trotsky] must lie, and lie, and lie; until all men know him and despise him for the contemptible thing he has sunk to be.

Left Review, 3, 2 (March 1937), pp. 116–17.

2.12 Meaning of the Moscow Trials

John Strachey was not officially a member of the CPGB and *Left News* was not one of the party's journals. Both, however, served the influential Left Book Club and, through this medium, promoted the Communist worldview. Strachey, Dutt once pointed out, was more useful to the CPGB in an independent role.[3] Certainly in reviewing a verbatim report of the 1938 Moscow Trials as an independent Strachey's views carried more weight than those of an open Communist.

The Soviet Trials, review by John Strachey

[...] For the first time it is possible to attempt an evaluation of the meanings of the Trials.

[...] It was a profound tragedy that the men who stood in the dock ... had engaged in a conspiracy to overthrow the Soviet Government ... But this does not mean that the Soviet Government did not have to arrest these men; or that it had any conceivable alternative, when they had told their stories, but to shoot them [...]

The above statements are based upon the authenticity of the confessions of the accused. I believe that no one who had not unalterably fixed his mind to the contrary opinion could read the verbatim report of the trials without being wholly convinced of the authenticity of the confessions ... it contains internal proofs of authenticity which cannot be doubted by any reasonable person who takes the not inconsiderable trouble to study the matter [...]

Two major questions arise from, and are resolved by, a study of the reports of the trial. First, why did the prisoners confess, and second, and more important still, why did they commit the terrible acts to which they confessed?

As to the first question, I should have thought that the testimony of the prisoners themselves as to why they confessed might be allowed to carry some weight. And several of them were at great pains to explain exactly what had induced them to confess. Let us take the cases of Rakovsky and Bukharin [...]

'[...] For three months I [Bukharin] refused to say anything. Then I began to testify. Why? Because while in prison I made a revaluation of my entire past. For when you ask yourself: "If you must dies, what are you dying for?" – an absolutely black vacuity suddenly rises before you ... There was nothing to die for, if one wanted to die unrepented. And, on the contrary, everything positive that glistens in the Soviet Union acquires new dimensions in a man's mind. This in the end disarmed me completely and led me to bend my knees before the Party and the country ... suppose by some miracle you remain alive, again what for? Isolated from everybody, an enemy of the people ... completely isolated from everything that constitutes the essence of it [...]'

Well, if you can read even these ... tiny extracts from the final speeches ... and still believe that it is all a put up job ... I am afraid that you are not a very good judge of men.

[...] there remains the immense question of why these men committed their crimes.

[...] Bukharin had come to the conclusion that not only was it impossible to build up a Socialist society in the Soviet Union, but that it *was* possible for the Capitalists in the rest of the world to restabilize Capitalism by working along Fascist lines [...]

[...] profound defeatism ... was the basic motif of all the conspirators' treachery.

[...] the conspirators reasoning was something like this ... we must retreat; therefore we must transform the Soviet Union into a State Capitalist, and rich peasant, community. Therefore we must make terms with the Fascists ... This is the only hope, in the present world situation, for our survival at all.

But, the conspirators continued to reason, Stalin and the majority of the Communist Party ... will not see all this; they will not retreat ... Therefore he must be got rid of ... and we must replace them in the Government [...].

[...] They were in close touch, generally through Trotsky, with the German and Japanese Governments [...]

Left News, July 1938, pp. 885–91.

2.13 Hitler–Stalin

If the Moscow Trials disconcerted Communist sympathisers, the Hitler–Stalin Pact added further strains to the Popular Front coalition, as revealed here by new divisions in the Left Book Club.

Marxism and Democracy, by Lucien Laurat (Gollancz, 7s 6d. Left Book Club Choice for November), review by John Lewis

Just a year ago the Left Book Club issued Leonard Woolf's *Barbarians at the Gate*. It was the Club's first attack on the Soviet Union and it marked a reversal of opinion and policy in its leadership. How fast and how far that leadership has fallen is apparent in the current choice, which is one of a score of similar revisionist anti-Marxist books all designed to show 'What Marx Really Meant'.

We are familiar with the method. Begin by paying a tribute to the greatness of Marx (in other words, show your forged credentials), proceed to damn the Soviet Union and end by showing 'true' Marxism to be some form of accommodation to capitalism and collaboration with Labour leaders and their masters, the governing class.

Both [John] Strachey, who writes a long review article in the *Left News* to accompany the book, and [Victor] Gollancz are constrained to demur at some of Laurat's conclusions and describe one section attacking the Soviet Union as 'deplorable'. This pretence at a discriminating judgment will take in no one. They manifestly approve the general tenor and fundamental positions of the book. It is not this one section, but every page of the book which attacks Soviet Russia, and not only Russia but Communism as such and everything Lenin said and did.

It is amazing that Gollancz and Strachey should only now discover these 'errors'. All that they said about Russia, about Lenin, about Marxism, about Communist policy, must now be withdrawn or heavily qualified. Their disagreement on the single issue of the war broadens into a repudiation of the whole Marxist position. Their criticism of the Soviet–German pact leads them on to the side of the enemies of the Soviet Union. [...]

Daily Worker, 27 December 1940, p. 6.

2.14 Pollitt's appeal

Having defended Stalin's purges and show trials of the 1930s British Communists were required to support the campaign against Tito and so-called 'Titoites', which Stalin waged across the whole of Eastern Europe after 1948. Here Pollitt justifies the Soviet line on Yugoslavia, after the country's eviction from the Communist Information Bureau (Cominform) in which it had played a leading role since its foundation in October 1947.

On the situation in the Yugoslav Communist Party

There can be no question that the resolution of the Communist Information Bureau on the situation in the Communist Party of Yugoslavia has come as a profound surprise to the Party membership of every Communist Party in the world, and also to the general political circles everywhere.

I want to make it clear at the outset that the presentation of our standpoint this evening in no way seeks to dampen down the enthusiasm which all of us have felt for the constructive achievements of the Yugoslav republic; nor will it be an attempt to weaken the bond of friendship between the people of Britain and Yugoslavia: rather, it will be an attempt to show exactly what are the political criticisms which some of the most responsible leaders of Communist Parties in the world have felt it necessary to make in connection with the Yugoslav situation. [...]

We also, in trying to assess the situation, have to remember that in all the principle issues that have been raised there lies behind the criticisms and formulations of the Information Bureau the vast experience of the Communist Party of the Soviet Union, which, since 1917, has time and again had to deal itself with such questions [...].

The last point of the resolution draws attention to the fact that the Information Bureau was in agreement with the main line of the letters of the Central Committee of the CPSU to the Yugoslav Communist Party; it expressed the opinion that the Yugoslav leaders were now setting themselves up against the Communist Information Bureau; it indicated that the road is one which leads to the splitting of the united Socialist front against imperialism, that it is a road which can lead to the betrayal of the cause of international working class solidarity, and it indicates that, from an international point of view the Yugoslav leaders have passed over to nationalism. The Communist Information Bureau condemns such a policy, and the resolution declares that the Central Committee of the Communist Party of Yugoslavia therefore puts itself and the Communist Party of Yugoslavia outside the family of fraternal Communist Parties, outside the

United Communist Front, outside the Communist Information Bureau.
[...]

Therefore I am appealing to you – do not be on the defensive on this question. Do not apologise for what has taken place. It arises out of a difficult and complicated situation. But take the offensive, explain and attack.
[...]

Extracts from speech delivered at an Aggregate Meeting of the London Communist Party members on July 7 1948. *World News and Views*, 17 July 1948, pp. 295–301.

2.15 Titoites and spies

As the extracts show the accounts of how leading Communists in Yugoslavia had always secretly worked for fascism became increasingly bizarre. Yet the conflicts of the Cold War were real enough and the world was divided into two hostile camps. For Communists there were still reasons for optimism about the future of socialism because Communist parties were in command in China from October 1949 and throughout Eastern Europe, while the Soviet economy continued to expand and Western capitalism was confronted with a growing anti-imperialist revolt in the colonies, client states and dependent territories of the 'Third World'.

[...] history was to pick up Laszlo Rajk from the filth and obscurity of Vernet camp and thrust a new role upon him. He was to be taken from his humble political intrigues among the Spanish [civil] war veterans and made once more into a police spy ... Rajk was to be returned to Hungary to continue his work for the police from there. And he was to be returned on the orders and with the indispensable help of Hitler's Gestapo ... Immediately on his return Laszlo Rajk did two things. He reported to police headquarters, and he got in touch with the illegal Communist Party ... He himself was interned by the police to [provide him with] cover ... And thus Rajk spent the grim years between 1941 and 1944 in the comparative comfort of a Hungarian internment camp.

Derek Kartun, *Tito's Plot Against Europe: The Story of the Rajk Conspiracy* (London: Lawrence & Wishart, 1949), pp. 26–7.

2.16 Betrayal of Yugoslavia

James Klugmann joined the CPGB at Cambridge in 1933. During the Second World War he was employed by the Yugoslav Section of the Special Operations Executive. He also worked for the United Nations Relief and Rehabilitation Administration in Yugolsavia after the war. He knew Yugolsav Communists personally and could be regarded as an expert on the country.

[...] in the course of the Second World War the group of Trotskyists and agents inside the Yugoslav Communist Party gained still more commanding positions, and disguising themselves as leading Partisans used their positions to get rid of those opposed to them ... By the end of the war, the Tito clique had become the direct representatives of American imperialism. In the Soviet Union the great conspiracy of the imperialists which began with Kolchak and Denikin continued with Trotsky and Bukharin ... And the work of Trotsky and Bukharin is continued by the Titoites. The Titoite clique serves western imperialism abroad as the MI5 and FBI agents serve it at home.

James Klugmann, *From Trotsky to Tito* (London: Lawrence & Wishart, 1951), pp. 78–9.

2.17 Anti-Semitism denied

Here Klugmann addresses the issue of anti-Semitism in the purges and repression sweeping Eastern Europe.

The use of labour spies and agents provocateurs against the Labour Movement is as old as the battle of capital and labour ... with the great Soviet victory in the war against fascism ... these methods of penetration and disruption were intensified still further.

[...] the United States became the centre of imperialist disruptive and subversive activity ...

[...] In 1945 Czechoslovakia was liberated by Soviet forces helped by a courageous Partisan and resistance movement [...]

[...] February 20, 1948, was the day that imperialism had fixed to bring Czechoslovakia back into the 'Western Orbit'.

[...] An armed putsch had ... been prepared and the assurance of Anglo-American military intervention had been given ... [but] ... the imperialist plot was defeated [...]

[...] Benes and the reactionary politicians of February 1948 were not the only instruments of imperialism inside Czechoslovakia ...

The reserves were above all the group of conspirators ... brought together ... by Rudolf Slansky, former General Secretary of the Czechoslovak Communist Party, acting as an intermediary for American and British imperialism and destined by them to become Czechoslovakia's Tito.

[...] The Slansky plot was the parallel of the Rajk conspiracy in Hungary, the Kostov conspiracy in Bulgaria and similar plots in the other People's Democracies.

[...] The conspirators were a hotch-potch of elements hostile to the Party who for some reason or another, in some way or another, had sold out and become agents of foreign imperialism ... [agents of] ... the French Sureté National ... Gestapo ... British Intelligence ... They included former Trotskyites, Slovak nationalists, and Jewish bourgeois nationalists [...]

[...] the imperialists tried especially to brand the ... regime ... and the ... Party with the accusation of anti-Semitism ... The pretext was that they had managed to secure as agents in their conspiracy a number of ... Zionists.

[...] the Zionist leaders have always aimed to separate the Jewish people from their natural allies, the Labour movement ...

[...] It was not therefore an accident that side by side with Trotskyites and with Slovak bourgeois nationalists ... Jewish bourgeois nationalists were drawn into the Slansky plot.

James Klugmann, 'Lessons of the Prague Trial', *Communist Review*, March 1953, pp. 79– 86.

2.18 Soviet economic dynamism

The perception of Communist strength derived from the apparent dynamism and growth of the Soviet economy, as much as from Communist military might or the spread of Communist ideas. This was particularly true until the mid-1960s and it was a conviction by no means confined to the Communists and their sympathisers. Many Communists and socialists persuaded themselves that the dictatorial character of the Soviet regime would be transformed democratically in the longer run because of an economic growth that turned illiterate peasants into a modern, urban and educated citizenry.[4] Thus confidence that the Communist project was worthwhile – despite all the human sacrifice it entailed – was heavily dependent on Soviet economic dynamism; and that was often exaggerated as it is here.

[...] The basic feature of the world situation as a whole is the extraordinary sharpening of the general crisis of capitalism ... This deepening crisis finds expression in:

A. The growth of the anti-imperialist camp
(a) The *USSR* has become the strongest world power, the centre and leader of the camp of peace which comprises one-quarter of the surface of the globe ... If peace is preserved the Socialist country will ... catch up with and overtake the most developed capitalist countries within 10–15 years. The standard of living of the working people of the USSR has already surpassed the standard of Western Europe.
(b) The *People's Democracies* ... add another 100 million people to the 200 million of the USSR ... Their industrial output in 1950 was already nearly 20 per cent of European output ... their rate of growth exceeded far the rate of all capitalist countries.
(c) The victory of the *Chinese Revolution*, the heaviest blow against imperialism since 1917 ... [and] the encouragement and strengthening of the national liberation movement throughout the colonial world [...]

'New Features of Imperialism after the Second World War: A Discussion Statement for Conference', Saturday, 6 October 1951, Marx House, Clerkenwell Green, CP/CENT/ECON/1/2.

2.19 Backward capitalism, advanced socialism

1959 was a year in which a Conservative government was returned to power – for the third consecutive time – with its leader, Harold Macmillan, cheerfully telling the voters 'You've Never Had it So Good'. But the Communists continued to be as unimpressed by British economic performance as they were convinced by the superior Soviet economic successes.

[...] During 1959 it appeared that, for once, Britain was enjoying a boom phase without the normal consequences of difficulties with the balance of payments and the external currency reserves [...]

[...] The economic developments of 1960 have demonstrated the temporary nature of the 1959 boom conditions. It is clear that there is a persistent tendency ... [of] oscillations of state policies between expansionary and restrictive monetary measures – expansion accompanied by inflation followed by anti-inflationary measures breaking the expansion.

[...] In the meantime the regular 8 to 10 per cent per annum growth continues in the Soviet Union and spectacular advances have been made in China. Comparisons between the two political (sic) systems are now commonplace – to the credit of the ... socialist countries [...]

'Socialist Growth – Capitalist Stagnation: The 1960 Report of the Economic Sub-Committee of the Communist Party', nd 1960, CP/CENT/ECON/5/2.

2.20 Reluctant apology

Khrushchev's denunciation of Stalin and rehabilitation of Tito as a true friend and Communist embarrassed Communist leaders. The extract below gives an idea of the reluctance with which Pollitt and other leaders of the CPGB acknowledged what Khrushchev had said, their own complicity in past deceptions now exposed for all to see.

We in the Executive Committee of the British Communist Party, were misled by evidence that is now stated to have been fabricated, and we now withdraw our previous attacks on Tito and Yugoslavia – including the statement made by myself at the London membership meeting in 1948 and James Klugmann's book *From Trotsky to Tito*.

Harry Pollitt, *World News and Views*, 1956, p. 248.

2.21 The trial of the two Soviet writers, Sinyavsky and Daniel

In February 1966 Andrei Sinyavsky and Yuli Daniel were sentenced to terms of hard labour for publishing satires about Soviet Communism in the West. Andrei Sakharov was among the Soviet academics who protested publicly against this return to Stalinism under Leonid Brezhnev. Western Communists also protested, but in the CPGB's case dissent was noteworthy because of its novelty rather than its ability to go to the root of the matter.

The trial and heavy sentences on the two Soviet writers ... have caused great concern among friends of the Soviet Union [...]

[...] The Soviet Press attacks on the accused before the trial assumed their guilt. So did the Tass versions of what went on in court.

Since no full and objective version of the proceedings ... has appeared, outside opinion cannot form a proper judgement [...]

The court found the accused guilty, but the full evidence for the prosecution and defence which led the court to this conclusion has not been made public.

Justice should not only be done but should be seen to be done.

[...] The handling of this affair has done a greater disservice to the Soviet Union than have the works of Sinyavsky and Daniel [...]

Press release from John Gollan, 14 February 1966, CP/CENT/STAT/2/3.

2.22 Jews in the Soviet Union

The Sinyavsky and Daniel case highlighted the persistence of anti-semitism in the Soviet Union. If Soviet citizens like Yevgeny Yevtushenko could combine loyalty to the Communist project with honesty about this – as in his famous and popular poem of 1961 'Babiy Yar' – and publicly protest against the trial, Western Communists could not remain completely silent.

From its inception the Communist Party ... has consistently campaigned against anti-semitism in any form ... showing how [all forms of race discrimination] arise out of class society and that the ultimate solution ... will be found in a classless socialist society [...]

The old Czarist Empire ... was the worst hot-bed of anti-semitism in the world ... When it was overthrown ... giant strides were taken in resolving the national problem and eradicating anti-semitism.

The crimes against socialist democracy between 1948 and 1953 had an adverse effect on Soviet Jews ... and retarded the process of eliminating all forms of discrimination.

[...] We welcome the measures taken in the Soviet Union since 1953 to redress the wrongs which arose in the 1948–1953 period ... [but] ... The Executive Committee ... considers that it is impossible to take the view that in the historically short period of less than half a century, every vestige of anti-semitism among the population could be eliminated. Remnants of anti-semitism remain amongst individuals as do remnants of other reactionary ideas and attitudes against which there is and must be continuous struggle.

In the light of this, the Executive Committee asks ... that the ideological struggle against the remnants of anti-semitism be improved; that greater care should be exercised ... to avoid impermissible crudities ... which could be exploited by anti-semites to further anti-semitism ... religious freedom implies facilities to obtain ritual articles associated with religious worship ... facilities for obtaining some such articles are still insufficient [...]

Press Release 24 May 1966, CP/CENT/STAT/2/3.

Notes

1 See document 14 in HMSO, *Communist Papers* (London: HMSO, CMND 2682).
2 See Victor Madeira, 'Moscow's Interwar Infiltration of British Intelligence, 1919–29', *The Historical Journal*, 46, 4 (2003), pp. 915–35, and 'The Open Conspiracy of the Communist Party and the Case of W. N. Ewer, Communist and Anti-Communist', *The Historical Journal*, 49, 2 (2006), pp. 1–16.
3 See Ruth Dudley Edwards, *Victor Gollancz: A Biography* (London: Gollancz, 1987), pp. 236, 229–37.
4 See J. Callaghan, 'The British Left and the Unfinished Revolution: Perceptions of the Soviet Union in the 1950s', *Contemporary British History*, 15, 3 (Autumn 2001), pp. 63–83.

3

The problem of social democracy

The Comintern was launched in 1919 at a time when the Bolsheviks still believed that a revolutionary situation existed across Europe and the CPGB was formed a year later, very much a product of this revolutionary optimism. It is clear that many of those drawn to Bolshevism were impatient with the gradualist and parliamentary approaches of the social democratic parties. Some of them were initially resistant to Lenin's idea that the Communists should fight parliamentary elections and take advantage of Labour's federalist structures by affiliating to the larger party and conducting the struggle for Communism within it. What they wanted to do was build independent revolutionary parties that would have nothing to do with reformism and elections. Lenin's views prevailed of course. Even though the Labour Party rejected the first perfunctory calls for CP affiliation,[1] the Communists renewed their application to join at intervals until Labour adopted a constitutional amendment in 1946 forbidding affiliation to parties with separate programmatic commitments. In the meantime Labour took measures to ban Communists from individual membership of the Labour Party and from standing as Labour candidates (1924); to prevent Communists being elected as trade union delegates to Labour Party meetings (1925); and to proscribe organisations that included CP members (1933).[2]

The instruction from Moscow in 1920 was to build a 'united front' with Labour and trade union activists. The idea was that the Communists would attract Labour supporters to common struggles and in so doing expose the pusillanimity of the Labour leadership and its one-eyed dedication to parliamentarism. This would enable the Communists to grow at Labour's expense as disillusioned socialists turned to the CP. The united front would not have been necessary if the Communists had been the mass party and Labour had lagged behind. But the roles were reversed and it was the Communists who were starved of support. Lenin was in no doubt that the Labour Party was led by traitors to socialism and functioned within the working class as an agency of the imperialist state.[3] But it attracted most working-class activists in left-wing politics and these had to be prised away from it. In 1923 the Communists turned their attention to building support within the affiliated trade unions with the same purpose. The National Minority Movement, as it was called, combined rank-and-file organisation and demands for a struggle for state power, with condemnation of the union leaders who refused to take the measures that the Communists deemed appropriate.[4] The idea that a mass Communist Party would emerge in this way was dropped only after the defeat of the General Strike in May 1926. From that time the dominant view in the Comintern was that the workers were rapidly radicalising while the reformist leaders were assessed as useless. In 1928 the Communists persuaded themselves that Labour politicians and social democrats generally were no better than 'social fascists'. This led the CP into a phase of isolation from which it only emerged with the adoption of the Popular Front turn in 1935.

The zig-zags in Communist assessments of social democracy continued after 1935 but a measure of stability entered into CP calculations from 1946 until the 1970s when the party's main industrial effort was placed on the promotion of Communist leadership in the affiliated trade unions, the better to influence, and eventually control, the Labour Party (see chapter 9). When the strike wave of 1968–74 failed to promote this outcome the Party was forced to think again but was unable to find a coherent alternative strategy. Bitter differences on this issue contributed to the factionalism and demoralisation that contributed to its demise in 1991. Throughout its existence the Communist Party was bemused by the contrast between a theory that insisted on its indispensability and a reality that marginalised it in the political affections of the British working class. But never was this starker than in the 1970s and early 1980s when the Labour Party at last moved to the left and the CP found itself largely superfluous to the process.

3.1 The Labour Party

The first two articles in this section are testimony to continuing differences within the Communist leadership over the question of how to regard the Labour Party and how to overcome it. The first, written by Dutt from his home in Brussels, expects workers to turn away from Labour in disillusionment and wants the Communist Party to be ready to receive them. The second, written by Murphy, a former engineering worker, argues that there is a long way to go before any such estrangement and in the meantime the Communists will grow in number by virtue of their close association with the Labour left-wing. The first expects the Communist Party to grow independently of Labour, the second envisages absorption of, even fusion with, the Labour left-wing in the process of mass radicalisation.

The collapse of the MacDonald Labour Government brings the British working class face to face with the question of leadership in the sharpest form ... The bourgeoisie is stronger and more united and compact than ever before. The working class is disorganised ... and wholly unprepared to meet the new offensive that is directed against them [...]

[...] the Labour Party ... has shown itself to be ... by the final episode of the Zinoviev forgery ... in open alliance with the bourgeoisie ... it must be obvious to every worker that any opposition that may be put up in the new period will only be a sham opposition of words in the parliamentary manner.

[...] Against the Trade Unions the bourgeoisie will certainly wish to carry through the legislation already promoted by the Conservative Party, for limiting the action of Trade Unions in politics, restraining picketing, and possibly limiting or delaying the right to strike in 'essential services' [...]

On the other hand ... The increase in the Labour vote makes clear that the workers are still firm and even advancing. They are not conscious of defeat [...]

[...] It means that ... the masses are moving forward to struggle, and ... the Labour Party is compelled by its whole character and position to place itself in opposition to them. The process of *separation* of the workers and the Labour Party ... is carried a whole stage forward in the new period [...]

Thus a position is reached in which it is demonstrably visible to the workers ... that the *only* possible path of struggle ... is the mass struggle outside of Parliament ... The workers are therefore *compelled* to seek for a new leadership ... In this way a process of differentiation begins, in which 'left' leaders come to the front, and are themselves subjected to the test of events ...

The role of the Communist Party must be made clear to the British workers to be not simply the role of a propagandist force within the Labour Party and the trade unions ... The remains of the 'left-wing' of the Labour Party conception must be wiped out [...]

The situation of the new period is obviously favourable to the development of the left ... the constitutionalists and parliamentarians will be all the more under a cloud, not only because of their visible impotence, but also because of the shadow of the Labour Government's record and their failure in the elections. The principal part will fall to those trade union leaders who had already begun to mark themselves as a nascent 'Opposition' ... and of the miscellaneous militant elements in the Labour Party. This left will now be brought to the test of events ... (Hicks, Purcell, Cook, Maxton, etc.) [...]

[...] This was the experience of 1919–1921 ... But because there was no revolutionary party ... the whole outcome of that period was a complete frittering away of the revolutionary energy of the masses [...]

Against this danger the only safeguard of the workers is the Communist Party [...]

'British Working Class After the Elections', R. Palme Dutt, *Communist International*, 8 (1924), pp. 13–35.

3.2 A mass Communist Party

The Comintern's perspectives of revolutionary opportunities in Western Europe were revised after 1921. In Britain, however, the Communists, since their foundation, had been instructed to get closer to the unions and the Labour Party and to build revolutionary groups within them by working closely with the non-Communist left. In the unions the National Minority Movement was launched in 1924 for this purpose. In 1925 a National Left-Wing Movement was announced by Communists working within the Labour Party. These initiatives were in their early days when Murphy replied to Dutt with this article.

[...] The problem yet to be faced is – how is this left-wing developing and by what means can the Communist Party become a mass Party.

[...] I believe [Martinov][5] is quite right when he urges us to help in the development of a Left-wing ... the majority of members of our Party have been members of the Labour Party continuously by virtue of our trade union membership and payment of the political levy. Had it not been for this fact, we would have stood no chance of fighting the Labour Party leaders effectively with so small a membership as we have at present. The fact of the matter is that there has been no real mass leftward movement in the Labour Party that could be harnessed to challenge the present leadership … Comrade Dutt sees the Labour Party from the newspapers as one reading from afar … forgetting entirely that the Labour Party is a mass movement of which *we are a part* […]

He assumes that the workers are already conscious of the weaknesses of the Labour Party leadership, are conscious that it is leading them to disaster … The masses may rid themselves of the MacDonald leadership, and those who carry the banner of Liberalism, but that does not mean the end of the Labour Party … but a stage in the differentiation process when the Labour Party is increasing in strength as the workers become more class conscious.

It is in the midst of this … process that our Party … grows from strength to strength … 'left' leaders represent this development … They are not our leading enemies, but the indicator of where friendship for our Party lies. Our concern is for the winning of the masses whose sentiments and aspirations these people are attempting to voice […]

[…] the fierce discussions raging throughout the Labour Party are *not* the signs of decay, but the manifestations of life and vitality … It is out of this process … that our Party … will grow to a mass Communist Party.

How?

By continuing our demand for affiliation … as an independent workers' Party … as a mass movement grows [it is] inevitably destined to be driven closer and closer to our Party […]

[…] If we vigorously attack the 'left-wing leaders' we attack the mass with a similar outlook and drive them away from the Party … The 'left' forces are coming nearer … our task is … to set before them the fact that they [need] … a party formed not simply for parliamentary and propaganda purposes, but a party with its foundations in the factories, its units the factory groups, its purpose to lead in strikes, demonstrations, elections and in every phase of the political struggle, culminating in the seizure of power and the dictatorship of the proletariat […]

[…] The working class is only at the beginnings of its … education. The Labour Party will grow in numbers and strength … We … fight against splits in the workers' organisations, and become the one Party fighting for united working class action … It is through this process and by these means that the mass Communist Party grows from the foundations of the Labour organisations of this country.

Extract from 'How a Mass Communist Party will come in Britain', by J. T. Murphy *Communist International*, 9 (1925), pp. 13–15.

3.3 Red Friday

Bolshevik hopes initially focused on Germany where the war ended with a revolutionary upheaval that gave rise to the Weimar Republic in 1919. The Communist Party of Germany (KPD) attempted to seize power in March 1921 and as late as October 1923 hopes were revived that the KPD could come to power imminently by insurrection. After the failure of this 'missed revolution' the Comintern's attention was drawn to Great Britain. It was not the size of the CPGB that attracted interest but the scale of the collision brewing between the employers, the state and the trade unions.

The deflationary economic policies pursued since 1920 and the employers' wage-cutting actions promised a conflict in mining and the possibility of a generalised dispute, which the Communists interpreted as class struggle with revolutionary potential. A major conflict in coalmining was averted at the last minute only when the Conservative government announced on 31 July 1925 that it would subsidise miners' pay for nine months and establish a Royal Commission to investigate the problems of the industry. This was dubbed 'Red Friday' and was widely seen as a mere delaying tactic for the collision to come. The Comintern's Moscow-based leadership consistently over-estimated the revolutionary potential of these events and some British Communists, as the documents here show, encouraged the error. The industrial conflict is characteristically linked to the bigger, deeper malaise of capitalism.

The direct clash between the British Government and the united Trade Union Movement on July 30, 1925, which resulted in the Government deciding to beat a temporary retreat and postpone the conflict, is the first act in a new series of struggles [and] ... has given impetus to the development of working class consciousness; and a period of intense preparation for future struggles now begins [...]

'Red Friday' is the name which has been given to the settlement of July 31st, 1925 [...]

The current process of 'Revolutionisation' in Britain has been analysed in the Fifth Congress [of the Comintern] ... 'Red Friday' is the first action in this process [...]

The clash of 'Red Friday' is one of a series ... during the past fifteen years ... these clashes ... represent a continuous and ascending series which must inevitably deepen and expand in scope until they culminate in open revolutionary struggle [...]

[...] [They] ... are the reflection of the accelerating decline in British economic conditions and the consequent growing divorce between British capitalism and the working class.

[...] the foundations of British capitalism ... are being increasingly undermined.

[...] financial supremacy passed to America, the already shaky industrial position could no longer be maintained in the face of shrinking markets after the war and the accelerated development of new industrial powers ... The pivot of policy ... after the Armistice was ... the restoration of the Gold Standard ... accomplished by 1925 ... but a heavy blow was dealt to British home industry ... there was stagnation for five years [...]

[...] Alongside the decline of home industry has gone an expansion ... abroad; the Industrialisation of India, consciously undertaken ... and the building of a new empire in the Middle East ... the development of the Empire ... not only weakens home industry, but inevitably develops the colonies along the path of independence ... [and] ... destroys the traditional 'standards' of the British workers.

[...] this [is expressed] in continual intensification of the economic struggle over wages ... But this struggle inevitably develops a more and more revolutionary character ... the workers ... are driven to more fundamental demands of nationalisation ... This process is the economic basis of 'Revolutionisation'.

[...] the new economic position of the industrial workers ... is most sharply and cruelly expressed in the condition of the miners ... Since the war the miners have become the revolutionary vanguard of the British working class.

After the defeats of 1921 and 1922 ... the Communist Party did heavy work ... throughout the trade union movement to re-rouse the fighting spirit ... visible in the rapid development of the Minority Movement ... started in the summer of 1924 and the strong establishment of Communist influence ... throughout every part of the trade union movement to-day ... The Second Conference of the Minority Movement in August 1925 gathered representatives of 750,000 workers.

[...] But ... the most characteristic difference which showed itself in 1925, as contrasted with 1921 ... [is] the fact that there existed ... the elements of a central leadership in the trade union movement.

[...] [although] it is true that ... the Communist campaign for the placing of the centralised powers of the whole movement in the hands of the General Council, pursued continuously over the past three years, was not yet successful ... The miners unreservedly placed themselves in the hands of the General Council ... On July 24th, on the summons of the General Council, a Special Trades Union Congress was held. The solidarity of the movement was declared behind the miners ... This was the turning point.

[...] through the direct intervention of the General Council, the common will of the movement had triumphed over the opposition to a United Front.
[...] The first lesson of Red Friday is ... the lesson of the power of working class solidarity [...]
[...] The second lesson ... is ... the necessity of effective immediate preparations for the certainty of future struggles.
[...] Unification is necessary, not only at the centre, but throughout the working class. This can be achieved on one basis – the factory Committees.

Extracts from 'Red Friday and After', by R. Palme Dutt, *Communist International*, 16 (1925), pp. 64–88.

3.4 1926

Even after the defeat of the General Strike the Communists continued to talk of an advancing mass radicalisation among the working class, which was said to be far advanced beyond the political ambitions and mentality of the Labour Party and trade union leaderships. Here the Comintern's representative in Britain, John Pepper (also known as József Pogány, born József Schwartz) realises that the Labour Party is still a rising force, however, and qualifies the revolutionary perspectives for Britain associated with the Comintern under Zinoviev's presidency.

[...] the General Strike and the miners' struggle signify a decisive turning point in the history of Great Britain.
[...] In domestic politics there appears a sharpening of class antagonisms hitherto unknown in England.
[...] The paralysis of coal production has its effect in the paralysis of heavy industry ...
[...] Stoppage of coal production, vanishing iron and coal production, a decimated textile production ... the British trade balance is becoming more and more unfavourable.
[...] The basic fact of the British situation is that the Government has lost its character of being 'above the battle' in the eyes of the broad masses. What was formerly only said by the Communists, that the Government is but a class government of the bourgeoisie, is now being repeated by the leaders of the Labour Party and also by the Liberal Party.
[...] For the first time the working class sees in surprise the skeleton of the

dictatorship of capital under the soft flesh and fat padding of 'democracy'. [...] The whole Conservative policy is now directed towards the offensive against the proletariat, towards smashing the Labour movement.

[...] The petty bourgeois masses which in 1924 went over to the Conservative Party are now beginning to desert the Conservative Party.

[...] [This] has not led to a growth in the prestige of the Liberal Party ... the General Strike and the miners' struggle have hastened extraordinarily the process of disintegration in the Liberal Party which has been going on for years.

[...] At the beginning of 1926 Sir Alfred Mond ... left the Liberal Party and joined the Conservative Party ... 'The only question today is Socialism versus Individualism, and the Conservative Party is a better instrument for the combating of Socialism' [he said].

[...] Another influential member of the Liberal Party, Hilton Young, likewise [said] ... 'I see only one chasm in our present-day politics. On one side individual liberty and prosperity based on constitutional methods. On the other side Socialism' [...]

[...] The influence of the Labour Party is growing. Its mass influence has been extraordinarily strengthened during the last six months.

[...] broad strata of the petty bourgeoisie are also beginning to see in the Labour Party the representative of their interests ... It intends to be reckoned with as not only a Party of the trade unions, but it would like to appear as a universal party of the broad masses of voters. This explains also the Labour Party leadership's expulsion policy against the Communists.

Differentiation in the Labour Movement

For some years we have been observing the crystallisation of a Left Wing in the British Labour movement ... tremendously hastened and intensified by the General Strike and the miners' strike ... The 'Left' leaders went over to the side of the Right Wing ... But millions remained on the Left, especially the masses of the Miners' Federation [...]

[...] This situation foreshadows two alternative possibilities. The first ... is that the bourgeoisie and its Conservative Government will try to smash the Labour Movement by force ... and thereby prevent a parliamentary victory and a Labour Party majority. This perspective would ... establish the Communist Party as a mass party [...]

Another possibility is ... for the Labour Party to win a decisive victory at the next elections.

The question of a second Labour Party Government would then become the question of the day ... A more powerful Left Wing has already crystallised ... it can only be a question of ... time before this Left Wing will transform itself into a Communist one ... under the direct leadership of the Communist Party.

The final struggle between the Labour Party leadership and the Communist Party for a majority of the Labour movement would begin.

Extracts from 'Britain's Balance-Sheet for 1926', by John Pepper, *Communist International*, 15 December 1926, pp. 5–13

3.5 The new phase

Between 9 and 25 February 1928 the 9th enlarged Plenum of the Executive Committee of the Communist International announced that the capitalist system was entering its final period of collapse. *Pravda* had already stressed the widening gap between the leftward moving working class and a rightward moving social democracy. For Britain these arguments were familiar fare since the General Strike. Here Dutt, an enthusiast for what would become known as the Third Period, is quick to call for a tougher independent stance, including candidates opposed to Labour at the forthcoming general election.

[...] In Britain [the] general situation ... takes on a special character and raises special problems because of the peculiar character of the Labour Party, which is at once the instrument of the reformist bureaucracy moving more and more completely to the right, and still holds the mass of the workers in its grip by its control of the mass organisations of the trade unions. How at once to maintain contact with the masses, and to realise the new and sharpened leadership required by the new period and the leftward movement of the workers, is the problem of the British Communist Party.

This problem takes on a specially urgent character with the approach of the General Election, which makes necessary the clear laying down of the Communist Party line and of its relation to the Labour Party [...]

1. The new phase of the British Labour Movement
The new phase which the British Labour movement is now going through, a phase of sharpening issues between revolutionaries and reformists, is the sequel to the victory of the bourgeoisie over the General Strike and the miners, their successful intervention in China and break with the Soviet Union, and their successful imposition of the Trade Union Act to bind and consolidate their control over the working class before the revolutionary forces grew stronger. The period since the General Strike up to the present

thus bears on the surface the character of a whole series of victories of the bourgeoisie and depression of the working-class movement; it is only below the surface that may be discerned the growing contradictions and insoluble problems of British bourgeois policy on the one hand, and on the other the growing unrest in the working class.

[...] In the face of ... extreme reaction, the leftward move of the workers, developing continuously in the past five years, has not been checked; on the contrary, all signs show that it is developing more deeply and with increasing power. The defection of the pseudo-left leaders so far from shattering, has helped to strengthen and clear the leftward movement. The cleavage between the reformist bureaucracy and the mass of the workers is deeper than ever before ... The new intensity and ferocity of the capitalist and reformist repression is itself evidence of the strength of the forces it is intended to repress.

[...] the strongest possible independent political leadership of the Communist Party becomes of ever more essential importance to save the working class from being dragged as a body in the wake of reactionary imperialist politics, to raise ever more clearly the banner of the only possible alternative leadership to the Labour Party reactionaries, and so to carry the movement a stage forward in place of the stagnation and decay threatened by the reformist machine discipline.

But the realisation of this independent political leadership raises the question under present conditions of a new stage in the Party line. Up to the present, our Party, while maintaining criticism of the reformist leadership both within the Labour Party and in general agitation and propaganda, has refrained from directly fighting this leadership in the political field, has left them a free field at elections and advocated support, has endeavoured to secure the adoption of Communists as Labour candidates, and in the demand for affiliation has expressed its readiness to accept the constitution and discipline of the Labour Party. This policy was based on the conditions of the early stage of the Party, on the stage of the development of the mass movement eight years ago, and on the conditions of the Labour Party as it was then.

[...] The question now arises whether the time has not come to advance to a new stage, a stage of direct and open fight against the reformist leadership of the Labour Party, while continuing to the maximum extent the policy of the united front from below with the workers in the Labour Party.

* * *

This question is made immediate by the General Election. The Labour Party will be running candidates in practically every constituency of importance ... Unless the Communist Party is prepared to fight official Labour candidates it will for practical purposes not be able to fight at all, and will not be a direct factor in the election. On the other hand, the running of

Communist candidates against official Labour candidates will undoubtedly mean in practically every case (since the British electoral system does not permit of alternative votes, second ballots or the like) that the division of the working-class vote will assist the open capitalist (Liberal or Conservative) candidates ...

[...] Between 1920 and 1928 a whole process of development has transformed the situation. This can be seen most rapidly from a survey of the position as regards the factors governing the situation in 1920.

First, the Communist Party has won a definite measure of mass support, on the basis of a series of years' systematic work in the mass organisations of the working class and participation in every aspect of the daily struggle. Its press has a steady circulation of over 50,000; through the Minority Movement it is able to influence a million trade unionists. Its problem now turns on the best means to organise this growing mass influence; and this problem will be found to turn on the necessity to advance from a secondary position to independent leadership. The primary task is no longer how to find a line of contact for the Communist Party with the masses, but how to strengthen its political leadership.

Second, the Labour Party has now advanced beyond the stage of the formation of a government, and the character of its leaders in office has been fully exposed. The primary task is now no longer to assist their advance to office in order that they may expose themselves, but to overthrow them on the basis of the exposure that has already taken place and is daily continuing [...]

'The New Phase in Britain and the Communist Party', by R. Palme Dutt, *Communist International*, 15 March 15 1928, pp. 130–40.

The reader interested in the CP's position on the Labour Party between 1928 and 1951 should now look at chapters 5 to 7 covering 'The New Line', 'Popular Front Communism' and 'The CPGB'.

3.6 The British Road to Socialism

The Cold War was exceptionally fierce in 1951 when the CPGB adopted a new programme committing it to a parliamentary and peaceful road to socialism. Written with Stalin's active involvement[6] the thinking that created the *British Road to Socialism* in some ways represented Soviet wartime aspirations for peaceful coexistence with the USA and Britain, but also Stalin's often-expressed conviction that the Bolshevik road was inappropriate in the West.[7] The Communists celebrated national roads to socialism and repudiated violent revolution. The Comintern had already been dissolved in 1943 as proof of Moscow's good intentions. Pollitt provided an early indicator of where this thinking was leading when he published *Looking Ahead* in 1947. Nevertheless worsening international relations between the former allies, culminating in the Korean War, complicated the picture. By 1951 the British Communists – anathematised as agents of a foreign power as never before – were, paradoxically, isolated advocates of broad coalition politics.

[...] The enemies of Communism accuse the Communist Party of aiming to introduce Soviet Power in Britain and abolish Parliament. This is a slanderous misrepresentation of our policy. Experience has shown that in present conditions the advance to Socialism can be made just as well by a different road. For example, through People's Democracy, without establishing Soviet Power, as in the People's Democracies of Eastern Europe.

Britain will reach Socialism by her own road. Just as the Russian people realised political power by the Soviet road which was dictated by their historical conditions and background of Tsarist rule, and the working people in the People's Democracies and China won political power in their own way in their historical conditions, so the British Communists declare that the people of Britain can transform capitalist democracy into a real People's Democracy, transforming Parliament, the product of Britain's historic struggle for democracy, into the democratic instrument of the will of the vast majority of her people.

The path forward for the British people will be to establish a People's Government on the basis of a Parliament truly representative of the people.

Such a People's Government would:

Break the power of the millionaire monopolists and other big capitalists by socialist nationalisation of large-scale industry, the banks, big distributive monopolies, insurance companies and the land of the large land-owners, and introduce a government monopoly of foreign trade.

Introduce a planned economy based on socialist principles aimed at fundamental social change.

Transform the existing unequal imperialist Empire into a strong, free, equal association of peoples by granting national independence to the colonies.

Make Britain strong, free and independent with a foreign policy of peace.

Break the political hold of the capitalist class by democratic reform, democratic ownership of the press, the people's control of the B.B.C. and the democratic transformation of the Civil Service, Foreign Office, Armed Forces and Police, the Law Courts and the administration of justice.

The essential condition for establishing such a people's power is the building up of a broad coalition or popular alliance of all sections of the working people: of the organised working class, of all workers by hand or brain, of professional people and technicians, of all lower and middle sections in the towns, and of the farmers in the countryside.

[...] The present leadership of the Labour Party is disrupting and demoralising the Labour Movement by its poisonous propaganda of collaboration with and capitulation to capitalism, and its betrayal of every principle on which the British Labour Movement was formed.

In order, therefore, to bring about a decisive change in Britain, the millions of workers in the trade unions, co-operatives and individual members' sections of the Labour Party will have to use their political and industrial strength to make it impossible for either the right-wing Labour leaders or the Tories to carry on their present pernicious policy. They will have to rouse all the working people and progressive sections for active struggle against the present policy of surrender to American political and economic interests, against the war preparations and the wars in Malaya and Korea, against the two years' conscription, the calling up of reservists, and the rearming of Germany and Japan. Such a struggle is also necessary to secure higher wages and salaries, more houses, schools and hospitals, the raising of benefits and pensions, and on all issues which affect the people. It is through this struggle that the unity of all workers by hand and brain, of professional people and farmers, can develop into a movement strong enough to defeat the rich and their defenders in the Labour Party and to ensure peace and a future for all working people. Because of this working class unity, the United action of all sections of the working-class movement – Labour, trade union, co-operative and Communist – is the vital need [...]

The British Road to Socialism (London: CPGB, 1951).

3.7 To defeat Social Democracy

Increasingly, Communist analysis in the 1950s emphasised the role of Labour's leadership – parliamentary and trade union – in corrupting the party. The implicit message, often made explicit, was the need for a Marxist (that is, Communist) leadership within the Labour Party – one that would emerge as the organisation was radicalised in struggle.

[...] With the First World War of 1914 and above all the October Revolution of 1917, the general crisis of capitalism began. The removal of a great area of the world from imperialist exploitation, the ever-growing national liberation struggles of the colonial peoples of the British Empire, the rapid growth of American imperialism and its increasing pressure on its chief imperialist rival – Britain, have led to a deepening crisis of British imperialism.

[...] more and more, the old positions of British imperialism have been *undermined*. Their capacity to buy off a stratum of the working class with bribery and concessions becomes progressively weakened ... the American loan and 'Marshall Aid' ... have partially offset the declining super-profits from the colonies; therefore the right-wing Labour leaders are the most abject quislings to America. *But the ideas of Social Democracy, which have grown up in decades of British capitalist development, do not melt away ... by themselves spontaneously or automatically. They have to be driven out by the experience of the workers themselves in struggle against capitalism and by long, patient and persevering ideological explanation.*

To lead this struggle for the defeat of reformism, of Social Democracy, is the task of the Communist Party, and today, when the material basis for Social Democracy is so deeply undermined, is the historic opportunity for developing this struggle.

[...] The right-wing Labour leaders in Britain sometimes boast that they are practical men, that they are not interested in 'high-faluting theories', that they solve problems as they come, unlike the rigid continental doctrinaire socialists.

[...] But this boasting of absence of theory, or contempt for theory, merely disguises the fact that Social Democracy, whatever form it takes, in its more Right or 'Left' varieties, is a form of the theory of the ruling class.

[...] The British reformist socialists from the early days of the Fabian Society, through Ramsay MacDonald right up till today, have taught that the working class would advance to 'Socialism' gradually and peacefully within the framework of existing capitalist society.

[…] The Social Democrats teach that the State is neutral, is above classes. […] Some of the Social Democrats pay lip-service to the class struggle but reject it in practice. Others deny it altogether. None of the Social Democrats accept the need for the dictatorship of the proletariat. Today the right-wing Labour leaders have come to the denial of the existence of classes.

[…] The Social-Democrat theoreticians teach that foreign policy is not a question of class policy but something that is above classes, that is 'national'. They therefore preach and practice 'continuity' in foreign policy, i.e. continuation by a Labour Government of Tory foreign policy.

From the very beginning, in an open or a more concealed fashion, they justify imperialism and colonial exploitation.

[…] The Social Democrats see reforms as an end in themselves, not as a part of the struggle for the ending of capitalism.

[…] The right-wing Labour leaders come out even more openly as the defenders of the decaying imperialist system and as the opponents of the new socialist world.

[…] They come out as the open defenders of the greatest and most reactionary imperialist country in the world – American imperialism – and of its policy of aggressive war in the Far East and against the U.S.S.R. and the People's Democracies. They renounce national sovereignty and accept the subordination of Britain to U.S. imperialism […]

[…] The successive Labour Party programmes more and more openly omit even the general expression of the aim of Socialism. Socialism is redefined as a moral and not an economic concept. The 'mixed economy', which is to consist of 80 per cent private capitalism and 20 per cent state capitalism, is more and more openly proclaimed as the Social-Democratic aim.

[…] The study of the theory and practice of Social Democracy shows that it is not some well-meaning but misguided trend within the working-class movement but in fact the direct means by which capitalist ideas and influence are maintained within the working class, the main agency by which the workers are held back from active struggle against capitalism.

Therefore, it is not possible successfully to develop the fight against capitalism, it is not possible to achieve working-class unity for this fight, without defeating the influence of Social Democracy in the British Labour Movement. The fight against Social Democracy is an essential part of the fight for working-class unity, the fight for peace and for Socialism.

[…] the greatest danger is not to make a clear distinction between the right-wing Labour leaders and the false doctrines that they preach on the one hand, and the masses of honest working people still under the influence of Social Democracy on the other. The increased struggle against Social Democracy, which the present situation necessitates, equally necessitates an increased effort to win contact, fraternal personal relations and united action with men and women in the Labour Party, trade unions and co-operatives. There is no contradiction in these two tasks. Communists know that the differentiation within the Labour Party will grow, that the rebellion of the masses against their right-wing leaders and their policy will intensify. They work in every way to aid and to speed up this differentiation, to help the membership of the Labour Party to understand that their right-wing leaders are following a path of catastrophe, to understand that united action with the Communists is necessary in the fight for peace, independence, democracy and living standards. To fail to make this distinction is sectarianism, and dooms all our efforts to failure.

[...] The fight to end the influence of Social Democracy in the British Labour Movement sharply puts before the British Communists the task always outlined by Marx, Engels, Lenin and Stalin, the task of fighting for the union of *Socialism with the mass Labour Movement.*

Social Democracy and the Fight For Working Class Unity (London: CPGB, 1951), by Central Education Department, pp. 3–16.

3.8 The way of advance

Communists could see that the key to power within the Labour Party was an alliance of the left-wing activists in the constituencies and the trade unions. Evidence that this was 'The Way of Advance' was supplied in 1954 by John Gollan, Harry Pollitt's future successor as General Secretary of the party.

[...] There has never been a period in the history of the Labour Party where there was not a 'left' movement. The enormous significance of the position now is that this struggle is taking place at a time of acute crisis in British imperialism and after the experience of six years of Labour rule.

This crisis of Labour policy is not the consequence of rearmament or the electoral defeat of 1951. It follows from the entire reformist right-wing policy and was already clearly visible in 1947 and 1948 [...]

[...] Broadly speaking, the struggle of the militant forces in the Labour Party and the trade-union movement [...] is a struggle to decide whether the Labour movement is to follow a militant, working-class socialist policy or continue along the lines of class collaboration and administration of capitalism. These are the issues which have repeatedly dominated successive Trades Union Congresses and Labour Party Conferences.

At the 1953 Douglas TUC these policies received two to three million votes and, at the Labour Party Conference, one and three-quarter to two million votes. And the outstanding new feature of the 1953 Margate Labour

Party Conference was the emergence of a powerful group of important trade unions with a vote of around one and a quarter million, including the engineers, electricians and railwaymen, in alliance with the majority of constituency parties. This alliance will grow and develop and is the key to the transformation of the situation in the Labour Party.

These new developments are causing the utmost concern to ranks of the official Labour and trade-union leadership, and in particular the latter.

[...] in the tradition and pattern established, above all by Ernest Bevin, the dominant right-wing trade-union leaders are in permanent association and collaboration with the employers, the capitalist state machine and the Government, whether it is Tory or Labour [...]

The threats of the Labour Party leaders, the expulsions and purges, bans and proscriptions have not been enough. The right-wing trade-union leaders, therefore, have increasingly resorted to the threat to split the Labour Party, to 'withdraw the Unions from the Labour Party if the left-wing forces will not capitulate [...]' This creates the dilemma for the right-wing leaders. They are looking ahead to the time when this expanding group of progressive unions, allied with the left forces in the constituency parties, could well win a majority in the Labour Party Conference.

[...] these leaders see the day approaching when the union vote in the Labour Party will prove a progressive force. Hence their dilemma.

[...] This then is a situation full of the greatest political possibilities [...]

John Gollan, *The British Political System* (London: Lawrence & Wishart, 1954), pp. 172–75.

3.9 Socialism in Britain

The second version of the *British Road to Socialism* was very much more reconciled than the first to the need for the Communists to find class allies and to work with the Labour left. Even though there was no practical prospect for the CPGB's affiliation to the Labour Party, it was still routinely invoked.

[...] The forces exist which, if united and determined, can guarantee victory. The workers in industry and agriculture, with their families, constitute fully two-thirds of Britain's population. The security and future prospects also of other sections of the people are closely bound up with those of the industrial workers. The great majority of clerical and professional workers, teachers, technicians and scientists, working farmers, shopkeepers, self-employed, and small business men, are victims of the reactionary policies of Tory big business at home and abroad.

A working class united in action for progressive aims will win the support of many of these professional workers, small business people and working farmers [...]

An alliance must be built up between the working class and these sections of the population, in the fight for peace and social progress, and against all attempts to maintain capitalism at the expense of the national interests. Such an alliance, headed by the working class, is an essential condition for the establishment of a real Socialist Government to build a Socialist Britain.

[...] There is no conflict between the Communist Party and the Socialist members of the Labour Party, trade unions or Co-operative movement. We all are working to end capitalism and win socialism. We all realise that it can only be achieved by the industrial, social and political struggles of the working class. Up and down the country, we work together in factories, streets, villages, in offices and at universities, fighting against policies we consider wrong, and for policies that will strengthen the movement and help the advance to socialism.

The Labour Party was founded as an alliance of all working class organisations, political, trade union and Co-operative, to fight for the common interests of the working class.

But when in 1920 a number of Left organisations, including the British Socialist Party which was affiliated to the Labour Party, merged to form the Communist Party, the new Party was refused affiliation to the Labour Party. By this step, and further bans and exclusions since, the right-wing leaders have sought to eliminate the influence of the organised Left in the movement, and to pursue policies which in practice have served the interests of British capitalism rather than the interests of the working class.

In spite of these measures, and of similar measures directed against Left opinion in the Labour Party itself, the influence of the working class policies put forward by the Communist Party has grown within the Labour movement. There is a widespread feeling of the need for a new militant and socialist Labour policy that will rally the movement against the class enemy. This is shown among both the trade unions and the Labour Parties locally, and their joint efforts have already succeeded in changing some aspects of Labour policy. The trade unions are the decisive force in the Labour Party, and every progressive step in the trade union movement strengthens the Left and progressive tendencies in the Labour Party.

But the Left in the Labour movement is still divided, and therefore unable to exert its full strength. It is in the interests of the whole movement to end this division.

In seeking to overcome the present divisions in the Labour movement, the Communist Party has only one motive – to strengthen the organisation

79

and class outlook of the movement, so that it uses its power as its founders intended.

The removal of the bans and proscriptions directed against the Communist Party is the first step in restoring unity to the movement. This could lead to further steps towards unity, including the possibilities of affiliation, and eventually of a single working class party based on Marxism when the majority of the movement has been won for the Marxist outlook [...]

The British Road to Socialism (London: CPGB, 1958).

3.10 A united party of the working class

Jimmy Reid introduced the third redraft of the *British Road to Socialism* to the 30th Congress of the CPGB in 1967, highlighting the problem of 'right wing social democracy' in relation to the question of how the party could 'contribute to the changing of the balance of forces inside our labour movement'. Reid was emphatically of the view that socialism in Britain would be democratic, pluralistic, devolved and parliamentary. But there was need for only one working-class party.

[...] A main aim of the left, socialist forces, is to end the domination of the right wing and its ideology in our Labour Movement. To unite and weld our great working class into the solid foundation for the wider popular alliance ... dedicated to the socialist transformation of Britain.

Implicit in our whole approach is that we Communists seek to advance to Socialism in company with all left, progressive, socialist forces.

[...] The unity we seek to establish is not confined to the immediate struggle, but is an alliance to go over into socialism, and will be the basis for the broad alliance of the British people.

[...] Our aim of socialism is shared by many members of the Labour Party and working class movement. With a common aim, we have a common interest in unity and the co-ordination of our efforts.

[...] In 1946 the constitution of the Labour Party was changed to rule out the future affiliation of our Party. For this reason we have not placed ... the question of affiliation as a campaigning issue [...]

[...] The mass base of the party is the trade unions, composed of workers whose elementary class interests conflict with the political aims of the right wing leaders.

Our Party ... plays a major role in the struggle for left policies in that movement [...]

As for our future association with the Labour Party, this will be determined in the course of the struggle. But we think it would be wrong to tie us to the view that it must be in the form of affiliation.

[...] The draft programme puts it correctly in terms of the developing left struggle breaking the right wing control ... A stronger Communist Party is necessary to facilitate this process.

Of course we also want to see the circumstances maturing which would make possible in this country a single united party of the working class based on Marxism [...]

Speech by James Reid introducing on behalf of the Executive Committee the redraft of *The British Road to Socialism*, at the 30th Party Congress 1967, CP/CENT/CONG/16/07.

Notes

1 See M. Durham, 'The Origins and Early Years of British Communism, 1914–24' (unpublished PhD thesis, University of Birmingham, 1982); R. Challinor, *The Origins of British Bolshevism* (London: Croom Helm, 1977).

2 See J. Callaghan, *The Far Left in British Politics* (Oxford: Blackwell, 1987), pp. 31–2.

3 R. A. Archer (trans.), *Second Congress of the Communist International, Minutes of the Proceedings* (London: New Park, 1977), volume 2, thirteenth session, 6 August 1920 'On Entry into the British Labour Party', pp. 183–4.

4 J. Hinton and R. Hyman, *Trade Unions and Revolution: The Industrial Politics of the Early British Communist Party* (London: Pluto Press, 1975).

5 Alexander Martinov, 'Lessons of the Elections in England', *Communist International*, 8 (1924).

6 See George Matthews' article, 'Stalin's British Road', *Changes*, 23 (September 1991), pp. 1–3.

7 See on this *The Diary of Georgi Dimitrov, 1933–1949* introduced and edited by Ivo Banac (New Haven: Yale University Press, 2003), for example pp. 13, 156–7, 271.

4

The British Empire

The Communists saw the Soviet Union as an anti-imperialist state at its foundation and in its subsequent behaviour. Lenin's *Imperialism the Highest Stage of Capitalism* (1916) provided the authoritative analysis of imperialism for the Comintern and the Bolshevik leader's conception of imperialism was in many ways the core rationale for a Communist movement separate from social democracy. British Communists learned at the 2nd Congress of the Comintern in 1920 that they were expected to actively promote anti-imperialism in the British colonies and dependencies, as well as at home.[1] In words, Communists struggled to bring British imperialism to the attention of British workers and to refute theories of imperialism, which gave it a conspiratorial or psychological foundation or which dressed it up in notions of trusteeship. They did this with propaganda and analyses of the Crown Colonies of Africa, as well as the Indian Raj, the Middle East and China and they devoted more space to these matters in their publications than any other socialists in the inter-war period. In deeds, they made attempts to seek out revolutionaries abroad and to found revolutionary groups, where possible, in Britain's colonies and dependent territories. India became the focus of these activities because it was at once the most important of Britain's possessions, both economically and strategically, and also the most receptive field for the Communist message. In the whole of Africa it was impossible to establish Communist politics anywhere outside South Africa and the Maghreb before 1945. National movements had yet to develop and the socio-economic foundations for effective intervention by the Comintern were often completely absent. The Middle East was little better, with Palestine and Syria partial exceptions. But in India a powerful nationalist movement arose after the First World War. The British Communists were required to assume responsibility for nurturing the Communist component of this national struggle in India itself.

Some British Communists eagerly took a special interest in India and developed an expertise in relation to it – such as the brothers Clemens Dutt and Rajani Palme Dutt; Shapurji Saklatvala, elected Labour MP for Battersea North in 1922 and again in December 1923; and Percy Glading, Ben Bradley and Philip Spratt who actually worked in India to establish trade union and Communist organisations in the 1920s. Members of the British party established organisational connections with exiled Indian revolutionaries in Berlin and set up agitational bodies in Britain such as the Workers' Welfare League of India and the League Against Imperialism.[2] Spratt and Bradley began work in Bombay in 1927 to establish trade unions among the textile workers and with a view to creating Workers' and Peasants' Parties (WPP) as legal cover for the Communist movement.[3] The wave of Communist-led strikes in 1928 and the creation of WPPs in Delhi, Meerut, Gorakhpur, Jhansi and Allahabad signalled the progress made. So did the police crackdown, which led to the arrests of 32 militants in March 1929 and the beginning of the Meerut Conspiracy Trial. The case lasted almost four years. Severe sentences were passed in January 1933, providing plenty of propaganda material for British Communists, as well as evidence of their activities on the subcontinent. Communism in India was ultimately strengthened by the trial.

Communist policy on the subcontinent was ultimately determined in Moscow and subject to the considerations of the factional struggles within the Soviet Communist Party as well as the perceived needs of Soviet diplomacy. But in the early 1920s there was considerable scope for individuals with apparent expertise to have a large say on both broad policy and its practical implementation. The Bengali intellectual M. N. Roy – an early Comintern authority on the Indian struggle – is a case in point.[4] But British Communists also developed their own distinctive views on India concerning the pace of industrialisation, the development of classes and the prospects for socialism.[5] Such independence of thought on these matters was finally suppressed at the 6th Congress of the Comintern in 1928. But day-to-day links between the CPGB and the nascent CPI remained important until after 1945 when a much bigger CPI emerged and India became an independent state.

Far more durable than the Comintern (which was dissolved in

1943) was the importance to the Communist ideology of the theory of imperialism that had supplied a large part of the rationale for the Comintern's existence. Under Stalin's guidance this was developed into a theory of the 'general crisis of capitalism'. This argument retained Lenin's theory of the necessity for imperialist wars, the super exploitation of colonies and the tendency of monopoly capital to stagnate within the advanced capitalist countries. But it added new emphases concerning the strength (and growth) of the socialist bloc and the rise of anti-imperialism in the colonies. There is no doubt that Communists expected that the loss of colonies would seriously weaken the advanced capitalist countries. When this failed to materialise, theories of neo-colonialism provided the explanation; though nominally independent, former colonies remained dependent in many ways on foreign capital and its institutions (such as the International Monetary Fund), which continued to hold back their progress. By the mid-1960s theories of neo-colonialism had begun to revise Lenin's original theory but, while often ingenious and illuminating, they could never recapture the simplicity or drama of the founding Communist perspective which envisaged the decay and overthrow of empire as an ingredient in the rise of socialism and the socialist movement.

4.1 Modern India

Founded in July 1921 under Rajani Palme Dutt's editorship (which he retained for the next 50 years) *Labour Monthly* was nominally independent of the CPGB and probably financed directly from Moscow.[6] From the beginning it concerned itself with world politics as well as the British scene. This was one of the first articles on India, reflecting the British Communists' argument that the subcontinent was rapidly industrialising, a thesis developed by Dutt in *Modern India* (1927).

There is a vague idea that India is an agricultural country [...]

But fifteen per cent of a population of three hundred million makes up a number of forty-five million people in India living by industrial and commercial activity ...

[...] there has now grown up an economic inter-relationship between Britain and the East which cannot be given up without disaster to the industrial workers of Britain ... The growing strength and demands of Labour in Great Britain created an interest for the British manufacturer to start manufacturing a limited amount of output in India. This in the course of years opened the eyes of the Indian bourgeoisie, who adopted modern industrialism for their own gain and in direct rivalry against the European concerns ... The European owner ... was soon reduced to the necessity of extending and consolidating his concerns in India ... He now finds that with a wise manipulation of his affairs ... he can obtain a controlling advantage over British Labour at home, by creating a rival cheaper group of Labour in India.

[...] The Dundee jute workers do not yet realise the urgent need of making the Bengal jute workers, as well as the Bengal jute growers, a part and parcel of the British Jute Workers' Federation, demanding a six-hour day and £5 a week minimum wages, whether the factory be in Dundee or Calcutta. The wages in Bengal jute factories are registered by the Government Commission at 14s a *month* [...]

[...] The British worker desires his wages to be increased and safeguarded ... if the Indian workers' wages do not rise appreciably, and the British wages aspire to rise continually, the Indian worker cannot be the customer of the British worker ... the neglect of effective working-class solidarity abroad has reacted ruinously on the home position of the workers.

[...] as the [First World] war developed ... definite measures were taken in 1916 to found in London a joint body of Indian and British Trade Unionists and Socialists (the Workers' Welfare League of India of London), with the definite object of bringing about a working connection between the workers of India and the workers of Britain in the same industries, and of demanding an approximation of legislative and economic standards for workers of both countries [...]

[...] [in India] the definite step was taken of establishing the All India Trade Union Congress. The first meeting of this congress took place in Bombay in the autumn of 1920 [...]

[...] the Workers' Welfare League of India ... has been duly accredited by the Indian Trade Union Congress as its representative [...]

[...] In Indian eyes the Amsterdam International is largely discredited by its imperialist associations; and at present the balance of opinion leans towards the Red Trade Union movement [...]

Shapurji Saklatvala, 'India in the Labour World', *Labour Monthly*, 1, 5 (November 1921), pp. 440–51.

4.2 Imperial responsibilities

While Saklatvala suggested in the previous piece that British workers could be out of a job if they neglected to make common cause with Indian workers, this article gives expression to the view that British workers were politically backward because enough of them benefited materially from imperialism. It is also concerned to drum home the Leninist lesson that anything that weakens imperialism is to be supported.

The Communist movement of this country has before it heavier responsibilities than the movement of any other country except, possibly, the United States. It has got to fight, not only the industrial magnate at home, but a tremendous imperial system which holds within its direct rule one-quarter of the human race ... for which Britain is the central citadel and arsenal [...]

[...] The British Empire is the knot which socialism in this country will have to unravel if it is to succeed.

[...] why is it that this country, which by all seeming should be the first and most socialistic in character of the whole working class movement, is actually weaker ... than any other important country in Europe?

[...] the livelihood of the workers of this country is bound up in that economic system known as the British Empire ... the ordinary worker ... is appreciably better off than the workers in other countries in Europe, and not least in revolutionary countries ... He feels that he has something to lose. He regards revolution as a hazardous experiment. And so, while ready to push to the utmost to better his share against the master class, he is not willing as yet to endanger the whole system.

What is going to change this position? ... It is experience ... The war has torn aside the veil for millions to reveal the ghastly realities of the system under which they lived. If that lesson is not enough, war will return ... on a more terrific scale, until the lesson is learnt.

[...] The masses that are subject to the British Empire are not yet fully proletarian in character ... But ... their consciousness of economic misery is supplemented by their consciousness of national or racial subjugation.

[...] for the purposes of the tactical struggle against imperialism, the point at issue is not between bourgeois and proletarian movements, but between revolutionary and non-revolutionary movements. This should be the determining factor in our attitude to Sinn Fein ... it has nothing to do with the development of Communism in the country concerned, which should be treated as an entirely separate question.

John Langland, 'Our Imperial Responsibilities', *Communist Review* (June 1921), pp. 4–8.

4.3 Blowing-up India

Saklatvala helped one the CPGB's more successful agents in India, Philip Spratt, by introducing him to a variety of contacts in Delhi, Aligarh and other places while visiting the subcontinent in 1927. Here Spratt recounts his early days working for the party.

[...] The British party is usually treated as negligible, but in fact, through its followers in the unions and its intellectual sympathisers, it has considerable influence. [...] Especially since the Nazis destroyed the German party and seamen's union, the British party has taken considerable part in organising the communist control of international communications through the seamen and dockers. Most important of all, perhaps, is the work of the British party in spreading communism in the colonies.

[...] it was not as an expert that I was sent to India. I was chosen because I was unknown to the police, and my job was to be that of a messenger and reporter [...] I was 24, with no ties, and in the full flood of enthusiasm for the cause. I jumped at it.

My principal messages were that the Communist Party of India should launch a Workers' and Peasants' Party as legal cover, and that members should get into the trade unions and obtain leadership of them [...]

[...] Early in December, 1926, Clemens Dutt took me to Paris [...] after two or three days of waiting about in deserted cafes, I left by the train for Marseilles on my own. There I boarded the P. and O. liner *Kaisar-i-Hind* for Bombay.

[...] Two British Communists had come to India before me. [...] I had met one of them casually in London. He was an engineering worker named Glading, who had come about 1925 and returned shortly without making any contacts. [...] Another I now met in Bombay. He was a Scottish coalminer named George Allison, who had been sent direct by the Red International of Labour Unions ... Allison was arrested ... on the charge of entering India with a forged passport. He was sentenced to eighteen months imprisonment and at the end of it was deported.

[...] When I arrived there were fifteen or twenty nominal members ... In Bombay there were four [...]

Some of these members and near-members understood the doctrine as well as I did, yet there was no activity ... I reported this to Dutt, and when Bradley arrived, at the end of 1927, he told me, in a tone of reproach, that my report had been taken as a criticism of Allison [...]

[...] In March, 1927, I went to Delhi for a session of the All-India Trade Union Congress. Under pressure from Allison and myself the communists had begun infiltrating this body [...]

[...] I returned to Bombay about August, 1927, and within a few days was arrested and put in jail, bail being refused ... they finally made up their minds to accuse me of nothing more than sedition, on account of a pamphlet entitled *India and China* which, following ... instructions, I had written and published [...]

[...] Soon after my release I attended a session of the A-I TUC at Cawnpore. This was a far bigger gathering than that at Delhi, and more communists and allies took part. The work was going ahead [...]

[...] The WPP was the only 'front' organisation in India in my time. We tried to infiltrate the Congress, trade unions, youth leagues, and so forth, and used deceit in doing so, but we did not normally deny or even conceal that we were communists ... The chief aim ... was to obtain 'legal cover' ... It was only incidentally that we deceived the public [...]

[...] There were many strikes in 1928, and members of the party ... contrived to gain the leadership of some of them. We also tried in a number of instances to bring about strikes [...]

[...] In Bombay the party group ... were highly effective, and they had the cotton mills completely tied up for five or six months. As a result, or so we heard, the Millowners' Associations of Bombay and Calcutta appealed to the Government to rid them of the nuisance, and the Government decided to launch a conspiracy case [...]

Philip Spratt, *Blowing-Up India: Reminiscences and Reflections of a Former Comintern Emissary* (Calcutta: Prachi Prakashan, 1955), pp. 28–49.

4.4 The Meerut Conspiracy Trial

The Meerut Conspiracy Trial heard evidence linking the British Communist leaders to subversion in India. Among the accused were Philip Spratt and Ben Bradley who had gone to the subcontinent in order to assist in the creation of Communist organisations. The author of this appeal to delegates at the 1931 Labour Party conference was Reginald Bridgeman, a former diplomat who left the service in 1920 after a visit to India converted him to the Communist view of imperialism. Though never an open member of the party, Bridgeman remained at the head of the League Against Imperialism throughout the twists and turns of Comintern policy – a sure sign that he felt himself to be under the party's discipline.

The British Empire

September 29th, 1931.

Dear Comrade,

For more than two-and-a-half years 31 members of the working class have languished in the tropical jail of Meerut, India, and according to our information, they will complete their third year in the jail. Of the accused, 3 are English comrades, the other 28 are Indian Trade Union and Labour leaders, and 5 of these were, at the time of their arrest, members of the Executive Committee of the All-India Trade Union Congress.

[...] It was during the Baldwin regime that the accused were arrested, 29 of them on the same night, in different parts of India, on the specially framed charge of 'conspiracy' and 'waging war against the King'. Their trial is the greatest state trial ever held in India, and it is remarkable in many respects ... The very place, Meerut, chosen for the trial, illustrates the determination of the Government to preclude a trial by jury, because there are no facilities for a Jury trial in this small town, which is over 800 miles from Bombay and 900 miles from Calcutta, and its recommendation would seem to be that all the arrangements there are of a primitive character, so much so that the judge has had to take down the whole of the evidence in the case in longhand [...]

It has been pleaded by the late Labour Government that the responsibility for the trial and for the procedure rested with the Baldwin Government [...]

Lord Irwin, who had refused to permit the discussion of the arrests of the Indian Trade Union leaders in the Legislative Assembly, staked his Vicereign on the maintenance of their trial. The Labour Cabinet, faced with the menace of the Viceroy's resignation, should they direct the trial to be dropped, decided that it should continue, and so preserved the continuity of the policy of Imperialist oppression.

In this Meerut 'Frame Up' which reflects the anti-combination spirit of the Trades Disputes Act of 1927, the dropping of its repeal in 1931, and has its counterpart in China in the recent smashing of the Pan-Pacific Trade Union in Shanghai ... the accused persons have been charged with 'Conspiracy together with others to deprive the King Emperor of his Sovereignty', and, inasmuch as the offence with which the accused are charged is punishable with transportation for life, it has been argued that they must clearly be dangerous persons and that therefore they should not be admitted to bail. The real political significance of the Meerut Trial can be gathered from the opening speech, of the Crown Counsel, the late Langford James, which was a violent diatribe directed not so much against the accused as against the Soviet Government [...]

During the period 1920–29, both the industrial working class and the peasantry in India, driven under the lash of wage cuts, rationalised exploitation, usury and exorbitant landlords, began to organise – with and under the leadership of the accused – against this brutal exploitation. During these nine years there were 1,739 disputes involving 3 and one-quarter

89

million workers, and the aggregate number of days of struggle amounted to 84 and one-quarter million. Of these strikes 783 were directly caused by attacks on wages; 141 related to bonus payment; and in nearly every one of them Trade Union Recognition was stipulated ... Despite the brutal strike-breaking methods of the Government, which used Gurkha troops against the strikers, not to mention the importation of Pathans, the workers were completely successful in 285 disputes and partially successful in 291 disputes.

The epic struggle was the six months of strike of 150,000 cotton-textile workers in Bombay in 1928 against 'speeding up' by means of the more-looms-per-weaver plan, and a 7 and one-half per cent reduction in wages. During this period the workers in face of great odds formed their own union – the Girni Kamgar Union – which, although not a bona-fide union in the eyes of Messrs. Citrine and Joshi, had 60,000 members according to the Government statistics. Ultimately the strikers were persuaded to return to work on the *status quo* pending a Commission of Enquiry (Fawcett Commission). In March, 1929, three days before the Commission made known its findings, the whole of the Executive of the Girni Kamgar Union was arrested, with others, on the charge of 'Conspiracy against the King' and despatched under armed guard to Meerut.

[...] The British Section of the League against Imperialism asks the delegates to the Scarborough Conference of the Labour Party, some of whom have tabled resolutions on the Meerut Case, to see that a full discussion of these resolutions takes place. We ask the members of the British working class to see that the action of the Labour Government in prosecuting Labour and Trade Union leaders in India is repudiated with the same determination that the workers in Seaham and the members of the N.U.R. have repudiated the action of Messrs. MacDonald and Thomas for their anti-working-class action in effecting national economies at the expense of the unemployed.

Always remembering that the Government of India is the Prosecution in this case and that the Secretary of State for India has supreme authority, not only over the Government of India and the Legislative Assembly, but over the Viceroy as well, the British Section of the League against Imperialism asks you to demand that the present Government shall unconditionally release all the Meerut prisoners, who after two-and-a-half years' imprisonment have had nothing proved against them, but who have already undergone a longer term of imprisonment than if they had been convicted of a well-proven charge of robbery with violence. We ask you to go back into every working-class organisation to interest our class in this 'case' and so create such an agitation that the Government will be forced to release these workers and thereby assist the Indian workers and peasants to vindicate their unconditional right to organise their own trade unions and working-class organisation against the exploitation and persecution of the workers which exist under imperialism.

Do not forget that Mr. Gandhi, although he did not include in his amnesty for all political prisoners the Meerut prisoners, some of whom had been his close associates as members of the working Committee of the Indian National Congress, and five of whom were members of the Executive Committee of the All-India Trade Union Congress at the time of their arrest, has explained to the unemployed workers of Lancashire that their poverty 'dwindles into insignificance' in comparison with the poverty and pauperism of the largest unemployed army in the world, the starving masses in India,

Yours fraternally,
R. Bridgeman,
Hon. Sec. British Section – League against Imperialism. 23, Great Ormond Street, London, W.C.1.

Open Letter to the Delegates to the 31st Annual Conference of the Labour Party at Scarborough, 5–9 October 1931 (Working Class Movement Library).

4.5 Meerut sentences

The Meerut case resulted in extremely harsh sentences as highlighted here by Percy Glading, one of the first British Communists to visit India with a view to promoting links with groups sympathetic to the Comintern.

[...] The sessions judge at Meerut has sentenced twenty-seven people to 175 years' imprisonment, and one other to life imprisonment. In passing sentence the judge ... stated:

> The International, from 1924, endeavoured to create a revolutionary situation in India by instigating and assisting Communists in India ... The methods included antagonising capital and labour and creating Workers' Parties [...]

[...] The charge against the prisoners is taken from the official statement:
[...] That there exists in Russia an organisation called the Communist International. The aim of this organisation is, by creation of armed revolution, to overthrow the existing forms of Government throughout the world and to replace them by Soviet Republics subordinate to, and controlled by, the central Soviet administration in Moscow.

That the ultimate objective of the said Communist International is the complete paralysis and overthrow of existing Governments in every country (including India), by means of general strike and armed uprising [...]

[...] The attitude of the Labour Party and the Trade Union Congress can be seen by the policy of 'continuity' pursued whilst they were in office ...

[...] the Secretary of the British Trades Union Congress ... covers up the callous tyranny and ... supports stark naked exploitation of the workers and peasants in India [...]

Percy Glading, *The Meerut Conspiracy Case* (London: CPGB, 1932), pp. 1–19.

4.6 The imperialist epoch and war

Here Dutt explains the nature of inter-imperialist conflict. It is a reminder that though he was writing at the time when the Popular Front against fascism was already Comintern policy, Communists had inherited a theory that regarded imperialist powers as equally bad.

[...] *The foreign policy of a given State is a function of its inner system of class-relations*, and not vice versa. The existing conflict between the imperialist Powers in possession and the 'dynamic' or challenging imperialist Powers cannot be understood except in relation to the dynamic of imperialism as a whole and its drive for expansion, which leads to the present insoluble problems and contradictions of inter-imperialist relations. The foreign policies and the wars of the capitalist States can be traced through three main stages, corresponding to the stages of capitalist development.

First, the epoch of mercantile capitalism, when the early capitalist forms were still breaking through the bonds of feudalism, when capitalist trading preceded the capitalist organisation of production, and the home market was still undeveloped; the wars of this period were mainly wars to overthrow the old feudal, local barriers and establish centralised States, or wars of colonial conquest, for trade and plunder, laying the foundations of early capitalist accumulation.

Second, the epoch of industrial capitalism, when the colonies were regarded as of doubtful practical value; capitalist production was organised, the home market was developed, and the mass production of cheap goods broke down all barriers; the wars of this period were in the main wars to establish the modern nation-States or areas of the home market, or exceptional colonial wars to break down special barriers to the free entry of goods, as in the British Opium Wars on China.

Third, the epoch of imperialism or monopoly-capitalism, when the colonial question becomes the central question of foreign politics and war, since each monopolist grouping strives to secure exclusive domination of the maximum area of exploitation, for the control of raw materials and markets, and for the export of capital. The continuous accumulation of capital seeking outlet, and expansion of productive power, and the limitations of consumption within the conditions of capitalist class-relations, with the consequent recurrent menace of depression and a falling rate of profit, lead to a continuous drive to expansion for new areas to open up and exploit, both as a market for the export of capital and for the accompanying export of goods, mainly production goods, railways, etc., and to a lesser extent consumption goods, and drawing in return raw materials extracted from the native population which is compelled by all manner of coercive means of the State power to labour for starvation prices. This whole process leads to the realisation of imperialist 'super-profits' or a higher rate of profit on the basis of colonial exploitation, and the corresponding development of the whole social structure of the metropolitan country on this basis. The accelerating advance of this process of expansion leads to the rapid division of the whole available world between the handful of imperialist Powers. Then, in the era of fully developed imperialism, begins the battle for the re-division of the world between the rising monopolist groups whose possessions do not correspond to their potential rate of expansion, and the monopolist groups already in possession of the maximum areas and subject populations. This struggle constitutes the theme of modern imperialist war, of which the first round began in 1914, and the second round threatens to-day. This ceaseless and perpetually renewed struggle develops continuously out of the conditions of imperialism. *The particular expression of this conflict at any given stage, the struggle between the so-called 'satisfied' and 'dissatisfied' imperialist Powers, between the so-called 'Have' and 'Have-Not' Powers, is only the reflection of the law of the inequality of capitalist development, and continuously arises anew out of each new 'solution'.* The Liberal pacifist theories of a peaceful solution of this struggle within the conditions of imperialism by a re-distribution of colonies, international control of colonies, freedom of access to raw materials, etc., arise from a failure to understand the workings of imperialism, and represent in the end the basically false assumption of the possibility of a static relation of forces between rival monopolist groupings of capital, developing at different rates, with different degrees of development of the productive forces, etc. In particular, they fail to understand the purpose of the colonial policy of imperialism, and break down because they endeavour to apply the conceptions of industrial capitalism, of freedom of buying and selling, to the conditions of imperialism or monopoly-capitalism, whose essential character is the striving for exclusive domination of a given area of exploitation [...]

What of the imperialist Powers in possession who find themselves con-fronted with the attack of the challenging Powers? Are they to be regarded as 'satiated' and therefore basically and permanently 'pacific' Powers? This is the theory of the apologists of British imperialism. But this theory fails to take into account that no imperialism is ever 'satiated'; the drive for expansion is ceaseless, if the possibilities are present. The simplest proof of this is the role of British imperialism before and after 1914 ... scheming ... to extend its influence in Persia and the Middle East, conducting mili-tary operations in Somaliland and Tibet, pressing forward policies of parti-tion and joint spoliation in China, preparing with extreme diplomatic skill the war against German imperialism, and crowning its victory in that war by absorbing another two million square miles of territory ... The only difference in the position of British imperialism, representing the Powers in possession, is that its problems of defending its already enormous posses-sions are more complicated, that any new war is therefore more hazardous for it and only to be undertaken with extreme care ... and that the type of war it is likely to organise, apart from minor colonial wars, will rather be a war of coalition to strike down a rising rival or menace before that menace is too strong. This is the maximum measure of the 'pacific' role of British imperialism [...]

R. Palme Dutt, *World Politics, 1918–1936* (London: Gollancz, 1936), pp. 181–4.

4.7 The problem of Pakistan

From 1942, while the Indian National Congress suffered repression for its campaign of civil disobedience, the Muslim League and the CPI were free to operate in British India. It was during this period that the CPI came out in favour of the Muslim League's demand for Pakistan, on the grounds that the subcontinent contained numerous incipient nations, of which this was one. Here Dutt expresses open opposition to this departure from previous Communist policy, but only in the most tortuous way consistent with the customary appearance of unity.

[...] In accordance with the plan inherited by the Labour Government from its coalition predecessor, and rejected by all Indian political organisations, the Viceroy, in association with the Cabinet Mission, after the completion of the elections in April, will enter into negotiations with the Indian political parties with a view to including their representatives in a new Executive Council and setting up the proposed 'constitution-making body' to draw up a new constitution for India.

[...] This political conflict will coincide with the grave and growing economic disorganisation, reflecting years of war and maladministration and the bankruptcy of the old governmental machinery, and the prospects of impending famine on a scale even more terrible than in 1943. The stormy conflicts in Calcutta and elsewhere, with government use of troops and firing, and the demonstrations for national freedom among the Indian armed forces, are a signal of rising tension.

[...] the election results so far available (the main provincial election results are still to come) ... reveal a considerable eclipse of minor sectional groupings, and the general tendency of the electorate to concentrate around the two main political organisations which stand for the aim of independence: the National Congress, the principal organisation of the national movement, with an overwhelming majority in all general seats, and an overall majority for the country as a whole; and the Moslem League, with a decisive majority in the special Moslem seats.

[...] both the Congress and the Moslem League proclaim the aim of Indian independence. But the Congress stands for a united India with a high degree of autonomy for the constituent parts. The Moslem League demands partition ... and insists that this must first be agreed by the Congress or granted by British imperialism before independence is conceded [...]

The growth of the Moslem League to a wide mass following among Indian Moslems is a recent development of the past decade. In the 1937 elections the Moslem League was only able to obtain 4.6 per cent of the total Moslem votes [...]

During [its] first three decades the Moslem League remained a narrow communal organisation, appealing mainly to the upper-class Moslem landowners ... The 1937 elections revealed its weakness. Its membership figures were never published.

What causes have led to its growth to a mass following in the recent period? Several factors may be distinguished.

First, the political ferment of the past decade has drawn new masses ... into the first forms of political consciousness [...]

Second, there have been tactical mistakes of the Congress leadership ... (election of Bose as President and expulsion of Bose; passivity during the imperialist phase of the war; policy of neither helping nor opposing the war effort; individual satyagraha; the ill-starred August resolution at the moment of the Japanese advance, followed by arrest of the leadership, difficult conditions of illegality and sporadic disorders, disclaimed at the time by the leadership and subsequently acclaimed as a national struggle) and neglect of social mass leadership in the war conditions of economic difficulty and famine ... weakening the appeal of a united national movement during this period.

Third, within the Moslem League there developed a younger radical section pressing a democratic programme against the resistance of the older reactionary leadership on top, and in certain districts and provinces, as in the Punjab and Bengal, conducting an active fight on social and economic mass issue [...]

Fourth, the wider mass extension of the national movement brought to the surface new forms of national consciousness reflecting the varied national elements of the Indian people; and in the case of those national elements, especially in North-Western India, whose religious faith was Moslem, the slogan of Pakistan reflected, albeit in distorted form, and gathered up this newly developing national consciousness. This clearer emergence of the multi-national character of the Indian people, with the advance of the national movement, had been foreseen by Stalin when he wrote in 1912:

> In the case of India, too, it will probably be found that innumerable nationalities, till then lying dormant, would come to life with the further course of bourgeois development.

[...] With regard to the six Provinces designated to constitute Pakistan ... it should be noted that the total population is 107 millions, of whom the Moslems constitute 59 millions, or 55 per cent [...]

[...] Is there any evidence that the majority of the population of these territories desire the establishment of a separate State of Pakistan rather than an All-India Federation? There is no evidence and can be none, failing the holding of a plebiscite [...]

[...] The demand for Pakistan was first adopted by the Moslem League in 1940 ... Mr Jinnah ... demands that the separation must first take place by the action of the British Government without consulting the wishes of the population. He further demands that any plebiscite must be confined to the Moslem 55 per cent of the population, which would mean that 28 per cent of the population (51 per cent of 55 per cent) could determine the issue for the whole population.

[...] the demand for Pakistan ... becomes a reactionary obstructive tactic which plays into the hands of imperialism to delay Indian independence and prevent a democratic solution of the Indian question ... This should not, however, blind us to the genuine national content behind the Pakistan demand.

The Communist Party of India has the credit of having first discerned in 1942 the genuine national element concealed within the Pakistan demand and explaining its measure of support among wide sections of the Moslems. The Report of G. Adhikari in the autumn of 1942 ... made this valuable theoretical contribution [...]

[...] Prior to this Report the Indian Communists, in common with the rest of progressive national opinion in India, laid the main emphasis on exposing the reactionary character of the Pakistan programme'.

[...] The Report of G. Adhikari brought out for the first time clearly the developing multi-national character of the Indian people ... and showed the political conclusions which must be drawn from this:

> Every section of the Indian people which has a contiguous territory as its homeland, common historical tradition, common language, culture, psychological make-up and common economic life would be recognised as a distinct nationality with the right to exist as an autonomous state within the free Indian Union or Federation and will have the right to secede from it if it may so desire ... Thus Free India of tomorrow would be a Federation of Union of the various nationalities [...]

The tactical reasons for this sympathetic approach to the supporters of Pakistan among the Moslem masses in order to win them for the united all-India national front are understandable. But there is some danger of consequent misinterpretation of the position of the Indian Communists as supporters of 'Pakistan' (meaning an idealised conception of Pakistan entirely at variance with the official programme of Pakistan put forward by the Moslem League), when in fact Pakistan means the official programme of the Moslem League as basically opposed to the programme of national self-determination put forward by the Communist Party.

[...] Hence it is essential ... to distinguish this from the reactionary official Pakistan programme of the Moslem League ... the Pakistan programme makes no mention of the varied nationalities recognised by the Communist programme ... The Communist Party calls for seventeen Constituent Assemblies, based on seventeen alleged nationalities [...]

Second, the Pakistan movement is not a federation of recognised national movements of nationalities. It is a movement of the Moslem League for the constitution of a Moslem State, with the determining factor as religion, not nationality.

Third, it is doubtful if it is correct to speak of 'Moslem nationalities' ... and the identification is dangerous and plays into the hands of Pan-Islamism.

Fourth, the Moslem League is not a national movement of certain nationalities occupying certain parts of India. It is a communal organisation organising Moslems as Moslems in all parts of India, just as the Hindu Mahasabha organises Hindus as Hindus [...]

[...] Congress-League unity is of vital importance at the present time in order to enable the India people to present a united national front and defeat the attempts of the imperialism to play on the divisions between organisations.

R. Palme Dutt, 'India and Pakistan', *Labour Monthly* (March 1946), pp. 83–91.

4.8 The partition of India

Dutt registers his opposition to the partition of India and is able to invoke P. C. Joshi, the CPI's General Secretary, in his support – the CPI having corrected its earlier advocacy of Pakistan in the course of 1946. Dutt visited India for the first time in March of that year and met with the Communist leaders in the course of his four-month stay. But if this episode is evidence of his influence it was among the last of such occasions. The CPI had become a mass organisation in an independent country, forced to make its own policy in the absence of any firm line from Stalin. In 1948 Joshi and Dutt were denounced as 'utterly reformist' as the CPI was steered towards an insurrectionist policy under the leadership of B. T. Ranadive.[7]

The Mountbatten Plan proposes the partition of India and the speedy transfer of responsibility ... to Indian Governments for the sections of divided India.

Formally, the Plan does not lay down the partition of India but ... in practice ... [it] means partition, including almost certainly the partition of the Punjab and Bengal.

The position of the Princes' States is left unchanged ... they can join either grouping or proclaim their independence and establish their separate relations with Britain ...

[...] on a very rough estimate Pakistan would represent about one quarter of India, covering mainly agricultural, feudal and industrially undeveloped, but strategically important territory ...

[...] This Plan ... has received the assent of the leadership of the major political organisations in India and in Britain ...

[...] On the other hand J. P. Narain of the Indian Socialists, and P. C. Joshi on behalf of the Indian Communists, have sharply criticised the Plan as involving the dismemberment of India, and as not representing a real transfer of power, and have opposed acceptance [...]

[...] Moscow Radio drew the conclusion [that] ... 'British ruling circles mean to maintain their economic, political and military positions in India, whatever her future constitutional structure may be'.

[...] Imperialism can no longer govern India in the old way ... Even the desperate attempts to divert the popular upsurge into fratricidal channels of communal strife have only deepened the crisis ... the Cabinet Mission Plan erected its entire structure on separating Hindus and Moslems in statutory fixed compartments of its so-called 'constituent assembly' and counterposing Congress and League in an uneasy balance of mutual impotence and antagonism. The resultant accentuated conflict spread the hell of communal violence through many areas of India.

[...] partition is a great evil for India. It represents no lasting solution, but contains the seeds of future conflicts. The delimitation of frontiers holds the possibilities of endless discords [...]

Partition ... encourages particularism, reaction and communal antagonism ... and provides a fertile ground for the disruptive intrigues of rival imperialist powers to gain a foothold in India.

[...] a solution of the multinational problem has already been powerfully demonstrated, not only in the case of the USSR, but more recently in the experience of the Jugoslavian People's Federal Republic. Such a union will undoubtedly prove the final solution also in India [...]

The working-class movement ... has alone ... maintained its ranks untouched by communal divisions ... The magnificent unity achieved through the All-India Trade Union Congress and the All-India Peasant Federation must not be broken.

[...] The international aspects of the new situation ... are of far-reaching importance ... Already ... Indian representatives in the United Nations, under the guidance of Nehru as Foreign Minister, have been able to take a courageous stand, independently of British reaction, over the issues of South Africa and Palestine. The combined leadership of the Soviet Union, India and the progressive democratic countries has even been able ... to rally a majority against the bloc of reaction represented by the United States, Britain, South Africa, etc. ... The world is looking to Indian representatives abroad to carry forward this progressive role [...]

R. Palme Dutt, 'The Mountbatten Plan for India', *Labour Monthly* (July 1947), pp. 210–19.

4.9 *The Crisis of Britain and the British Empire*

When he introduced a new draft of the party programme at the organisation's 30th Congress in 1967, Jimmy Reid invoked Dutt's magnum opus on British imperialism to explain Britain's relative economic decline since 1945.[8] Published in 1953 Dutt's analysis linked the future of socialism in Britain with the collapse of imperialism and continued to regard British economic problems as symptoms of a bigger, longer crisis of the imperialist epoch itself.

[...] The Empire remains the permanent unspoken assumption of British politics [...]

[...] the maintenance and protection of the vast overseas interests and spheres of domination of British finance-capital; the complex manoeuvres and myriad political forms in ceaselessly changing conditions to counter the challenging tide of insurgent national sentiment; the precarious balance of relations, economic, political, and strategic with the stronger advancing American imperialism; the deep-set hostility to the new triumphant world of socialist and anti-imperialist popular advance extending to over one-third of humanity; the conflict between the strategic requirements of super-rearmament for the maintenance of these interests and the limitations arising from inner economic decay – all these constitute the inner essence of modern British ruling class politics on the world arena [...]

This common foundation of imperialist interests is also the basis of the essential unity of official policy of the two ruling parties and their leadership ... this essential unity is repeatedly revealed on all major imperial and strategic issues [...]

[...] In the broadest sense the crisis has been endemic since the first world war. It manifested itself in the long depression, the loss of markets, the collapse of the pound and the advent of the second world war.

But since the second world war the crisis has taken on a peculiarly acute, switchback character ... it took the grim form of the Dollar Crisis and the Balance of Payments Crisis ... Then followed the Devaluation Crisis of 1949. By 1950 the Raw Materials Crisis, associated with the Korean War ... And by 1951 the Balance of Payments Crisis had returned.

[...] The crisis which is affecting Britain in so many and varied forms is not temporary or accidental. It is an integral part of the era of social change through which we are living ... On the broadest canvas, the crisis of Britain is only part of the general crisis of capitalism and imperialism, which has developed continuously since the first world war and the first victory of the socialist revolution in Russia [...]

[...] The special crisis of Britain and Western Europe is the crisis of the imperialist system, upon which the economy of these countries has been built up, and which is now approaching bankruptcy.

[...] the entire social-economic structure of these countries ... and the entire political structure of so-called 'Western democracy' ... have been built upon this basis. Imperialism has been the grand permanent assumption underlying equally Toryism and Labour Reformism, and finding expression in all the peculiar features of what is currently (and inaccurately) termed 'Western civilization', 'Western democracy', the 'Western labour movement' and the 'Western way of life' [...]

R. Palme Dutt, *The Crisis of Britain and the British Empire* (London: Lawrence & Wishart, 1953), pp. 19–24

4.10 Neo-colonialism

Britain and France had withdrawn from colonialism in Africa by the mid-1960s but leaders of the newly independent states complained of neo-colonialism exercised through the structures of economic power of advanced capitalism. Communists agreed with them.

[...] It was not so much a question of the formal granting of independence which worried the imperialists – though even that was a retreat which they would have preferred not to undertake; rather it was a determination to prevent, at all costs, the emergence of independent governments in Asia and Africa that would represent the most consistent anti-imperialist forces, and especially the workers and peasants. Where such forces were led by Communists, the counter-revolution was waged especially ferociously [...].

[...] it is evident that as far as motives were concerned, the Western powers had every intention after 1945 of re-establishing the essential pattern of colonial rule which had existed in Asia and Africa prior to the war. And for more than a decade they strove to that end. It was only the changed world situation and the strength of the national liberation movements themselves which compelled colonialism to retreat.

[...] It is in this new situation of dying colonialism that neo-colonialism appears as a major phenomenon in the world [...]

[...] In those territories such as Cuba, or North Vietnam, where working class power has been established, it has been possible to dig up the roots of imperialism and prevent the operation of neo-colonialism [...]

In a certain sense, neo-colonialism is not an entirely new phenomenon, Lenin pointed out that 'finance capital is such a great, it may be said, such a decisive force in all economic and international relations, that it is capable of subordinating to itself, and actually does subordinate to itself, even states enjoying complete political independence'. Lenin subsequently emphasised the necessity 'to explain to and expose [...] the deception systematically practised by the imperialists in creating, under the guise of politically independent states, states which are wholly dependent upon them economically, financially and militarily' [...]

[...] For the United States, the method of controlling a country without exercising direct political rule has been a long-standing one. For decades American imperialism pulled the strings in Liberia, determined its policies and ran its economy. The entire constitutional system was modelled on that of the United States.

It was above all in Latin America, however, that the United States fashioned and practised this tactic ... real power [...] resided firmly in Wall

Street and Washington, acting through a most fearsome and corrupt brood of dictators [...]

[...] The Western powers have understood that in this new epoch they can only have influence in the new states by operating via the new social forces which have been thrown up into positions of power by the national revolutions; and this means, above all, the new élite – the petty-bourgeoisie, the intelligentsia, the new administrators, technicians and military leaders, and the emerging indigenous capitalist forces.

If, as we have seen, the old system of colonial rule was, in essence, an alliance between external imperialism and local pre-capitalist forces, then neo-colonialism generally represents a new alliance, one between external imperialism and sections of the local bourgeoisie and petty-bourgeoisie [...]

Jack Woddis, *Introduction to Neo-Colonialism* (London: Lawrence & Wishart, 1967), pp. 28, 43–56.

4.11 Problems of independence

In 1980 Woddis, while invoking theories of neo-colonialism to explain Africa's ills, is now giving more emphasis to structural problems within the independent states themselves, not least the incipient multinational character of many of these states, as well as the diversity of the paths being taken after formal independence.[9]

If one looks back over the whole period since 1945 certain things stand out. [...] the most obvious fact is the rapid collapse of the old imperialist system of direct colonial rule which formerly saw the armies, police, judges and civil administration of the Western powers in direct control over vast regions of the world.

Secondly, one can clearly observe the very great difficulties experienced by these developing countries in following up the winning of national independence by liberating themselves from imperialist control and exploitation, and thus being in a better position to tackle the poverty and misery which is still the lot of so many of their citizens.

Third, despite these difficulties there has been the development of a process, especially in the last few years, of several countries passing over from independence to revolutionary changes which have challenged or, in some cases swept from power, dictators and social strata which have acted as imperialism's internal ally. The most obvious recent examples have been Iran and Nicaragua.

The fourth striking feature is the great diversity of the paths being followed by these scores of separate states which make up what is sometimes termed the Third World. The relevance of different national roads of development is not limited to Europe. Developments in, for example, Iran, Ethiopia, Nicaragua, El Salvador, Jamaica, Yemen, Grenada, Iraq, India and Tanzania indicate only too well the rich variety of circumstances, of political and social alliances, of forms of struggle, and of institutions and organisations which are emerging in these countries. They are in no sense following preconceived blue-prints or particular models of social revolution [...]

[...] The changes taking place in the Third World demonstrate very clearly that although the trend to put these countries on a new progressive path persists in one degree or another, it nevertheless encounters very great obstacles. These stem from imperialist legacies and continued imperialist pressures. They also stem from the nature of these societies and their stage of development. Yet many acute problems also arise owing to weaknesses within the ranks of the liberation forces, weaknesses which are themselves a consequence of the class character of their organisations and leaderships, and of their political experience [...]

[...] Firstly, there is the problem of ending imperialist exploitation and overcoming the distortions in the economy arising from years of colonial and feudal domination. This *economic* task, and the building of viable economies capable of beginning to overcome the poverty and social backwardness inherited from imperialist control, is, in a sense, the central *political* question facing developing countries [...]

[...] The exploitation, the robbery by big transnational companies continues, sometimes admittedly in new forms [...]

[...] Of course, economic backwardness, and the continued economic exploitation and robbery of the developing countries by imperialism, need economic solutions. But they cannot be solved by the elaboration of economic measures alone. Basically, it is not a technical problem but a political one.

To bring about basic economic changes from which the mass of the people will benefit, changes which mean real liberation from imperialism, and which help to open up a perspective of advance to socialism, it is necessary for there to be a state representing the power of the people, a state based on forces which have a concept of tearing up the roots of imperialism, a state with its sights set clearly on socialism [...]

[...] This raises another key problem facing the developing countries, namely, the lack of political power in the hands of the people, the lack of their direct involvement and participation in deciding their country's affairs, the lack of democratic organisation and initiative from below. It is not only that many developing countries have one-party systems which are based on a denial of democratic freedoms to the majority of workers and peasants (I am excluding from this argument the existence of one-party states where the single party is primarily the expression of the aspirations of the workers and peasants as, for example, in Angola, Mozambique and Guinea-Bissau).

It is not only that many developing countries are under military governments which permit the legal functioning of no political party at all or, at best, only that party (or parties) which they, the military, allow to exist. The fact is that even where many formal democratic rights exist there is often a 'paternal democracy', if one can use such a contradictory term, or a 'guided democracy' as Sukarno called it, in which the power of the people to decide questions of policy and the nation's course are very much restricted if not denied [...]

[...] In Africa the national question is particularly complex and pressing. There are over 40 independent African states, some with very small populations. Most contain a considerable number of different nationalities and ethnic communities [...]

[...] It seems to me that many of these African states are multi-national or, at least, in a very early stage of formation as a 'nation', with the continued existence of a number of different ethnic communities, separated by language, cultural patterns, history, 'tribal' or nationality loyalties and links. There is therefore a very complex problem facing many new states, namely that of uniting all these different communities within the frontiers of a single state and providing a stable basis for co-operation between them all [...]

Jack Woddis, 'Political Strategy in the Third World', *Marxism Today* (August 1980), pp. 9–14.

Notes

1 See J. Callaghan, 'The Communists and the Colonies', in G. Andrews, N. Fishman and K. Morgan (eds), *Opening the Books: Essays on the Social and Cultural History of the British Communist Party* (London: Pluto, 1995), pp. 4–22.

2 Jean Jones, *The League Against Imperialism*, Occasional Papers Series No. 4 (London: Socialist History Society, 1996).

3 Jean Jones, *Ben Bradley: Fighter for India's Freedom*, Occasional Papers Series No. 1 (London: Socialist History Society, nd, probably 1995).

4 See his articles and those of his wife Evelyn in *Labour Monthly*, February, July and October 1922 and February 1924. Also M. N. Roy, *The Future of Indian Politics* (London: Bishop, 1926).

5 See J. Callaghan, *Rajani Palme Dutt: A Study in British Stalinism* (London: Lawrence & Wishart, 1993), pp. 82–109.

6 Ibid., pp. 42–4.
7 Ibid., pp. 224–30.
8 Speech by Jimmy Reid introducing the third redraft of *The British Road to Socialism*, 30th congress of the CPGB 1967, CP/CENT/ CONG/16/07.
9 The argument is taken further by the independent Marxist thinker Basil Davidson in *The Black Man's Burden: Africa and the Curse of the Nation-State* (London: Times Books, 1992).

5
The New Line, 1928–35

The 'New Line' unfolded by the Communist International from 1928 was inextricably bound up in the consolidation of Stalin's political authority, a process completed by the end of the decade. In the Soviet Union, Stalin's faction was the ideological force behind the 'left turn' of the first Five Year Plan. This policy of mass collectivisation, ruthless oppression of the peasantry and vertiginous industrialisation was designed to eliminate not only the New Economic Policy, which tolerated vestiges of a market economy in the Russian countryside in the name of greater productivity, but also the rival political faction, under Bukharin, associated with it. The essential function of the 6th Congress of the Communist International, held in the summer of 1928, was therefore to impose a New Line on the global economic situation in synch with Stalin's vision.

Recent history, the Comintern announced, could be divided into three periods. The first period of 1918–23 was one of capitalist crisis and spreading revolutionary activity culminating in the consolidation of the Russian revolution and the establishment of the Communist International. The second period, 1923 to 1928, opened with the defeat of the revolutionary movement in Germany, and was defined by a partial stabilisation of capitalism and necessarily defensive strategies from the international proletariat. Contradictions in the capitalist system, ran the analysis, now heralded a 'Third Period' of economic destabilisation, inter-imperialist wars, possible attacks on the Soviet Union, and 'gigantic class battles'. This era of capitalist crisis and renewed revolutionary opportunity called for the rapid modernisation and consolidation of the Soviet economy and the decisive revolutionary leadership on the part of Communists throughout the world.

The New Line dictated that Communists outside the Soviet Union should break decisively with those former labour movement allies who advocated social democratic or constitutionalist policies. In a position that had first surfaced in the PCI in the early 1920s, it was argued that those who duped the working class with reformist ideologies were propping up decaying capitalism – considered to be mutating into fascism – and deserved to be denounced as 'social fascists'. Communist parties were to see themselves as the unique and true representatives of the proletariat, and alone should lead the new 'class against class' stage of revolutionary struggle.

In terms of the CPGB, this Comintern-sanctioned sectarianism brought to power a new leadership of Stalin's men, centred around theorist and hard-liner Rajani Palme Dutt – who optimistically shared the Comintern analysis of a new revolutionary mood in the British working class – and Harry Pollitt, a former boiler-maker and experienced industrial organiser appointed as party General Secretary in August 1929.[1] The CPGB's 11th Congress held in November of that year saw, in effect, a purge of the party old guard. A Central Committee comprising twenty-three new members was elected, ten of whom had held no previous office. The rapid promotion of this new generation, many from the zealous leadership of the Young Communist League, marked a decisive turning point in the party's history.[2]

The dominant mood of the 'class against class' period was a self-righteous and ultra-leftist isolationism adrift from British political realities but fuelled by eternal vigilance against the 'Right danger' of former and current comrades still mired in reformist assumptions. Harry Pollitt uncompromisingly called for 'war to the death' against the Independent Labour Party';[3] in the general election of May 1929 Communists applied the logic of the New Line and contested Labour seats. Even Pollitt's humiliating defeat, in which the wheels literally came off his campaign vehicle and he trailed former and future Labour Prime Minister Ramsay MacDonald by over 33,000 votes, failed to reorient the party.[4] Historians of communism in Britain have been rightly critical of a period – graphically characterised as one of 'drastic internal self-mutilation' by one commentator – pointing out that isolated political successes, such as the National Unemployed Workers Movement through which communists organised 40,000 members in the early 1930s, were those least in step with the New Line.[5]

Though the period was indeed one of delusional insularity in which Comintern projections rather than British historical realities shaped policy, the New Line's impetus to forge an independent political culture likely to generate radical working-class consciousness also jump-started some striking, if occasionally fanciful, initiatives.[6] The most enduring legacy of the class against class period was undoubtedly the party's *Daily Worker* newspaper, from hereon its public face. Launched in part through the indefatigably energies of rank and file activists on 1 January 1930 and edited by the journalistically inexperienced but ideologically dependable New Liner, twenty-seven-year-old Bill Rust, the paper crystallised the period's confident, independent mentality in the name of reflecting and promoting a Communist reading of the world.[7] The period also saw parallel developments in Communism's cultural sphere including education, with a spreading network of district schools and study groups.[8] From 1928 Communists came to control the British Workers' Sports Federation, an organisation that resisted the capitalist 'penetration' of sporting events and promoted worker-led activity independent from encroaching commercial circuits.[9] Emboldened by the New Line, some cultural activists came to advocate an aggressively and earnestly 'proletarian' mode of literature, while the small but burgeoning Workers' Theatre Movement performed a break with 'bourgeois' conventions of naturalistic theatrical representations in favour of experimental agitprop didacticism.[10] Communists also attempted to harness the medium of film to the struggle: workers' film societies were set up to screen programmes of Soviet films; alternative newsreels were created to counter the ubiquitous, capitalist news media.[11]

5.1 Comintern's New Line

The 6th Comintern Congress was held between July and September 1928. Delegates unanimously adopted its 'Theses and Programme', which formally implemented the New Line.

After the first imperialist war, the international labour movement passed through a series of phases of development, reflecting the various phases of the general crisis of the capitalist system.
    The first was the period of extremely acute crisis of the capitalist system, and of direct revolutionary action on the part of the proletariat. This period

reached its highest point in 1921, culminating on the one hand in the victory of the USSR over the forces of intervention and internal counter-revolution, and in the consolidation of the proletarian dictatorship and the establishment of the Communist International; and on the other, in a series of severe defeats for the Western European proletariat and the beginning of the general capitalist offensive. This period ended with the defeat of the German proletariat in 1923.

This defeat marked the starting-point of the second period, a period of gradual and partial stabilisation of the capitalist system, of the 'restoration' of the capitalist economy, of the development and expansion of the capitalist offensive, and of the continuation of defensive battles fought by the proletarian army weakened by severe defeats. On the other hand, this period was a period of rapid restoration in the Soviet Union, of important successes in the work of building socialism, and also of the growth of the political influence of the communist parties over the broad masses of the proletariat.

Finally came the third period, the period in which capitalist economy and the economy of the USSR began almost simultaneously to exceed their pre-war levels (the beginning of the so-called reconstruction period in the Soviet Union, the further growth of socialist forms of economy on a new technological basis).

For the capitalist world, this is a period of rapid technical development, and of the accelerated growth of cartels and trusts, one in which a trend toward State capitalism can be observed. At the same time it is a period of intense development of the contradictions in the world economy, operating in forms determined by the entire course of the general crisis of capitalism [...]. This third period, in which the contradiction between the growth of the productive forces and the contraction of markets becomes particularly accentuated, will inevitably give rise to a fresh era of imperialist wars among the imperialist States themselves; wars of the imperialist States against the USSR; wars of national liberation against imperialism; wars of imperialist intervention and gigantic class battles [...]

In determining its tactical line, every communist party must take into its calculations the given internal and external situation, the relation of class forces, the degree of stability and strength among the bourgeoisie, the level of militancy and the preparedness among the proletariat, the attitude of the middle strata, etc. The party determines its slogans and methods of struggle in accordance with these conditions, starting from the need to mobilise and organise the masses as widely as possible at the highest possible level of that struggle. [...]

When the revolutionary tide is rising, when the ruling classes are disorganised and the masses in a state of revolutionary ferment, when the middle strata are inclined to turn towards the proletariat and the masses display their readiness for battle and sacrifice, it is the task of the proletarian party to lead the masses to a frontal assault on the bourgeois State. This can be achieved by propaganda in favour of transitional slogans on a rising scale [...], and by organising mass actions, to which all branches of the party's agitation and propaganda must be subordinated, including parliamentary activities: among such actions are strikes, strikes combined with demonstrations, strikes combined with armed demonstrations, and finally the general strike, combined with armed insurrection against the State power of the bourgeoisie. This highest form of struggle follows the rules of the art of war and presupposes a plan of campaign, offensive fighting operations, and boundless devotion and heroism on the part of the proletariat. [...]

The proletariat of the Soviet Union controls all the decisive key economic positions; it is methodically squeezing out what remains of private capital in the towns, whose share in the total economy declined very steeply in the last phase of the New Economic Policy; the proletariat is obstructing in every way the expansion of the exploiting strata in the countryside which grow out of the development of a commodity and money economy; it is supporting the existing Soviet farms and promoting the foundation of new ones; it is incorporating the bulk of simple commodity producers among the peasantry into the proletarian system of economy, and so into socialist construction, by means of rapidly developing cooperative organisation, which, in a proletarian dictatorship where socialist industry plays the leading part in the economy, is identical with the development of socialism.

Sixth Comintern Congress: 'Theses and Programme', in Jane Degras (ed.), *The Communist International, 1919–1934: Documents* (London: Cass, 1971), II, pp. 455–6, 509–10.

5.2 The New Line in Britian

Founded in 1921 with Moscow's encouragement, and edited by key CPGB theoretician, Rajani Palme Dutt, *Labour Monthly* was a journal sharply attuned to Moscow's political mood. In this document Dutt uses his 'Notes of the Month' editorial to anticipate the contours of the New Line, formally adopted by the CPGB a year later.

The future of the Labour Party is the central question to-day, both of the British working-class movement and of the entire British political situation. In the General Strike the highest point was reached of the struggle of the working class, acting through the trade unions, to impose its will on society.

The failure of that attempt revealed the shortcomings of the trade union machine, and laid bare the dominating issue which no trade unionism can solve – the conquest of political power. Henceforward, a deadly blow is struck at the old trade union exclusivism and self-sufficiency: on the one hand the trade union bureaucrats are increasingly compelled to drop their airs of feudal independence and take refuge under the wing of the Parliamentary Labour Party leaders; on the other hand, the revolutionary industrialists are increasingly compelled to recognise the primary task of building a revolutionary political party. But at this point the Labour Party endeavours to stand forward as the medium of the new period, as the means of the conquest of political power through Parliament. [...]

How far is the Labour Party still serving as a means to draw and organise the backward masses of the workers into some elementary form of political expression, however limited, for their class? Or how far has a point been reached, with the development of the class struggle, with the increasing domination of the Right Wing leadership, and with the moving of the masses to the left, when the machine of the Labour Party has become primarily and overwhelmingly a means to hold back and stifle the political expression and advances of the working class, and to tie the workers as a body to corrupt reactionary politics, which a considerable mass-section of the workers has outgrown? In what way is the growing revolutionary consciousness within the working class to find political expression, in proportion as the avenues of expression through the Labour Party become increasingly closed to it through the tightening discipline of the reformist machine? And at the same time, how is this independent political expression, which is of paramount necessity in the present situation, to be most effectively combined with the task of propaganda and organisation within the wider masses of the Labour Party, as in the trade unions, to win them to a revolutionary consciousness and policy? It is obvious that on these questions heavy issues hang. Discussion of these questions is urgently important in all bodies of the militant working-class movement. It is obvious that the militant Left Wing within the working class and within the Labour Party will have to face these issues, and will not be able to maintain a permanently static attitude in the face of a rapidly changing process and situation, but will need to take into survey the whole line of development, and endeavour with clear eyes to see the future. [...]

The fight for independence only becomes real when it becomes the positive fight for revolutionary working-class politics against the whole reformist-democratic tradition of co-operation with capitalism. This is the stage to which the whole militant Left Wing needs to advance. It is necessary to cease looking backward to the dead (and largely imaginary) ideal of an old-time purity and independence of the Labour Party, and look forward instead to the revolutionary working-class future in which alone true political independence, only partly achieved in the transitional stage of the Labour Party, can become fully realised. It is necessary to go beyond a merely negative defensive opposition to the reformist Right Wing leadership, who are themselves continually taking the offensive and intensifying the fight against the Left, and instead to advance to the offensive against them. The revolutionary Left must lead. The workers cannot afford to lose the measure of hard-won independence in politics they have in the past gained at the expense of so many battles, by being now in the day of their growing strength dragged at the tail of the coalitionist Labour leaders into the support of capitalism and the stultification of all their fight. The duty of the guardianship of that independence lies with the revolutionary Left. In the political as in the trade union field, whatever the attempts of the reformist leadership at coalition and class-co-operation, the fight must go on. [...]

Rajani Palme Dutt, 'Notes of the Month', *Labour Monthly* (January 1928), pp. 5–22.

5.3 Class against class

Applying the logic of the New Line to electoral politics, the CPGB challenged Labour Party candidates in the general election of May 1929, and secured just 50,000 votes from twenty-five constituencies. In this section of the election manifesto, that decision is explained.

Our changed attitude to the Labour Party
Prior to the formation of the Labour Government in 1924, the Communist Party, although the leaders of the Labour Party were as treacherous then as now, advised the working class to push the Labour Party into power whilst sharply criticising and exposing the leaders of the Labour Party. To-day this policy is no longer possible for the following reasons. The situation of 1929 is entirely different from that of the years prior to the General Strike and the Labour Government of 1924. In the years immediately after the war the Labour Party, in spite of its anti-working class leaders, was forced by the pressure of the workers into action against the Tories and Liberals, [...]. The Labour Party also had not yet become a closely knit party with a single discipline. [...]

The Labour Government exposed the Labour Party Leadership completely. It proved the Communist Party criticisms to be correct. The 'Minority' Labour Government was nothing more than a coalition with the Tories and Liberals. The Labour leaders 'led' the General Strike only to betray it in the face of the challenge of the State. The General Strike raised the question of class power – which class shall rule in Britain. The Labour Party leadership of the General Council of the Trade Union Congress were against the struggle for power. They stood for capitalist power against working-class power. They co-operated with the Tories in the defeat of the General Strike, but from within. They denounced the General Strike and propagated against it. They developed the offensive against the Communist Party and the revolutionary workers who stand for the working-class struggle for power. [...] It is now no longer possible for the Communist Party or trade unions to bring pressure to bear on the Labour Party from within. It is a completely disciplined capitalist party.

The Communist Party, as the party of the working class, must of necessity therefore explain to workers in deeds as well as words the completely changed situation, and set before the workers the means of advancing to socialism.

These are the reasons for the Communist Party's exposure and denunciation of the Labour Party as the third capitalist party, and why it puts forward its candidates against the Labour Party and selects its leaders for especial challenge.

Class is against class. The Labour Party has chosen the capitalist class. The Communist Party is the party of the working class.

Class Against Class: the General Election Programme of the Communist Party of Great Britain, 1929 (London: CPGB, 1929), pp. 9–10.

5.4 The right danger

The Communist Party held two congresses in 1929, in the course of which the New Line and its key personnel were formally inaugurated. As well as mapping new priorities, this congress document gives a sense of the inner-party sectarianism and in-fighting unleashed in the process.

Independent role of the party

The Communist Party is the most resolute vanguard of proletarian class struggle. In the present period of capitalist rationalisation, of worsening conditions for already low standards of the working masses [...] the Communist Party is the only force capable of leading the working class in its daily struggle for elementary and vital demands, against the war danger, against preparation for a new redistribution of colonies and territory, i.e., against imminent danger of war, and for the liberation of workers' organisations from the grip of employers and the State. [...]

The Labour Party, notwithstanding its social composition, is a third bourgeois Party. [...].

The principal tasks of the Communist Party

The principal tasks of the Communist Party, in its independent class fight for the leadership of the workers, are to rally the workers for:

(i) The fight against the war danger;

(ii) The struggle in defence of the revolutionary movement in the colonies;

(iii) The fight for the independent leadership of the Party in economic struggles [...];

(iv) The fight for the trade union unity on the basis of democracy and the replacement of the Labour lackeys of the capitalist class by militant revolutionary leadership;

(v) To carry on its independent electoral fight against the Baldwin Government and the bourgeois Labour Party under the slogan of the struggle for the revolutionary Workers' Government. [...]

In carrying out its main political tasks the chief danger confronting the Party is the right danger, which results from an over-estimation of capitalist stabilisation, of the strength of the reformist bureaucracy, lack of faith in the activity and consciousness of the working-class, nationalism in the Party, excessive formalism in trade union work, failure to recognise that the bureaucracy will attempt to take away all trade union rights from Communists and left workers and to split the unions in which Communists have influence; unclear understanding of the independent role of the CP and in a half-hearted attitude towards application of the new Party line.[...]

The New Line: Documents of the Tenth Congress of the Communist Party of Great Britain, held at Bermondsey, London, 19–22 January 1929 (London: CPGB, 1929), pp. 77–8.

5.5 The *Daily Worker*

The *Daily Worker* was formally launched on 1 January 1930. This editorial article, from the first edition, outlines the vision behind the venture.

Daily Worker: your paper

Will fight social fascist labour government and lead revolutionary struggles

Fight and work and write for it!

To-day the *Daily Worker*, organ of the Communist Party and the voice of the entire working class, makes its first appearance. After years of persistent effort the *Workers' Life* has fulfilled its role and developed into a daily newspaper, the first working-class daily in the history of the British working class.

The publication of the *Daily Worker* is an historical achievement – the sharpest expression of the independence of the revolutionary workers from the influence of the Social-Fascist leaders of the Labour Party and trade unions and the surest proof of the determination of the revolutionary working class movement to carry on a bitter daily struggle against the triple alliance of State, employers and Social Fascist bureaucracy.

New methods of struggle

The *Daily Worker* has come out at this moment because the working class cannot go forward without it. The transformation of the economic and political life of this country ushered in by the mighty struggle of the General Strike is compelling the working class to change its forms and methods of struggle and to develop new organs of struggle entirely independent of and against the treacherous trade union and Labour Party leaders.

The *Daily Worker* is a new and powerful weapon of struggle which every day will give the lead to action, co-ordinate the scattered actions of the working class and develop them into a united and invincible class movement against the capitalists and their 'Labour' Government. [...]

A class paper

The *Daily Worker* will be a class paper of the struggle against the Labour Government, exposing its policy of starvation and rationalisation at home and bloody reaction and imperialist war abroad. The *Daily Worker* will show that every struggle, however small, must at the same time be directed against the Labour Government if it is to succeed and serve to rally other workers. Our paper – the paper of all the workers – will unite the struggles at home with the mighty revolutionary movement of the colonial masses who are dealing hammer blows at British imperialism.

The *Daily Worker* will be a paper for the revolutionary independence of the colonies because the colonial workers and the peasants are the strongest allies of the British workers and without this united front the overthrow of British imperialism will be only a dream. [...]

The *Daily Worker* will fight the danger of a new imperialist war, it will expose the war manoeuvrings of the Labour Government against the Soviet Union and mobilise the masses for the defence of the Workers' State. It will be the only paper to give the truth about the Soviet Union; it will have unrivalled sources of information about the life of the Russian masses and the marvellous achievements of the Five Year Plan for the construction of Socialism.

The *Daily Worker* will breathe the spirit of internationalism. From all quarters of the world the revolutionary masses will pour the news of their struggles into our columns.

The worst enemies

The capitalists and their lackeys will resort to every means and vile trick in order to smash us. The Labour Government will use all the resources of the State and the millionaire *Daily Herald* in order to smother the clear voice of the workers. [...] We are up against every conceivable difficulty. Our enemies are amazed that we have the audacity to begin and they do not think we will carry on. We are faced with the most highly organised Press ring in the world and surrounded by a mesh of regulations designed to preserve the monopoly of the millionaire Press. On every hand we meet with heavy costs despite our endeavours to run on the barest minimum.

To win out in this herculean task demands enthusiasm, energy, self-sacrifice and determination on the part of every reader.

We are confident and optimistic because we rely on the invincible class spirit of the workers. The slimy Press octopus cannot break us. We will go forward in spite of all. We are a *new* paper, with nothing in common with the traditions of Fleet Street journalism. The *Daily Worker* will be a co-operative production of all its readers.

It will be *your* paper, the paper of every worker. Our *Daily Worker* will be like a great family; every reader will be a member playing his part in making the paper strong and influential. It will be your paper, therefore write and fight for it.

Tell your mates about it, carry it into the factories and plant it there in that excellent soil. Criticise the mistakes we make.

Worker correspondents

The *Daily Worker* will be a paper of worker correspondents. There will be no room for professional truth stranglers. The network of worker correspondents will penetrate into the factories, mines and mills and bind the *Daily Worker* so close to the masses that it will reflect all their movements and feelings.

The *Daily Worker* has come out because thousands of workers generously gave their pennies and shillings; its continued appearance is assured because we know that we can reply upon the workers to continue their financial support. The Fund will be the barometer which will show the degree of our support amongst the workers. Every penny given to the *Daily Worker* Fund is a nail in the coffin of capitalism.

Unsigned, *Daily Worker*, 1 January 1930.

5.6 Class fiction

Occasionally the *Daily Worker* published short fiction; during the 'class against class period' this tended to advance ideas of a separate 'proletarian culture' based on Soviet models. Here 'A. P. Roley' – a pseudonym drawing attention to the 'proley' or proletarian authenticity of its creator, Manchester railwayman George Chandler – imagines the exploited class extracting its vengeance.

Humanity moving
Clack, clack, clackerty, clackerty. The clogs and heavy boots ring out their rhythmic chorus as the river of industrial humanity moves along the cobbled bed.

The banks are formed by staring hoardings, urging our weary souls to spend our surplus income – if any – on somebody's pale ale or someone else's bread and confectionary.

Overhead, low clouds having broken their hearts on the nearby hills, pour their grief impartially on young girls, whose eyes are still bright with the ideals and hopes of children, and grandmothers whose souls are seared in the grim industrial machine.

This steady forward movement of the stream of animal life is a perfect example of the working of the mass mind. One thought from several thousand brains, one urge, and that, the minute hand of a comparatively tiny clock, driving us forward in time to slip a blue piece of cardboard into a wooden box, and with the click of the time stamp becoming a piece of human machinery within the walls of the compound.

Clack, clack, clackerty, clackerty
Each clack a step nearer to the welcome lights that blaze in the factory yard, for even the light and warmth of the factory is welcome when it means shelter from a relentless, drizzling rain and a keen, gusty wind of a winter's morning.

Would that it was a shelter from the equally relentless struggle against the economic blizzard that blows with increasing severity through our lives.

Slowly but surely the minute-hand of the factory clock reaches the vertical and then forms an angle with the hour-hand below.

As it rests on the zero the harsh, strident call of the buzzers shriek above all other sounds – a fresh work-day has commenced.

Hands reach up and pull at long wooden levers switching the endless belts on to driving wheels.

Drillers shield their eyes with their disengaged hands as tools bite deeply into metal. Lathe workers direct the cooling flow of oil and soap water on to heated cutting tools and anxiously watch the uncurling swarf, for swarf is springy and can snap back and cut deep.

Tiny boys hurry here and there amid the chatter of machines carrying cans or staggering with bars of warm metal.

Girls in their teens risk finger and eye in the weaving sheds as they hastily adjust faulty shuttles. Old women clutch tightly at their breasts as they perform methodical tasks and suck the humid diseased-laden air into withered lungs.

Overlookers stalk severely up and down the aisles and foremen sit ponderously at their desks gently digesting their rising meal, some of them weaving dreams of the time when promotion will extend their hours of sleep.

Directors just grunt in their beds and turn over.

We may just look two hours ahead as sleek limousines will draw up outside the porticoed office entrances and plutocracy will climb asthmatically down to waddle in the holy of holies inscribed 'Private'.

And over all, over and above the rain clouds, over the clouds of factory life – and death – over the clouds of capitalist industrial depression, gathers a still greater and menacing cloud, a cloud that holds rending lightning – for the people who arrive at the factory last and work in the room inscribed 'Private!'!

When this cloud bursts, hope and joy will be written, where sadness and suffering now appear.

This cloud is named, 'Working-class solidarity'.

A. P. Roley, *Daily Worker*, 19 January 1930, p. 6.

5.7 Class sport

Here George Sinfield, a prominent activist in struggles for workers' sport, outlines the movement's genesis, and the recent success of Communists in securing control over the British Workers' Sports Federation (BWSF), of which Sinfield was president.

The Workers' Sport Movement

Since the launching of the *Daily Worker*, on January 1, the British Workers' Sports Federation has received more attention and publicity than ever before in its history.

The discussion around the advisability of the publication of bourgeois sport in the columns of the *Daily* has simultaneously proved that right throughout the country revolutionary workers are alive to the great importance of the workers' sport movement, and has also proved beyond doubt that the development of a great mass workers' sports movement can be visualised within a reasonable period of time.

The *Daily*, too, has been the means of awakening greater interest and enthusiasm amongst the membership of the BWSF itself, and, incidentally has provided a long overdue stimulus and encouragement that will lay the sure foundations so necessary for its rapid development, and for enabling the workers' sport movement to become an integral unit of the revolutionary workers' movement.

The significance of this fact is enormous, more so probably than is immediately seen on the face of it. The workers' sports movement will be the means of generating a constant source of energy, stamina and revolutionary fervour, such as proved the case in the U.S.S.R., Germany, Czechoslovakia, and in other countries. [...]

In this country it was not until 1923 that a real start was made. A group was inaugurated in London in that year, and has been in existence ever since, though not without experience of certain inevitable difficulties.

In the first place, we had to meet and combat hostility to the idea of a workers' sports movement from almost all who happened to be outside our own particular sphere.

Secondly, the BWSF, from 1923 to 1928, was under the control of a junta of social-democratic officials whose actions were consistently directed against the development of a real workers' sports movement. [...]

In April, 1928, the first National Congress of the BWSF was held in Birmingham. The Congress elected in the place of the old officials, who actually represented nobody other than themselves, an entirely new and militant leadership. Since that Congress our development, without being sensational, has shown a steady progress. [...]

But the main task of the BWSF in this period is to make a drive to the factories, mines and rail depots, &c. We must struggle to set up, wherever possible, sports clubs in these enterprises. We must carry on the constant struggle against the boss-subsidised clubs, tearing them away from the support of the boss, and exposing to the workers the role and nature of such clubs, in their utilisation for the furthering of the general attack on wages and conditions and the imposition of rationalisation. We must point out clearly and consistently the aims of bourgeois sport which endeavours to subdue and weaken the class-conscious response of the workers to the capitalist attack. [...]

The visit to this country in the spring of the Soviet football team provides the BWSF with a wonderful opportunity of putting these plans of development into immediate operation. The team will in all probability play games in London, South Wales, Shipley, Newcastle, Fife and Glasgow. [...]

Red Sports Day, which will be held in Victoria Park, London, E., on April 26, will be linked up with the Russian tour, and is a project of similar importance. The success of Red Sports Day is already assured if the indications to hand are any criterion at all. We hope to arrange for the Russian footballers to take part in the many events, and if this is possible, then Red Sports Day will have an added attraction.

We do not expect the habitual pot-hunters to compete in the competitions. Our aim is to provide some genuine sport for the workers of London, and, if possible, to get representation from the provinces as well. [...]

It is on the above plan of activity and basis of development that the BWSF will organise its Second National Congress, representative of every club in the Federation.

We are convinced that, constituted in this way, the Congress will be a real one, will breathe the desires of actual membership of the BWSF, and will positively sow the seeds for the creation of a mass revolutionary sports movement in this country.

G. W. Sinfield (National Secretary, British Workers' Sports Federation). *Labour Monthly* (March 1930), pp. 167–71.

5.8 Staging the struggle

The Workers' Theatre Movement (WTM) was a product of the New Line, envisaging a separate, proletarian culture opposed to 'bourgeois' theatrical traditions and embodying instead the radical impulses of the militant working class. This document is from the first edition of WTM's monthly journal, *The Red Stage*.

The growth of the Workers' Theatre Movement
The issue of a monthly Journal by the Workers' Theatre Movement marks a big step forward, and is a good indication of the growth of our movement.

The fact that we feel strong and confident enough to run our own printed paper is a sign that we have developed from the day when we consisted of a few scattered groups working along very loose lines.

To-day, we are a rapidly growing body with groups springing up all over the country – groups coming into existence faster than the central organisation can cope with them.

Dramatising the struggle

Our value as a means of exposing the capitalist system and its supporters in all their brutality, hypocrisy, lying knavery, is undoubted.

By means of our sketches, written, produced and acted by workers, we are able to show our fellow-workers (the fellow whom the press refer to as 'the man in the street'), the meaning of the present crisis and the attempts to delude the workers into sacrificing lives for their bosses and bankers. By means of our sketches [...] we endeavour to give in dramatic form the day-to-day struggles of the workers; the frantic efforts of the financiers and statesman [sic] to pull their system off the precipice of destruction. And, side by side with the pictures, we portray the vigorous and energetic life of the Russian workers in their triumphant battles toward Communism.

The class stage

You may be amazed at our audacity in bringing the Theatre on to the street. But our stage, comrade reader, is situated wherever workers gather together, in work or pleasure. Our stage is the open street, the borrowed lorry, the trade union branch room, the meeting platform. We disdain the spotlights, limelights, 'stars' and other trappings of the bourgeois theatre. Our only spotlight is a Workers' Britain: our only star – the five pointed badge of the Soviet State.

As the movement recognises our worth, so will the WTM. become greater and more effective – a vigorous weapon in the class struggle.

Our organisation is not merely confined to this country. All over the world the Workers' Theatre Movement is helping the revolutionary movement – in many places in the teeth of bitter persecution. Such a deadly weapon is the Workers' Theatre Movement in Germany that in many places it is completely banned. In the Soviet Union, our brother organisation fights for the workers' State against the prejudices of the relics of Czarism, against the enemies of the Soviet Union, and helps to inspire the workers to greater achievements for the Five Year Plan.

A word to those within our ranks. We want our paper to reflect the life and activity of the WTM and this can be done by reporting its activities. In this way we can make our paper a leader in our struggle to build a stronger WTM in Britain.

And to those outside our ranks – a welcome awaits you in our organisation. Join up to-day!

Unsigned editorial, *The Red Stage: Organ of the Workers' Theatre Movement*, 1, 1 (November 1931), p. 1.

5.9 Projecting the struggle

For Lenin cinema was the most important of all the arts; for Stalin, 'the greatest means of mass agitation'. Compared with the state sponsored triumphs of Soviet cinema, incursions by British Communists in the medium of film were, to say the least, fragmentary. This document describes one attempt to bring radical film to the working class.

Films in the streets
The new film section of the Workers' Theatre Movement, on Sunday evening in the East End of London, gave the first practical demonstration of the potentialities that lie in the use of small film as the medium through which it intends to develop interest in its work.

With the aid of a car loaned by a comrade a section of the film *Soviet Russia Past and Present* was actually exhibited to audiences outside their homes in this densely populated area.

The apparatus used was a small projector of the box type containing its own screen, and power was obtained through a generator connected directly with the accumulator of the car.

The effect was quite presentable, but owing to slow running a large amount of flicker was noticeable. A strong battery would easily obviate this, and as an experiment the young men who evolved and presented the 'show' are to be congratulated on the pioneer work which will lead to big developments.

Here is the new medium which will add yet another weapon of intense cultural and propaganda value. Nothing of the sort within so reasonable a financial outlay has been possible before in the scope of the workers' movement, and realms of possibilities are opened up.

We understand that this is only one of the plans on which the recently formed film section of the WTM hope to organise interest in the film as an invaluable medium in the class struggle.

Daily Worker, 3 August 1933.

5.10 Film propaganda

Ivor Montagu, son of Lord Swaythling, began his career as a zoologist and did research for the British Museum on expeditions to the Hebrides (1922), Slovenia and Croatia (1923), the Caucasus (1925) and Sicily (1927). Increasingly devoted to film-making and Communism, he made frequent visits to the Soviet Union, where he met film-makers including Sergei Eisenstein. Montagu travelled with a group of such film-makers, including Eisenstein, through Europe and the United States in 1929–30, and briefly worked with Eisenstein in Hollywood. The Communist Party was under surveillance by MI5, of course, from the 1920s. The document below – a letter from G. A. Atkinson of the *Daily Express* to the Commissioner of Immigration at Ellis Island, New York – shows that Montagu was already regarded as a dangerous Communist. Atkinson's concerns reflect contemporary perceptions of the power of film and recognition of the Communists' early appreciation of it.

7 July 1930
[…] As a cinema editor of the *Daily Express* and *Sunday Express*, a post which I have filled for some eleven years, it has been my duty from time to time to check up the activities of Moscow plotters in this country in connection with their elaborate scheme of film propaganda.

During these investigations I have acquired a fairly extensive knowledge of Moscow activities in general.

One of the most dangerous and, in my position, the most cunning propagandist in this direction is the Hon, Ivor Montagu […] Montagu, for the best reasons known to himself, has recently removed to America and has obtained a post in Paramount (Famous-Players-Lasky) organization, where he is now working in association with S. M. Eisenstein, another extremely clever Moscow propagandist.

Montagu has very influential connections in social and financial circles, in addition to considerable private means, but instead of following the brilliant career marked out for him, he has turned aside to devote the whole of his energies and not considerable [sic] intellect to the fomentation of industrial revolt.

I know enough about him to be in a position to advise you to deport him without delay. Listen to no explanations, excuses or denials. Believe nothing he says or anything that may be said to you in his favour. No effort will be spared to protect him, but it is a matter in which you should be ruthless. Deport him bag and baggage. We understand him here, and know how to deal with him.

If you care to have your London representatives to call on me, I shall be pleased to show him my file of information.
With compliments
Yours faithfully, G. A. Atkinson.

CP/IND/MONT/1/1.

Notes

1 John Callaghan, *Rajani Palme Dutt: A Study in British Stalinism* (London: Lawrence & Wishart, 1993).

2 Willie Thompson, *The Good Old Cause: British Communism 1920–1991* (London: Pluto, 1992), p. 45.

3 *Which Way for the Workers? Harry Pollitt versus Fenner Brockway* (London: CPGB, 1932), cited in Kevin Morgan, *Harry Pollitt* (Manchester: Manchester University Press, 1993), p. 82.

4 Harry Pollitt, *Serving My Time*, 2nd edn (London: Lawrence & Wishart, 1941), pp. 278.

5 Thompson, *Good Old Cause*, p. 43; Kevin Morgan, *Harry Pollitt* (Manchester: Manchester University Press, 1993), p. 77; Francis Beckett, *Enemy Within: The Rise and Fall of the British Communist Party*, 2nd edn (London: Merlin, 1998), pp. 36–45.

6 Matthew Worley, *Class Against Class: The Communist Party in Britain Between the Wars* (London and New York: I. B. Tauris, 2002).

7 See Alun Howkins, 'Class Against Class: The Political Culture of the Communist Party of Great Britain, 1930–35' in Frank Gloversmith (ed.), *Class, Culture and Social Change: A New View of the 1930s* (Brighton: Harvester, 1980), pp. 208–40; Kevin Morgan, 'The Communist Party and the *Daily Worker*' in Geoff Andrews, Nina Fishman and Kevin Morgan (eds), *Opening the Books: Essays on the Social and Cultural History of the British Communist Party* (London: Pluto, 1995), pp. 142–60.

8 Worley, *Class Against Class*, pp. 200–3.

9 Ibid., pp. 208–13.

10 Andy Croft, *Red Letter Days: British Fiction in the 1930s* (London: Lawrence & Wishart, 1990), pp. 31–55; Richard Stourac and Kathleen McCreery, *Theatre as a Weapon: Workers' Theatre in the Soviet Union, Germany and Britain, 1917–1934* (London and New York: Routledge & Kegan Paul, 1986), pp. 200–8.

11 Bert Hogenkamp, *Deadly Parallels: Film and the Left in Britain 1929–39* (London: Lawrence & Wishart, 1986); Don Macpherson (ed.), *British Cinema: Traditions of Independence* (London: British Film Institute, 1980).

6
Popular Front Communism, 1935–39

Adolf Hitler's rise to power, consolidated in his election as German Chancellor in January 1933, transformed the European political landscape. Though the Comintern would never explicitly revoke the Third Period sectarianism that had disorganised the left and helped to smooth the Nazis' path to power, the following couple of years witnessed a reorientation of political strategy away from isolationism and towards the building of anti-fascist coalitions. In 1934 the Soviet Union joined the League of Nations, signalling a willingness to form alliances with bourgeois states; in July of that year the French Communist Party cemented an alliance with the socialists. The 7th World Congress of the Communist International of 1935 spelt out the new reading of the political scene. The key address was given by Comintern General Secretary Georgi Dimitrov, a hero of anti-Nazi struggle in Germany, who presented a new global situation in which moribund capitalism was 'seeking salvation in fascism'.[1] Dimitrov urged Communists to build alliances with all who opposed fascism, even those who remained committed to bourgeois democracy.[2]

The political benefits of taking a leading role in the struggle against fascism were already apparent to the CPGB. Co-ordinating resistance to rallies and marches organised by Oswald Mosley's British Union of Fascists in 1934 had re-grounded the party within the broader labour movement, and created the momentum for further political unity with those recently denounced as 'social fascists'. In Britain attempts to form a viable electoral Popular Front alliance like those in France and Spain would run aground on deeply entrenched suspicions (the Labour Party would eventual expel Sir Stafford Cripps and Anuerin Bevan for persisting with their campaign for unity). But nevertheless, during the late 1930s the Communist Party would become the dynamic core of anti-fascist activity in Britain.

When the Spanish Civil War broke out in July 1936, the party co-ordinated military volunteers through the British Battalion of the International Brigade: between a third and a half of the 2000 British volunteers who fought in Spain were Communists, including many of the 526 killed. The party was also central to co-ordinating relief for the Spanish people through the Aid for Spain initiatives.[3] Though it still had fewer than 20,000 members, its steadfast commitment to what became seen as the frontline of international anti-fascist struggle added lustre the party's reputation.[4] The readership of its ideologically softened *Daily Worker* reached 200,000 in this period.[5]

The Communist Party had proved inhospitable to intellectuals during the 'class against class' period:[6] Dutt had famously instructed them to cure themselves of any delusions of superiority with party legwork.[7] Popular Front period thinking, by contrast, frequently emphasised the importance of intellectual and cultural struggle to protect and develop humankind's cultural riches from the ravages of fascist barbarism; these years saw Communist cultural activity enjoy a profile unimaginable a decade before.[8] Literary figures such as Edgell Rickword, Christopher Caudwell, Randall Swingler, Sylvia Townsend Warner, Stephen Spender and Cecil Day Lewis joined the party, as did composer Alan Bush and classicist George Thomson. These new members subscribed to the analysis that intellectuals must now choose between a decaying capitalism turning to fascism or a different political future rooted in the working class. The party's atmosphere in turn became more accommodating to a radicalised intelligentsia willing to break from traditional class allegiances. The most famous cultural initiative of the period was the Left Book Club, essentially a vast reading group with its own publishing house. Launched in 1936 and dominated though not openly controlled by Communists, at its height the Left Book Club numbered 57,000 members; many of these were active in the 1500 reading groups who met to discuss titles ranging from Palme Dutt's *World Politics 1918–1936* (1936) to George Orwell's *The Road to Wigan Pier* (1937) and A. L. Morton's *A People's History of England* (1938).[9] Parallel initiatives on the cultural front included the Artists International Association, which promoted and co-ordinated the work of visual artists opposed to fascism, and Unity Theatre, which established a permanent base in London's King's Cross, and whose very name signalled its Popular Front priorities.[10] The key cultural journal of the 1930s was the vibrant *Left Review* (1934–38), a Communist-dominated publication shaped by an ethos of Popular Front inclusiveness, which would carry contributions from many of the major British writers of the 1930s.[11]

Dimitrov's analysis had argued that each nation's progressive cultural and political traditions should be developed by Communists to resist the bogus nationalism promoted by fascism;[12] in line with this devolved Popular Front logic, Communism in Britain sometimes took a patriotic turn. The outlines of a better future were now to be detected in the patterns of the nation's past, and Harry Pollitt made time to review books by Communists exploring England's instructive, longstanding radical traditions.[13] Communists put on pageants plotting English history as a narrative of resistance to ruling class oppression culminating in themselves. These performances, which paraded through Britain's major cities, insisted that Communism grew organically from England's deep-rooted radicalism; the fundamental contradiction concealed here was that British Communism was always part of an international movement whose course was ultimately determined by the need to defend the lodestar of proletarian revolution, the Soviet Union. That agenda forcefully broke back into the frame on 23 August 1939 when the Soviet regime, diplomatically isolated by the major Western powers, signed a mutual non-aggression pact with Hitler, thereby subordinating the anti-fascist cause to the interests of self-preservation. The implications of the volte-face, which are unravelled in the next chapter, brought to an abrupt end Popular Front Communism.

6.1 Working class against fascism

The new political line was formally adopted at the Comintern's 7th World Congress, held in Moscow in August 1935. This is from the official report of Comintern General Secretary Georgi Dimitrov.

[...] With the outbreak of the present and most profound economic crisis, the sharp accentuation of the general crisis of capitalism and the revolutionisation of the toiling masses, fascism has embarked upon a wide offensive. The ruling bourgeoisie is more and more seeking salvation in fascism, with the object of instituting exceptionally predatory measures against the toilers, preparing for an imperialist war of plunder, attacking the Soviet Union, enslaving and partitioning China, and by all these measures preventing revolution.

Imperialist circles are endeavouring to place the *whole* burden of the crisis on the backs of the toilers. *That is why they need fascism.* [...]

They are striving to forestall the growth of the forces of revolution by smashing the revolutionary movement of the workers and peasants by undertaking a military attack on the Soviet Union – the bulwark of the world proletariat. *That is why they need fascism.* [...]

Comrades, as was correctly stated by the Thirteenth Plenum of the Executive Committee of the Communist International, fascism in power is *the open terrorist dictatorship of the most reactionary, most chauvinistic and most imperialist elements of finance capital.* [...]

Great Britain

In *Great Britain*, as a result of the mass action of the British workers, Mosley's fascist organisation has for the time being been pushed into the background. But we must not close our eyes to the fact that the so-called 'National Government' is passing a number of reactionary measures directed against the working class, as a result of which conditions are being created in Great Britain too, which will make it easy for the bourgeoisie, if necessary, to proceed to a fascist regime. [...]

The ideological struggle against fascism

One of the weakest aspects of the anti-fascist struggle of our Parties lies in the fact that they *react inadequately and too slowly to the demagogy of fascism*, and to this day continue to look with disdain upon the problems of the struggle against fascist ideology. Many comrades did not believe that so reactionary a variety of bourgeois ideology as the ideology of fascism, which in its stupidity frequently reaches the point of lunacy, was capable of gaining mass influence at all. This was a great mistake. The putrefaction of capitalism penetrates to the innermost core of its ideology and culture, while the desperate situation of the broad masses of the people renders certain sections of them susceptible to infection from the ideological refuse of this putrefaction.

We must under no circumstances underrate this fascist capacity for ideological infection. On the contrary we must develop for our part an extensive ideological struggle on the basis of clear, popular argument and a correct, well thought-out approach to the peculiarities of the national psychology of the masses of the people.

The fascist are rummaging through the entire *history* of every nation so as to be able to pose as heirs and continuers of all that was exalted and heroic in its past [...].

[...] Communist who suppose that all this has nothing to do with the cause of the working class, who do nothing to enlighten the masses on the past of their own people, in a historically correct fashion, in a genuinely Marxist, a Leninist-Marxist, a Leninist-Stalinist spirit, who do nothing to *link up their present struggle with its revolutionary traditions and past* – voluntarily relinquish to fascist falsifiers all that is valuable in the historical past of the nation, in order that the fascists may bamboozle the masses.

G. Dimitrov, *The Working Class Against Fascism* (London: Martin Lawrence, 1935), pp. 9–10, 39–40, 68–70.

6.2 Anti-fascist struggle in Britain

Though not a card-carrying Communist, former Labour MP and prominent Marxist intellectual John Strachey was a significant figure in the Popular Front period closely aligned with the Dutt, Pollitt and the party. A selector for the Left Book Club, he was also Secretary for the CPGB initiated Committee for Co-ordinating Anti-Fascist Activities. In this capacity he reports below on the Communist-led counter demonstration against Oswald Mosley's Hyde Park rally in September 1934.

The prospects of the anti-fascist struggle

An important and critical stage in the organisation of Anti-Fascist activities in Great Britain has been reached. The counter-demonstration of London workers in Hyde Park on September 9 marked the first appreciable success in securing the participation in the Anti-Fascist struggle of the large majority of the British workers who are accustomed to follow the official Labour Party and Trade Union leadership.

This was an event of very great significance; but it would be a mistake to over-estimate what has been accomplished. September 9 was only a beginning, and a comparatively small beginning at that. It is hardly too much to say that the object of the Anti-Fascist struggle at this stage is to prevent the natural and spontaneous desire of the workers, which certainly exists, to destroy Fascism while it is still weak, from being stifled by their leaders. And we must not think we have yet succeeded in this task. On the contrary, the official Labour and Trade Union leaders are very active indeed. The working-class struggle against Fascism is still very small compared to what it would be if it was encouraged, united, and organised, instead of actively discouraged, by those who possess nine-tenths of the apparatus of political and industrial organisation. [...]

We need not go into the motives of the national Trades Union and Labour Party leaders in making it clear, as they are doing, that they fear and hate Communism and revolutionary activity of any kind far more than they fear and hate Fascism. The important fact is that there are still very many perfectly sincere workers, both in the rank and file, and in the intermediate ranks, of the Labour Party who are held back from the Anti-Fascist fight by the illusions which their national leaders are active in confirming in their minds. It will not be denied that the Anti-Fascist struggle has as its primary task to reach and to convert these people. We cannot succeed unless we get the co-operation and active participation of the best elements of the British working class. If we do succeed in reaching these key men and women we cannot fail. [...]

It is vitally important that we should explain that Mosley's Fascism has not been killed; and that it cannot be killed, except by the full and united strength of the British working class; and that this unity has not yet been achieved.

Until and unless that unity is achieved, two things will always enable Mosley to keep his movement alive. First, his ability, to draw substantial funds from a section of the capitalist class and, second, the fostering care which the National Government section of that class bestows on his movement in its present undeveloped stage. September 9 was the perfect object lesson of how this process, so well described in the August resolution of the Central Committee of the Communist Party, works out in practice. Since this resolution may not be familiar to all *Labour Monthly* readers it will be well to cite its most significant passage:

> On one hand there is a tendency to see the issue of Fascism as the only issue of Mosley and the Blackshirts, and not to see the main weight of the Fascist offensive, which is being directly conducted by the National Government.
>
> On the other hand, there is a tendency to emphasise solely the Fascist offensive of the National Government, and to treat the Blackshirt movement as a politically negligent factor.
>
> Both tendencies are incorrect. Finance capital at present backs the National Government as its main weapon against Fascisation [...] but at the same time gives Mosley lavish support and utilises his gangs as a subsidiary weapon which will be rapidly brought to the front in proportion as the National Government proves insufficient and if the workers [sic] upward movement continues.
>
> The National Government offensive and the Mosley offensive supplement each other; the Blackshirts can only operate under the protection of the police, but at the same time can be used, and

subsequently disavowed, where it would be inconvenient to use the police.

It is essential to make clear to the workers the twofold character of the Fascist offensive, at once through the official State machine and through the open Fascist forces, the effective division of labour and interplay of both.

The understanding of this necessarily destroys the 'democratic' illusion, the illusion of the possibility of the legal bourgeois democratic opposition to Fascism.

The events of September 9 provided ocular proof of the perfect accuracy of this analysis. It would have been utterly impossible for Mosley in the present stage of his movement, before he has developed any important degree of mass strength, to have staged his military display at Hyde Park but for two factors. First, the determination of the Labour Party leaders that the full strength of the workers should not be used against him, and second, the formidable police protection which the National Government accorded him. [...]

John Strachey, *Labour Monthly* (October 1934), pp. 607–12.

6.3 Reorientation

Dutt uses his 'Notes of the Month' editorial to endorse the New Line.

We are entering into a period of big issues and big decisions, of rapid and far-reaching transformations in the world situation and in the international working-class movement, of responsibilities without equal for the political leadership of the working class. Never was there more need of cool heads, long views and unflinching audacity in action to be equal to the sharp and sudden changes of the world situation. The storm is breaking all round us. The consequences of the world crisis, of the bankruptcy of the old liberal social-democratic policies, and of the fascist offensive, are now unfolding themselves with lightning speed. World imperialism is openly advancing in every continent to the struggle for the new division of the world. In the forefront the fascist Powers are launching the war-offensives which they have ceaselessly prepared. The hour and the testing-time is here for the massing of all forces to defeat this offensive. On our present actions and decisions in the months before us depends the character of a whole future historical period, whether mankind must advance through the limitless blood and destruction of a new world war to the ultimate revolution, or whether we can yet succeed – we have still time, we have still the possibility, but not for long – in massing the front in all countries, in unity with the Soviet Union, to turn back the offensive of blood and terror and reaction, and advance rapidly to the struggle for power and the building of a new world. This and nothing less underlies the issues which are at present agitating the working-class movement.

The Seventh World Congress of the Communist International met at the turning point of this great transition from one period to another, and gave the leading line for a whole future period. This Congress, more than any Congress before, spoke for the whole human race, and showed the one way forward from the destruction, blood and terror that overhangs the world. The call of the Seventh Congress for the unity of all the working class masses without exception, for the unity of the overwhelming majority of the population in every country against the finance-capitalist oligarchies who are preparing to drown civilisation in slaughter and barbarism in order to maintain their sinking power, will echo and resound louder and louder through the coming period. What was the achievement of the Seventh Congress? The achievement of the Seventh Congress was above all that, at the moment of greatest urgency, when on every side in the working class movement there was gathering the sense of the imperative need of fresh vision and reorientation to meet the new issues of the day, the Seventh Congress, with the sweeping boldness and unsparing realism of Marxist-Leninist theory, faced completely the new world situation that is developing and all its implications, and drew therefrom with concrete and unequivocal clearness, in the midst of the enormously difficult and complicated issues of the present situation, the positive path forward for the working masses all over the world to extricate themselves from the dilemmas which the past period of reformist illusions has landed them, confront the towering new menaces which have consequently arisen to-day, and reach forward to win again the initiative and new advance of socialism in the world. [...]

Where before the dream of democracy was a counter-revolutionary opiate, to-day the fight for democratic rights against fascism has become a mass fight against the main attack of finance-capital. Where before the hypocritical talk of peace was a main weapon of imperialist enslavement, to-day the fight for peace against the new world war has become a fight of the masses, in unity with the Soviet Union, against the main drive of finance-capital. The old slogans take new meanings and pass to different sides of the frontier, according as the battle rages. The masses are awakening from the old illusions to the new conditions of struggle. The need of the hour is for the widest mass unity against fascism, against imperialist war, for the defence of the Soviet Union. The Seventh World Congress, in voicing this call, has voiced the deepest need of the masses throughout the world at the present stage. This line holds the key to the future. For Communism has seen that this present new stage of the struggle, this transitional stage of elementary fighting unity against the ferocious onslaught of dying capitalism is the historical path of advance of the main body of the workers, no longer only of the vanguard, from reformism to revolution.

Rajani Palme Dutt, 'Notes of the Month', *Labour Monthly* (October 1935), pp. 589–609.

6.4 Radical Englishness

Here London District organiser Ted Bramley describes 'The March of English History' of 20 September 1936, a carefully choreographed marched pageant in which Communist laid claim to the present and future by way of the radical past.

London's historical pageant: thousands march behind C. P. banners to Hyde Park

Last Sunday's march of thousands of Communists, organised by the London District Committee, was an unforgettable sight.

It was a blaze of colour – hundreds of red flags and banners interspersed with 85 gaily-painted banners depicting great figures and great events from Magna Carter to the present day.

The banners vividly recalled events in the struggle of the English people for peace and freedom and against poverty. As the demonstration marched past Victoria Station, Hyde Park Corner and Marble Arch thousands of people gathered to watch. The District Committee, which marched at the head, was greeted with the Popular Front salute and cheers. Cheer after cheer greeted the *ex-service men* wearing their medals and carrying red flags. In Hyde Park the District Committee mounted the platform, over which floated two huge red flags.

Thousands of people assembled there burst into applause as branch after branch marched past giving the impression of never-ending battalions of Communists. All eyes were on the banners depicting the events and figures of the past. Applause greeted each one as it came into view. Cheers for the early Socialist Pioneers – Robert Owen, William Morris, Keir Hardie, Marx and Engels – especially the banners revealing England's contribution to the international struggle. [...] As the more recent events came the cheering grew continuously. [...] Warmest of all for the leaders of the Communist Party, *Pollitt, Gallacher, Campbell* and the others. [...]

The result was amazing. Application forms were signed on the spot and *810 new members* gained for the Communist Party. [...]

It is an event deeply significant and full of promise for the English movement. [...] [T]he Communist Party is learning to speak to the English workers in a language they understand. [...] It is beginning to grasp the great and glorious tradition of the English people, and to use it as a mighty weapon against fascism and reaction. [...] Sunday's pageant was a story told in beautiful colours of the growth of Communism out of England's soil. [...] Communism is growing unmistakeably in London. Growing in influence, especially in the labour organisations. It is revealing itself as a legitimate heir of generations of great English fighters for freedom and progress. It is preparing and will lead the people forward to a free and merrie England.

Ted Bramley, *International Press Correspondence* 16, 44 (29 September 1936), p. 1201.

6.5 Singing Englishmen

The CPGB would enjoy a prominent profile in the British postwar folk music revival through individuals such as Ewan MacColl and A. L. Lloyd, and institutions such as Topic Records, the in-house record label of the Communist-dominated Workers' Music Association (WMA). The Popular Front period gave a significant impetus for Communist interest in cultural forms such as folk song – considered progressively national without being nationalistic. This article is an early exploration of the topic.

The past is ours: the people's own poetry

Few ideas are more deceptive, more calculated to undermine the self-confidence of the working class than the present-day conception of culture.

From our school days onward, we are taught to believe that humanity is a troop of beings incapable, in the main, of any real creative activity, especially artistic activity. In this troop, from time to time, there spring up as if by miracle, certain geniuses.

These are the thinkers, the inventors, the poets and artists.

Nearly always these geniuses come from the ranks of the middle-class intelligentsia. Occasionally they are from the aristocracy.

And how about the masses? 'Bah!' our teachers say, 'working-class poets and artists are so exceptional as to prove the rule that the masses are naturally inartistic, congenitally lacking in all those inner qualities of temperament and intelligence that make the artist and the poet.

This is, of course, the sheerest nonsense. Broadly speaking, the masses in most capitalist countries *do*, like their masters, lack any highly developed artistic sense. But far from being *natural*, this is a highly *artificial* state of affairs, as you see at a glance when you read a collection of folk poetry.

It is true that capitalism has put an end to folk-art, for the time being. But before this unnatural state of things arose, what wonderful poetry the workers were capable of!

Isolated by class barriers and often by geographical remoteness, as well as by their inability to read, the peasants were unable to become fully acquainted with the culture elaborated in the cities for the more privileged classes.

They were obliged to make up their own songs, and being unable to write, they could only hand them down by word of mouth.

The real author of the ballad is the people who have sung it, making their successive changes so that it corresponds more closely to their own feelings, tastes and preferences.

The people's poetry, so far as the English language is concerned, was always spontaneous. I mean, it was always the direct, and, unreflecting expression of passion, love, terror. The ballads told their story simply, but with terrific intensity that never slackened into reflection. [...]

Many of these ballads had their origins in the fourteenth and fifteenth centuries, but because they have undergone such alterations and amendments as they are handed down to each successive generation, it would be quite wrong to fix the age of a ballad dogmatically at four or five hundred years.

Even today the English ballad goes on developing, no longer, alas, in England, but in primitive communities of English origin and culture, such as in the Appalachian Mountains of the United States, or in Newfoundland.

My space is too limited to give more examples of this magnificent poetry. But surely the existence of such ballads and the splendid tunes to which they were sung emphatically disproves the theory that the masses are by nature unable to create artistically.

And, more than that, the superb quality of English folk poetry is a foreshadowing of what the masses will be capable of when they are at last free of the stultifying miseries of capitalist industrialism.

A. L. Lloyd, *Daily Worker* (10 February 1937), p. 10.

6.6 Left Book Club

Left News was the in-house magazine of the Left Book Club. Here the club's founder and leading light, publisher Victor Gollancz, takes stock of the first year's achievements.

Editorial

(A) Anniversary self-criticism
It would be easy, on this occasion of the anniversary of the Left Book Club, to congratulate ourselves on what has been achieved; and, indeed, the achievement, both here at headquarters and among the members, has been such as might excuse a large measure of congratulation. The mere statistics are staggering. Close on 50,000 members [...]; the distribution through the Club of between four hundred thousand and half a million books; between 500 and 600 local Groups in England, and others throughout the world – certainly nothing on a similar scale has ever been achieved in the past.

We think also we might fairly congratulate ourselves on the quality of the books – whether 'Choices' or 'Additional' and 'Supplementary' books – which have been sent to the members. [...]

While, however, we think that we may be pleased with the Choices we have given to members in the past, we are even more pleased with those which we shall be giving them in the future. It must be remembered that books take a long time to write and a certain amount of time to publish, and therefore in the early days of the Club the monthly programme could not reflect the scientific *planning* which is now taking place. From the first month such planning has been in progress: and now there are arranged, for a very long time ahead, books which the Selection Committee has *commissioned* as being on topics about which our members ought to have information – and commissioned from authors whom we believe to be the best people to write on these topics.

A good example of this scientific planning is to be found in the trio of books which is to be published from June Onwards. The first will be Allen Hutt's *The Post-War History of the British Working Class*, which will describe and analyse that history from the point of view of a Communist, and which leads up to a vigorous advocacy of the United Front. The second will be *The Labour Party in Perspective*, by C. R. Attlee, Leader of the Parliamentary Labour Party, which will deal with broadly the same topic from the point of view of official Labour. Finally there will be a brilliant book on *The People's Front*, by G. D. H. Cole, again dealing with this topic, but this time from a point of view that is neither Communist nor official Labour. [...]

To get back to self-criticism, we are acutely aware here, day by day, that we are only doing a small part of the work that we ought to be doing. The fact is that the never-ceasing development of the Club has, so to speak, taken our breath away, and we find ourselves with only twenty-four hours to get through the work of forty-eight. When we started the Club we had no idea of its potentialities: and now, a year later, we live in a real fear that, this marvellous opportunity having occurred, we are not taking full advantage of it. And we *must* take full advantage of it – we must follow up and consolidate every development and seize every opportunity. It is a matter partly of organisation, partly of constantly adding to our staff people particularly suited for particular jobs. I only want to say here that we are alive to the necessity of spending most of our waking hours in devising new methods of dealing with our problems.

[...] [B]efore ending this section of my Editorial, I should like to put to the whole body of the membership one very simple bit of arithmetic: if each new member of the Club would make himself responsible for obtaining *one new member only*, then I could announce in the next issue that the membership was, not 50,000, but 100,000. With 100,000 members we should be, I believe, the most powerful body of educated public opinion that any country has ever had. Will members really think this over very seriously?

Victor Gollancz

Left News 13 (May 1937), pp. 336–7.

6.7 Re-reading history

Here Harry Pollitt reviews Communist Hymie Fagan's history of the Peasants' Revolt, a Left Book Club monthly choice for August 1938.

Lessons of 1381 still thrill today
Nine Days That Shook England. By H. Fagan. Gollancz, 7s 6d., LBC Additional, 3s.

Never was a book so timely as this. A book that thrills, teaches, and, in the most skilful manner, connects the events around the great Peasants' Revolt of 1381 with the events of today.

There are so many so called revolutionaries, and armchair philosophers who so learnedly hold forth about the limitations of democracy, so long as it rests upon the basis of capitalist economy (as if no one only themselves were aware of this) that it is timely and salutary to read once again, in a new form, of the struggles of the past to win the beginnings of our democratic rights.

It has become so fashionable to hold cheaply that which we never had to fight to achieve ourselves. Here, way back in the 14th Century, were a band of men to whom hard work, sacrifice, suffering and life itself meant nothing; who did marvellous deeds that inspire everyone not only to defend democracy, but, through that defence, to advance to greater perspectives – to labour in the common cause as they have done before.

In this book we see unfolded all the disgusting corruption, lechery and debauchery that surrounded the Monarchy, State and Church at that time, and it is not absent today.

Shining like a jewel through it all is the heroism and incorruptibility of the common people, our people, your people, which has revealed itself again and again, especially in the history of these last few years. Wat Tyler, John Ball and William Grindcobbe were men who knew how to die like men, who, in their last moments, hurled defiance at their executors, pledged anew their faith and principles.

To read it all again is to see how little now, we give in our favoured conditions, compared to what they gave.

To read *Nine Days That Shook England* is to fan anew one's hatred of our own ruling class – [...]; it is to allow to sink in the mind the thought: 'Never trust or be deceived by the class enemy'. [...]

We have a right to be proud of our British heritage. We have the duty to prove worthy of it. We have the duty to learn from other countries, we have, above all, the duty to learn from our own history – a glorious history of struggle and sacrifice.

I emphatically recommend every reader of the *Daily Worker* to get this book. You won't put it down until you have finished it, and then, like me, you'll want to go out and do something about it.

For me, that is the test of any book in these days, when our whole future depends on how we can apply, in our conditions, the lessons of the pioneers, such as those who organised and led the Peasants' Revolt of 1381.

Harry Pollitt, *Daily Worker* (10 August 1938).

6.8 Unity?

Early in 1937 Communists were active in the short-lived 'Unity Campaign': the overarching objective was to draw the Labour Party towards the idea of a unified labour movement alternative to the National Government. Launched at Manchester's Free Trade Hall on 18 January, the campaign brought together the Communist Party, the Independent Labour Party and the Socialist League, a dissident fraction from the Labour Party centred around Stafford Cripps. Hostile to the initiative, the Labour Party threatened to expel those Socialist Leaguers who participated, and the campaign was soon dissolved. This is an extract from Pollitt's speech to the launch meeting.

Raises standard of united advance
Everybody recognises the seriousness of the present situation and the advance of reaction, Fascism and the danger of war.

It is a terrible reflection that never has the British Labour Movement been so unready as now to face this challenge.

The divisions in the ruling class, the contradictions and vacillations in its policy, would make our task easier if Labour were united. It is no use pretending that unity already exists within the Labour Movement. [...]

The position is more critical because of the many fears that have been expressed that 1937 might be the decisive year determining peace or war. [...]

Our key-note – unity!
When the Socialist League, Independent Labour Party and Communist Party reached agreement, it was for no narrow or Party aims. *It was for the salvation of the whole working class Movement of Britain.* There was no secrecy or conspiracy against the Movement. [...]

It is necessary in the first place to emphasise that the campaign is not in any way directed against the Labour Party.

On the contrary, its whole aim is to strengthen the movement by bringing all sections into what should be the united, all-embracing and, therefore, all-powerful Labour Party.

The Unity Campaign strives to hasten forward the unity of all forces for democracy and peace, against fascism and reaction, and for the workers' needs and demands. The Unity Campaign has as its central aim the achievement of working class unity, the strengthening of the Labour Party, and opposition to breakaways, splits, or the formation of new organisations.

The campaign is definitely intended to make the Labour Party the real united organisation of the British working class. [...]

For them and us
If the Spanish, French, Italian, German, Polish and Belgium workers can unite, why can't the British workers? If the Socialists and Communists in all the countries that we have mentioned have been able to find a basis of

common agreement and advance together against the class enemy, what is there to stop us doing the same in Britain?

Unity in Britain means Unity in the International Labour Movement. This means a new International situation. It strikes the heaviest blow against Hitler, Mussolini and Baldwin. It means victory in Spain, peace and democracy in Europe, and the possibility of speedy advance to Socialism.

Let us dedicate our every endeavour to this great end. To-night, in Spain, in trench, field and street, in mountain fastnesses and on bloody battle-fields, Unity is being cemented in the blood of the best sons and daughters of Spain. They have died that liberty might live. We cannot and dare not betray them.

Hitler and Mussolini are to-day rendering assistance to Franco because one of the major political aims is to destroy in Spain the developing movement towards Unity. They believe the defeat of Unity in Spain would strike a heavy blow against the growing development of Unity all over the world. They believe it would be followed by serious political crises in a number of other European countries, especially France, and therefore, they use the whole of the forces at their command to strike a blow against the Unity of the working class. The very fact that these bitterest enemies of peace, democracy and Socialism should go to such lengths in order to carry out their policy is truly the best recommendation that we need as to the advantages and benefits that can accrue from Unity within the British Labour Movement. [...]

Our greatest service

[T]he greatest service that we could render the Spanish people, the greatest blow that we can give to Franco, Hitler, Mussolini and Baldwin, would be if it were known to-morrow that Unity in the British Labour Movement had been achieved, for that Unity would at once call the united fighting power of the whole working class into action against the National Government, the employers and the landlords of this country. [...] It would speedily result in a new Government that would – in alliance with France, with the great and mighty Soviet Union, and with other democratic countries in Europe – completely change the present tense International situation. [...]

We ask you to pledge yourselves, along with us, to realise this great aim.

Let us end the policy of splendid isolation.

To-night opens the mightiest campaign for splendid unification the Labour Movement of Britain has ever seen.

Harry Pollitt, *The Unity Campaign* (London: National Unity Campaign, London, 1937), pp. 18–31.

6.9 Poetry and the struggle

Though not formally a member of the Communist Party until 1941, Australian born polymath Jack Lindsay was a key figure in Britain's 'cultural front' as a novelist, historian, essayist and poet. First published in *Left Review*, this poem was re-issued as a pamphlet, and then widely performed at demonstrations, meetings and in a more polished version by Unity Theatre.

On guard for Spain!

A poem for mass recitation

What you shall hear is the tale of the Spanish people.
It is also your own life.
    On guard, we cry!
It is the pattern of the world to-day ...

I speak for the Spanish People
I speak for the Spanish people to the workers of the world.
Men and women, come out of the numbered cells
of harsh privation, mockingly called your homes,
break through the deadening screen with your clenched fists,
unrope the bells that jangle in the steeple of the sky,
make the least gap of silence in the wall of day
and you will hear the guns of Spain.

Face here the map of your own fate, and say:
This suffering shall not be in vain.

Thus we plead with you our need.
Cannot you hear the guns of Spain? ...
[...]

For the war in Spain is war for the human future.
All that crawls evil out of the holes of the past,
and all that rises with love for the lucid warmth of the day,
meet in the grapple. In it meet
the evil and the good that swarm
in your inherited blood.
Yes, yours, and yours, and yours.

Listen, comrades,
if you would know our pride.
Have you ever faced your deepest despair?

Then what you see in the agony of Spain
is your own body crucified.

Listen, comrades, if you would know our pride.
Can you dare to know your deepest joy,
all that is possible in you?
Then what you see in Spain's heroic ardour
is your own noblest self come true.

Then, workers of the world, we cry:
We who have forged our unity on the anvil of battle
we upon whom is concentrated
the shock, the breath of flame
belched from the hell of greed,
we who are pivot of all things since we give
to-day the ground of courage and devotion,
the fulcrum of power to shift the harried world
into the meadows of the future's plenty,
we who have claimed our birthright, O hear our call.
Workers of the world, unite for us
that bear the burden of all.
You shall not hear us complain
that the wolves of death are ravening in our streets,
if you but understand, if your bodies flow
into this steel of resistance, this welded mass,
making you one with us, and making us
unconquerable. Workers,
drive off the fascist vultures gathering
to pick the bones of Spanish cities,
to leave the Spanish fields
dunged with peasant dead
that greed may reap the fattened crops.
Fuse your unity in the furnace of our pain.
Enter this compact of steel,
and then we shall not complain.

On guard for the human future!
On guard for the people of Spain!

6.10 Reminiscences of a younger world

Margot Kettle interviewed a number of her old comrades in the Communist Party in the course of 1983 as she did the research for a planned book, *Reminiscences of a Younger World*, which was never published. Here she interviews Gabriel Carrit, university friend of W. H. Auden. The trial Carrit refers to was of the Bundische Jugend in 1937. In May 1939 he won 32.6 per cent of the vote in a by-election as an anti-appeasement candidate.

[…] I remember, about my first year at Oxford, being consciously disgusted with party politics in England. I especially despised Ramsay MacDonald. But I was much more interested in political ideas. I used to listen to my friend, Wystan Auden, talking about Berthold Brecht, Ernst Toller, Marx and Freud. This introduced me to some problems of politics […] But after Oxford I went on a fellowship to Columbia University, New York, and quickly got much more actively involved in political affairs […] I turned back to the students and in particular to a lovely Jewish girl, Hilda Rubens, a clothing worker doing a part-time course […] she taught me the essentials of working-class politics. She took me to her branch of the Communist Party […] and so I joined […]
 […] Like many others I believed that the Russian revolution was producing paradise, that all the problems of poverty and backwardness and misery could be solved there. That was part of the reason why it was so attractive. If I and others like me had appreciated the problems of the first socialist revolution taking place in such a backward country we wouldn't have deceived ourselves so, with such serious consequences later […]
 […] I came back to mass unemployment, even of Oxford graduates […]
 I […] became National Secretary of the League of Nations Union Youth Groups […] Of all the people I knew at that time I think John Gollan was an exceptional man. He was Secretary of the Young Communist League […] I travelled to the Spanish War with him, to meet the Spanish Republican youth leaders and discuss how we in Britain could best help […]
 Again at Johnnie's suggestion, I travelled to Essen in Germany, where a group of right-wing youth leaders were on secret trial for opposition to Hitler. I broke into the court room and warned the judges that the eyes of the world were on them.
 […] The climax of all this political campaigning was for us the parliamentary by-election in the Abbey Division of Westminster in 1939, when the movement for a collective security pact against Hitler's aggression was reaching its height. Sir Richard Acland, MP, who was a prominent member

of the Liberal Party, suggested that the youth and student movement put up a candidate to stand for a non-aggression pact against Hitler, with the support of all parties who stood behind this programme. I was selected to be that candidate [...] Some of the members of the Cabinet, I was told, sent subscriptions to the election campaign [...]

CP/IND/KETT/01.

Notes

1 Georgi Dimitrov, *The Working Class Against Fascism* (London: Martin Lawrence, 1935), p. 10.

2 Ibid., p. 9.

3 See Lewis Mates, *The Spanish Civil War and the British Left: Political Activism and the Popular Front* (London and New York: I. B. Tauris, 2007).

4 The party had 5000 members in February 1934, and 18,000 in December 1938. Figures from Andrew Thorpe, *The British Communist Party and Moscow, 1920–43* (Manchester and New York: Manchester University Press, 2000), p. 284.

5 John Callaghan, *Rajani Palme Dutt: A Study in British Stalinism* (London: Lawrence & Wishart, 1993), p. 167.

6 For Communist intellectuals in this period, see John McIlroy, 'The Establishment of Intellectual Orthodoxy and the Stalinization of British Communism 1928–33', *Past & Present*, 192 (August 2006), pp. 187–226.

7 R. Palme Dutt, 'Intellectuals and Communism', *Communist Review* (September 1932), pp. 421–30.

8 See for example the significant Popular Front collection of essays on cultural questions, Cecil Day Lewis (ed.), *The Mind in Chains: Socialism and the Cultural Revolution* (London: Muller, 1937).

9 See John Lewis, *The Left Book Club: An Historical Record* (London: Victor Gollancz, 1970).

10 Lynda Morris and Robert Radford, *The Artists International Association 1933–1953* (Oxford: Museum of Modern Art, 1983); Colin Chambers, *The Story of Unity Theatre* (London: Lawrence & Wishart, 1989).

11 David Margolies (ed.), *Writing the Revolution: Cultural Criticism from Left Review* (London and Chicago: Pluto, 1998).

12 Dimitrov, *The Working Class Against Fascism*, pp. 68–74.

13 Harry Pollitt, 'Lessons of 1381 Still Thrill Today', review of Hymie Fagan, *Nine Days that Shook England*, *Daily Worker* (10 August 1938), p. 7; Harry Pollitt, 'History Points the Way to Unity', review of Allen Hutt, *The Post-War History of the British Working Class*, *Daily Worker* (16 June 1937), p. 4.

7

The CPGB, 1939–47

The international crisis that culminated in the Second World War exposed deep tensions between the Communist Party's identity as a British organisation – able to formulate radical policies in response to national events – and its overriding loyalty to the 'first workers' state', the Soviet Union.[1] Between the Second World War and the onset of the Cold War the party would make headway when those identities pulled in the same direction; at other moments it would find itself caught in impossible contradictions.

The party was at the core of the movement to create an anti-fascist Popular Front government, but was less clear about what line to take in the increasingly likely event of war against Hitler under Neville Chamberlain's National Government (1937–40). The issue broke to the surface over the question of conscription, which Chamberlain introduced in April 1939. Though the party initially opposed conscription from a government denounced for fascist appeasement, this position sat uneasily with ongoing calls for military alliance with the Soviet Union and France (where conscription was already in place). The line was changed after unambiguous intervention from Moscow the following month, an unwelcome diktat that provoked General Secretary Harry Pollitt to threaten his resignation.[2]

In the months following the conscription crisis a more coherent position took shape. The party campaigned for collective security through a military Anglo-French alliance with the Soviet Union, while remaining vociferously sceptical of Chamberlain's commitment to anti-fascism. As war draw nearer, the party assumed more bellicose tones, notably in Pollitt's pamphlet *Will It Be War?* (July 1939), which now inflected the progressive patriotism of Popular Front years with a proud emphasis on Britain's fighting traditions and spirit. It was a theme to which Pollitt warmed, and which would resonate through his next pamphlet, *How to Win the War*, published in mid-September.

By then, however, Pollitt's preferred line – a war on two fronts, against the men of Munich, against rampaging fascism – had been rendered obsolete by the Hitler–Stalin pact of 23 August 1939. A flourish of Soviet *realpolitik* not easily distinguished from the appeasement Communists had long denounced, the pact appeared a Comintern U-turn from internationalist anti-fascism to Soviet self-preservation. The *Daily Worker* initially presented the pact as a diplomatic triumph compatible with the ongoing Soviet alliance between France and Britain;[3] this gloss on events was soon overruled by Moscow, who insisted that the war should now be denounced as one of inter-imperialist rivalry.[4] The New Line fractured the Left Book Club, the most significant institution to emerge from the Popular Front's energies.[5] Behind closed doors, it also divided the very leadership of the Communist Party of Great Britain. Some of the Central Committee proved supple in their willingness to reflect the views of the Comintern; others were more recalcitrant. At the pivotal meetings on 2 and 3 October 1939, Harry Pollitt and veteran Communist J. R. Campbell voted against the New Line, and were removed from their posts as General Secretary and *Daily Worker* editor respectively.[6]

The symbolism of the pact was powerful, vividly dramatising the central conundrum of how the party's historical mission – to mobilise the working class against capitalism and towards self-liberation – was forever entangled in the interests of the Soviet Union, from where the CPGB's political authority ultimately derived. Its real impact on the Communist Party was, however, less severe than might be imagined. Party membership actually grew slightly during this period, despite the Russo-Finnish war in which Stalin used military force to shore up the border near Leningrad.[7] The day-to-day activities of Communists were not significantly altered by seismic national and international political events, which the party was, in reality, always too small to influence.[8]

Though the New Line formally remained in place for over twenty months, the fervour with which the war was denounced diminished once the so-called 'bore war' exploded into military crisis and Hitler swept through Europe. From January 1941 much Communist activity centred closer to home on a 'People's Convention', a coalition whose six-point charter included issues such as improving wartime living standards and protecting trade union and democratic rights. The popularity of such initiatives, which tapped into widely shared wartime discontent, ensured that the party remained on the radar of the Secret Services. The outright banning of the party was discussed in the corridors of power (the party duly made preparations to operate as an underground organisation); in one instance of especially vigilant surveillance a local amateur dramatic production staged by Communists was shut down;[9] less surprisingly the *Daily Worker* and a smaller CPGB publication, *The Week*, were suppressed on 21 January 1941.

Relief from this limbo paradoxically came with Hitler's invasion of the Soviet Union on 22 June 1941. The 'imperialist' war now imperilled the very existence of the 'bulwark of the world proletariat' and enabled marginalised Communists to fall in step with wartime feeling (the *Daily Worker* was permitted to resume publication on 7 September 1942).[10] The key political instincts of Harry Pollitt – summarised by his biographer as leftist patriotism, hatred of fascism and devotion to the Soviet Union – now crystallised into a single vision of a people's war and people's peace, and he was duly reinstated as General Secretary of the party.[11] From being a source of suspicion and an impediment to progress, the party's connection to the heroic Soviet Union suddenly became its key asset. Applications to join the party increased in proportion to the military feats of the Red Army (membership peaked at 56,000 in December 1942, compared with 17,500 in January 1940).[12] A new mood of constructive engagement took root in this context: the morale-lowering People's Convention was suspended; strikes damaging to wartime production targets were criticised; the party officially backed Winston Churchill's coalition government – a 'cornerstone of all human progress' according to the *Daily Worker*.[13] Taking the spirit of wartime coalition very literally, the party even refrained from pressing home its wartime popularity in electoral terms, standing aside from contesting parliamentary seats.

However, if the party appeared galvanised by this mood of wartime co-operation – a mood enhanced by Stalin, who dissolved the mistrusted Comintern in May 1943 – its leadership was caught off-guard by the depth of radical feeling the war had unleashed. The Labour Party's imminent electoral landslide was clearly not in Pollitt's mind in March 1945 when he proposed that the wartime coalition government should be extended to ease the country into peace. The party contested that July election on a programme that, in terms of domestic policy, largely overlapped with Labour's manifesto (Pollitt's election broadcast made no criticisms of Labour).[14] The party did not, however, share in the electoral spoils, returning just two MPs and losing its deposit in twelve of the twenty-one seats contested. The resulting post-mortem, in the form of the Party's 18th Congress that November, was unusually open. The pages of the weekly CPGB journal *World News and Views* and critical congress resolutions from local branches vented members' frustrations about inattentive top-down leadership, rigidly bureaucratic party structures and a wartime policy that lacked critical detachment from the political establishment.[15] Isolated political struggles seemed momentarily to re-ignite more militant traditions: Communists played a leading role in the mass squatting movement of 1946, in which homeless families defied the logic of property relations and occupied military bases, blocks of flats and even, on one occasion, a Bloomsbury hotel.[16] But from the leadership, the dominant tone of the period was not revolutionary or even consistently oppositional, but of constructive participation in the reforming priorities of the new Labour government. In an extension to the strategy of the wartime years, government candidates were endorsed in by-elections and trade unions were encouraged to be forever mindful of production levels. Pollitt detected in the wartime spirit – 'the many-sided effort and sacrifice of peoples and Governments, this tremendous new international cooperation' – the outlines of a better future; Dutt claimed that 'a new world is being born, not yet a Socialist world, but a tremendous advance toward Socialism'.[17] The essential political assumptions that framed this increasingly constitutionalist emphasis would later be codified into the party's new programme, *The British Road to Socialism* (1951). Before then, however, international events in the form of the Cold War would return the party to a more embattled position on the fringes of British political life.

7.1–7.2 Nazi–Soviet pact

These two items from the *Daily Worker* on 23 August 1939 give the party's immediate response to the emerging Nazi–Soviet pact.

7.1: Soviet's dramatic peace move to halt aggressors: Premier decides to recall commons on Thursday

The eyes of the entire world were turned on the Soviet Union yesterday.

Today von Ribbentrop, German Foreign Minister, is flying to Moscow to attempt to conclude a non-aggression pact between Germany and the Soviet Union.

As realisation of the significance of this master-stroke of Soviet peace policy dawned upon the world, it was seen as

> a shattering blow to the policy of the 'anti-comintern pact' on which past aggressions, particularly in Spain and the Far East, were based;

> a thunderbolt for the Chamberlain Cabinet, which has for long months been sabotaging the conversations for an Anglo-Soviet Pact in the hope of reaching another 'Munich' with Hitler;

> a demonstration before the world of the decisive power of the Soviet Union and of the results which can be achieved by a genuine stand against aggression.

The very first result of the announcement was the sudden collapse of the Chamberlain decision not to recall Parliament in accordance with public demand. [...]

Daily Worker (23 August 1939), p. 1.

7.2: Soviet–German talks victory for peace and socialism: blow to the fascist war plans and the policy of Chamberlain

Communist Party's statement

The following statement on the Soviet–German negotiations was issued yesterday by the Central Committee of the Communist Party of Great Britain.

The announcement of the Soviet–German trade and credit agreement and negotiation between the two governments for the conclusion of a pact of non-aggression represents a victory for peace and Socialism against the war plans of Fascism and the pro-Fascist policy of Chamberlain.

It represents the fiasco of Hitler's policy of aggression and of Chamberlain's policy of support for that aggression. But it places before the British people, in particular, the sharpest urgency for the conclusion of the Anglo-

Soviet Pact and the removal of Chamberlain.

The significance of this change in Nazi policy cannot be grasped unless we recall that the openly proclaimed aim of Hitler has been the crushing of Bolshevism. This was accompanied by the organisation of the anti-Comintern Pact, ostensibly aimed to bring about the complete encirclement of the Soviet Union. [...]

Hitler knows full well the power of the Soviet Union. Hitler has seen the moral and material aid that the people of the Soviet Union have given to the peoples of Spain, China and Mongolia. It is high time the same things were realised in all their significance by the people of Britain. [...]

The record of negotiations over the Anglo-Soviet Pact are a shameful page in British history. The Soviet Union took the initiative of getting the negotiations for an Anglo-Soviet pact opened. It was clear from the start that Chamberlain had no intention, if he could avoid it, of concluding a pact of mutual assistance with the Soviet Union. [...]

The keystone of the Peace Front is the Anglo-Soviet Pact. Lay this foundation now.

Away with the defeatism and craven hearts.

The British people will resist Fascism whether it comes from abroad or at home. But the price of success is also that the Chamberlain government shall be removed, and a government led by trusted representatives of the Labour movement shall come to power.

Central Committee, Communist Party of Great Britain.

Daily Worker, 23 August 1939, p. 3.

7.3 War on two fronts?

Issued the day before war was formally declared, this manifesto argues for a war on two fronts, against Chamberlain and against fascism.

War! Communist policy
Manifesto issued by the Central Committee, Communist Party of Gt. Britain, Sept. 2nd, 1939.

You are now being called upon to take part in the most cruel war in the history of the world.

One that need never have taken place. One that would have been avoided even in the last days of the crisis, had we had a People's Government in Britain.

Now that the war has come, we have no hesitation in stating the policy of the Communist Party.

We are in support of all necessary measures to secure the victory of democracy over Fascism.

But Fascism will not be defeated by the Chamberlain Government.

The first and most vital step to victory is a new Government in which the key positions are in the hands of trusted representatives of the people who have neither imperialist aims, nor latent sympathies with Fascism.

This is absolutely vital for any success in a war against Fascism abroad and the friends of Fascism in Britain.

Indeed, the essence of the present situation is that the people have now to wage a struggle on two fronts. First, to secure the military victory over Fascism; and second, in order to achieve this, the political victory over Chamberlain and the enemies of democracy in this country. These two aims are inseparable, and the harder the efforts to win one, the more sustained must be the activity to win the other. [...]

For unity and democracy

All the men of Munich Must Go. A New Government must come to power. There can be no real unity in Britain while the present Government is in power.

We call upon the Labour Party to renounce its alliance with the Chamberlain Government, and to use the power Labour has got to obtain a new Government.

Now the nightmare of war is upon us, we Communists cannot stand aside.

Our brothers and comrades are in the armed forces. Our homes, like those of all the working population, will be bombed and destroyed.

Our rights and liberties as a democratic people are in danger if Fascism is allowed to conquer. The victory over Fascism will also be a victory over the rich friends of Fascism Britain.

Never again must the destinies of our country be at the mercy of the rich.

To-day the British people are called upon to pay a heavy price for their toleration of Chamberlain and the policy of the dominant group of Labour leaders.

To-day the British people are called upon to pay a heavy price for their desertion of other democratic peoples which looked in vain for our help in their own struggle against Fascism.

Now tens of thousands of British soldiers and civilians will die in a war that could have been prevented if we had all acted together in the defence of these other peoples.

Remember these things now and direct your wrath not only against Hitler, but against the enemies of democracy in Britain. The stronger your anger against them the stronger will be your fight against Hitler and for the victory over Fascism.

Central Committee, Communist Party of Great Britain

Daily Worker (2 September 1939). Reprinted in Harry Pollitt, *How to Win the War* (London: CPGB, 1939), pp. 25–31.

7.4 How to win the war

Harry Pollitt's pamphlet *How to Win the War* was published on 14 September 1939, the same day that a telegram arrived from Moscow indicating that the war should be seen as 'imperialist', a line that the CPGB would adopt – after much acrimony – over the following weeks.

On September 3rd, 1939, Britain and France declared war on Germany. [...]
In a Manifesto printed in the *Daily Worker* on September 2nd, the Communist Party clearly stated its policy in connection with the war.

'We are in support of all measures to secure the victory of democracy over fascism.'

The Communist Party supports the war, believing it to be a just war which should be supported by the whole working class and all friends of democracy in Britain.

Why does the Communist Party support this war?
It has always maintained, and still maintains, that the fundamental cause of war is the capitalist system. Nevertheless, as the Manifesto states:

It has never hidden and never will hide its detestation of Fascism and its readiness to take part in any struggle, political or military, to secure the defeat of Fascism. For it recognises that the victory of Fascism represents not only a conquest of markets, colonies, sources of raw materials etc., it also leads to the forcible destruction of every democratic right and liberty that the working class has fought so bitterly, and at such cost and sacrifice, to win from its class enemies. [...] For if these democratic rights were lost, this would represent a defeat for the working class, which, long after time had healed the wounds caused by the grief and suffering that war brings, would involve the most bitter struggles and sacrifices in the future to retain those rights and liberties which are essential for the advancement of the working class and the achievement of a Socialist world, from which the menace of war will have been removed for ever.

These fundamental principles of liberty, peace and Socialism now at stake have determined the decision of the Communist Party. To stand aside from this conflict, to contribute only revolutionary-sounding phrases while the fascist beasts ride roughshod over Europe, would be a betrayal of everything our forbears have fought to achieve in the course of long years of struggle against capitalism. [...]

Harry Pollitt, *How to Win the War* (London: CPGB, 1939), pp. 3–4.

7.5 Volte-face

In this document Comintern loyalist Dutt uses his 'Notes of the Month' column to justify the about turn.

[...] Now that the war is here, under the conditions of Chamberlain's choosing, not of our choosing, what course must the British and French peoples, what course must the working-class fighters against fascism pursue? Though it is a war against Hitler, the spearhead of international reaction and the deadly enemy of the international labour movement, the fact must be faced that it is an imperialist war. This is not the war of the Peace Front against fascist aggression; for the Peace Front was never realised; the realisation of the Peace Front would have meant, not war, but peace. The British and French reactionaries are not fighting for democracy against fascism; or they would have stood by Spain and Czechoslovakia. They are not fighting for the freedom of small nations, or for the sanctity of treaties, or for the maintenance of peace against aggression. They have trampled all these principles under foot and shown in practice that they have no care for them. They are fighting for their own imperialist interests and nothing else. They are fighting because the further advance of Hitler-fascism, to the domination of Europe, to the south-east and to the Middle Eastern Empire, and to the demand for colonies, threatens the vital interests of British imperialism. They are fighting for the maintenance of the British Empire against a rival imperialism. And even though they have formally declared war, they still seek for a way out, for a basis of settlement that could divert the imperialist war, whose deadly menace to their own system they well understand, into the channels of counter-revolutionary war. They use the slogans of anti-fascism for their own dirty aims. They will pursue the war for their imperialist aims to reach an imperialist peace. On all these harsh realities there is no room for illusions.

The standpoint of the working class and of the democratic anti-fascists in relation to this war must be an independent standpoint, irreconcilably opposed to that of the imperialists. [...] Since the collapse of the aim of the Peace Front, through the failure of the Western democratic movements, and the consequent alternative path of the Soviet–German Non-Aggression Pact, we have entered into a completely new international political situation in which it would be self-destructive blindness to endeavour to operate with conceptions belonging to conditions which have vanished. We need to face the new situation, which will require the most careful review of all the problems by the working class movement. With merciless realism the working-class leadership of the Soviet Union has faced the new situation and seen how to utilise it to advance the interests of world socialism. The working-class movements of Western and Central Europe will need to face the situation, and the sharp problems raised by the war, with no less realism and audacity in defining their tasks and seeing the historical role which falls to them in the present developing situation. [...] The problems before the working-class movement are sharp and urgent. But the dilemmas of the imperialists are a hundred times greater. They can neither find their solution in peace nor in war. The Soviet Union grows immeasurably stronger. The basis of the fascist dictatorships is being undermined. Explosive situations develop in all the belligerent countries. The colonial peoples stir against their bonds and see before them new possibilities of advancing their struggle for liberation. The second imperialist war is the historical signal for mass awakening in the countries of Europe and in all the colonial countries, and for new advance to the goal of world socialism.

Rajani Palme Dutt, from 'Notes of the Month', *Labour Monthly* (October 1939), pp. 593–6.

7.6 People's Convention

This document spells out the context and priorities of the 'People's Convention', the party's key initiative in the period of its opposition to the war.

The People's Convention
The following call for the People's Convention to be held on January 12, 1941, for a People's Government has been issued by the National Committee, People's Convention [...]
   In these eventful days the whole future of our people is being decided. The full horrors of war are let loose on the peoples of Britain, Germany and other countries, and millions are looking into the future with anxious

concern. Our rulers have proved themselves bankrupt of constructive thought or action. The time has come for the people to unite in defence of their interests.

The present Government is a Government of the rich and privileged, ruling the country in their own interest and against those of the masses of the people.

Behind it are the ruling class, the Tory machine, the men of Munich, the friends of Fascism, whose policy built up the power of Hitler, brought the nation into war, and is diretcly [sic] responsible for the unpreparedness which has sacrificed scores of thousands of lives.

* * *

This Government stands rooted in the profit system. It is dominated by the Tory machine. It represents those natural enemies of the mass of people, the interests of big business and reaction. Such a Government can never defend the people.

The interests of the people must override the interests of those who prey on the people.

This Government, which represents the interests of profits must go.

In this hour of crisis, threatened by limitless danger and hardships, the people must make their will felt. The present Parliament, elected five years ago under entirely different conditions, is reactionary and unrepresentative. The formation of a coalition Government has wiped out the normal functioning of parliamentary opposition.

The work of the Labour Movement is paralysed because the leadership of the Labour Party is tied up with the Government, and in place of leading the opposition to it, shares the responsibility for the present evils. Vital issues, affecting lives and deaths of millions, will continue to be decided in secret over the heads of the people, if the people do not make their will prevail.

The people must unite to make their will felt.

* * *

As a step to the victory of the people's demands and the assertion of their power, their delegates must meet together in a Great People's Convention.

Following on conferences all over the country, and in accordance with declared will of those conferences, we, the undersigned, representing the most varied sections of the people, have united to call a People's Convention, to be held on January 12, 1941, which will be at once the climax of months of preparatory work and the prelude of a further mighty campaign. [...] [W]e propose, as the basis on which the convention is called and in preparation for the full platform which will be decided by the Convention, the following Six Points:

(1) *Defence of the people's living standards.*
(2) *Defence of the people's democratic and trade union rights.*
(3) *Adequate air raid precautions, deep bomb-proof shelters, rehousing and relief of victims.*
(4) *Friendship with the Soviet Union.*
(5) *A People's Government, truly representative of the whole people and able to inspire the confidence of the working people of the world.*
(6) *A people's peace that gets rid of the causes of war.* [...]

Labour Monthly (November 1940), pp. 601–2.

7.7 Second Front

This article, written by reinstated General Secretary Harry Pollitt four months after Hitler invaded the Soviet Union, calls for a military Second Front to relieve pressure on the Red Army. It also casts forward to the post-war order, detecting in collectivist and co-operative wartime production the outlines of a different Britain.

The way to victory
[...] What did Hitler hope to achieve when he attacked the Soviet Union? That by posing thus as 'the saviour of the world from Bolshevism', he would split the ranks of the people in the democratic countries.

The immediate formation of the Anglo-Soviet Alliance, as a reply to Hitler's invasion of the Soviet Union, was the first major political blow he has received since the start of the war. [...]

It is time we stopped admiring the Russians so much, and performed deeds alongside them that proved we are Allies, and prepared to sacrifice as much to smash Hitler as the Russians are doing.

Time we stopped so much loose talk about 'Russia's vast manpower and Britain's productive capacity' and realised that the day when other countries did all the fighting and dying, while we made munitions for them, has gone for ever.

This is why we not only have to send now to the Soviet Union all the planes, tanks and guns possible, but to create a Second Front that will show Fascism that the Anglo-Soviet Alliance is one of deeds and actions. [...]

The creation of a Second Front is a task which will involve great sacrifices and it is our duty to face them. [...]

If we are not prepared for such sacrifices to be made, then we have no right to expect others to continue to make the colossal sacrifices they are making now.

We have, also, no right to demand a Second Front, unless we are going to create a production front that can achieve the very maximum from the productive resources of Britain.

Despite all the sunshine stories to the contrary, the simple fact is that there is not a factory, mine or shipyard in Britain of any consequence where the workers employed in them are not aware of the possibilities that exist for a tremendous increase in their productive capacity.

The whole position has got to such a stage that when you mention the word Production, it only raises cynical comment or amused ironical adjectives.

It is caused by the appalling waste, inefficiency, lack of planning and control, wasted labour hours, lack of continuity in the productive process, the thousands of non-producers floating around factories, impeding production by their multiplicity of directives and so-called 'expert' opinions.

There is no single plan or control either in the allocation of contracts or the carrying out what are allocated.

This is a terrible position to have reached at a time when we are fighting for the whole future of humanity. But it can be remedied and quickly at that if the job is tackled with the necessary candour, thoroughness and relentless determination to smash down any barrier that stands in the way. [...]

This is why as in all things connected with the conduct and winning of the war it is so urgently necessary that the workers in the factories should feel their own power, and be confident in the exercise of that power. For it is upon what they do that the issue depends both now and in the future. Once men and women on the job are really angry at what they see going on, and fight to put it right, then things will begin to move and not before. And trade union conditions can be absolutely safeguarded and shop stewards, factory and trade union organisations as a whole considerably strengthened. [...]

We take the view that the workers who are going to win the victory over foreign Fascists and reactionaries will never allow any of the British breed to try it on after the victory has been won.

This is why while fighting to rectify every abuse that springs from capitalist mismanagement and profiteering, at the same time we have to get together in the factories as between one shop steward and another, between one trade union and another, and co-operate together in workshop practices and customs in such a way that nothing is allowed to stand in the way of all round increase in production. That skill, output, willingness to teach others, especially to make the fullest use of the army of women who are now coming into war industry shall be the intention of every worker, that the quality, quantity and rapidity with which we turn out the planes, guns, tanks, ships, shells and coal shall amaze the world. [...]

Harry Pollitt, *Labour Monthly* (October 1941), pp. 415–21.

7.8 Supporting the government

Daily Worker editor William Rust, formally an advocate of the 'imperialist war' line, here calls for ongoing constructive support of the Churchill government.

Labour and the government
The editor of the Daily Worker *shows that anti-fascist unity is still the primary task*

The heroism and sacrifice of the Red Army have brought us to the most glorious moment of the war – the turning point where joint offensive actions of the Allies can most certainly bring the Fascist enemy to its knees.

But what is our nation doing in these heroic days?

It is losing touch with the grim realities of the war and turning to all kinds of diversionary issues.

Hence the concentration on post-war blueprints, the bitterness about the by-elections, the desire to end national unity, the easy gossip about Labour leaving the government and the emergence of irresponsible and adventuristic political groupings.

One cannot contemplate this scene without shame and perplexity.

For at this moment when so many British men and women are turning their backs on the war, tens of thousands of Red Army men are dying for our cause and steeling themselves for the most desperate and bloodily ferocious round of the struggle. Listen to the stern, wise words of Stalin on the 25th anniversary of the Red Army. He is speaking to us as well as to them.

> The struggle against German invaders is not yet ended – it is as yet only developing and flaring up ... The Red Army has before it a grim struggle against a perfidious, cruel, and, as yet, strong enemy ... That is why there can be no place for complacency, carelessness or conceit in our ranks.

* * *

From Stalin's Order of the Day I turn to the letters of those Daily Worker readers who are horrified at our advice that in the interests of national unity they should vote for Government candidates in by-elections.

How can a Labour man vote for a Conservative? What a head-aching conundrum! How can capitalist Britain and Socialist Russia stand united against the common Fascist enemy? This is the real question.

We can vote for Conservative because our future as a people depends on holding together a Government that will continue an alliance which is the cornerstone of all human progress.

If the Nazis were at this moment directly threatening Britain, the posing of by-election conundrums would have but little attraction. But the illusion has grown up that we are no longer threatened, that the Red Army has won the war for us. [...]

But the war is not won. Britain is still threatened by Fascists. The hardest battles have yet to be fought. [...]

We want to see the Government and the country brought directly up against the most urgent question of the day – the opening of the Second Front in Europe. [...]

To-day all free men stand in profound admiration before the deeds and sacrifices of the Soviet People. What they dared to achieve springs from their confidence in their own united strength. The working-class movement in Britain, if it only has faith in itself, can also move mountains. Let us now display that faith. [...] Let the working class assume its real role as the leader of the nation.

William Rust, *Daily Worker* (27 February 1943), p. 2.

7.9 Transitions

Like his pamphlet *How to Win the Peace* (1944), Harry Pollitt's *Answers to Questions* (1945) struck a note in CPGB discourse far removed from the insurrectionist tones of *For Soviet Britain* (1935). In a constructive spirit, Pollitt enthusiastically endorsed the proclamations of post-war peace and mutual co-operation issuing from the 'Big Three' (Stalin, Churchill and Roosevelt) in their wartime gatherings at Tehran (1943) and Yalta (1945). And in a break from Leninist vanguardism, he envisaged such global peace and co-operation creating a context that might enable a gradual, peaceful transition to socialism.

Is a peaceful transition to socialism possible?
[...] There can be no doubt that the conditions created by the great political changes arising out of this war are now objectively more favourable for the peaceful transition to socialism than they have ever been, and Communists have always worked for precisely such a transformation.

Socialism will become the issue when the majority of the British people democratically decide that the time has come to replace capitalism by a socialist order.

Will they, the capitalist class, accept the democratic verdict of the people, or will they, as so often in the past, organise measures of violence against those who peacefully wish to transfer society from capitalism to socialism? The extent and nature of the democratic advance and transformation we can win now will decide. And the greatest guarantee of such advance is the unity of the Labour movement. [...]

We believe that the force and violence used in this war has brought with it results, which taken together, in the conditions of our time, constitute as great an advance for the workers of the world as the Russian Revolution did. We believe it has also settled the question of future wars. Likewise it has made it doubly difficult for the reactionary capitalist forces, after a war waged with extreme violence to defend democracy, to resort to violence to crush democracy.

The Communists have always endeavoured to avoid using force and violence. [...]

The aim of the Communist Party is to achieve a Socialist Britain, in which the public ownership of the means of production and exchange shall replace the existing capitalist system.

Only a Socialist Britain, co-operating with all other peoples of the world in close, friendly, free and equal association, will be able so to plan the use of all Britain's material, productive and scientific resources, that every citizen will be guaranteed security, the right to work, and leisure, a steadily rising standard of living, liberty and equal opportunity for a full and happy life. [...]

In striving to achieve these great aims, we are making the greatest possible contribution towards the possibility of a peaceful transition to Socialism, but we are under no illusions about the character of the political fight that will have to be made to win them, the outcome of which will be decided in accord with the economic and political conditions prevailing at the time.

Harry Pollitt, *Answers to Questions* (London: Central Books, nd [1945]), pp. 39–42.

7.10–7.11 Groundswell

These documents reflect the rank and file discontent with the party's leadership and priorities in the run up to the 18th Congress in November 1945. 7.10 consists of critical resolutions submitted for consideration at the Congress, 7.11 is correspondence printed in the party weekly, *World News and Views*.

7.10: [...] Party Policy

187. That this Congress considers that the results of the General Election showed that our Party under-estimated the deep political change among the people. We resolve, therefore, to considerably extend our mass activity and work among the People.
Portsmouth Branch [...]

190. That this Congress requests that a commission be set up to investigate the reasons for the recent loss in membership and loss of enthusiasm among members and to report on the reasons for any mistakes in policy which have contributed to this situation.
South Leicester Branch [...]

202. That the Labour movement needs an organised party, basing its action on the Marxist analysis of society; that our Communist Party can and should fulfil this role if it is functioning correctly; that mistakes made by our Party in recent years are due to:
(a) Lack of education of the members in Marxist theory.
(b) A tendency to stifle expression of minority opinion within the Party, which has encouraged on the one hand automatic acceptance of directives, and on the other, discouragement and cynicism.
(c) Incorrect political analyses by our leadership, resulting from lack of contact with the masses, and inadequate understanding of Marxism.
Milngavie Branch

Communist Party 18th Congress, November, 1945: Resolutions and Agenda (London: CPGB, 1945), pp. 49–59.

7.11: Comrade, – We wish to support [...] a more conscious approach to theory. 'Practice without theory is blind'; [...] revisionist theory [...] influenced Answers to Questions and cost us dearly in the General Election. [...]

Unless we realise that the social revolution is a world process which must be studied as a whole, we shall inevitably adopt the social-democratic view that socialism can be won by a progressive home policy alone. This has obvious bearing on our propaganda, as there is a danger that we shall underestimate the importance of forcing the radical change in foreign policy without which very little can be achieved.
Joan D. Smith (Nottingham University Branch)
H. F. W. Taylor (Beeston Branch)

World News and Views (27 October 1945), p. 335.

Comrade, – [...] Apart from the incredibly defeatist outlook which led to the Party's suggestion of collaboration with the Tories after the Election, over which the curtain of forgetfulness has been so markedly drawn, the Party obviously underestimated the swing to the Left and at the same time over-estimated the support for the Party as such. The working class, with their instinctive recognition of the class struggle, voted solidly against the Boss, while we were thinking in terms of Political Parties.

These and other mistakes derive from a basic theoretical weakness at all levels of the Party and the fight against revisionism is the first essential towards strengthening the Party.

S. Beechey (London, E.8)

World News and Views (31 November 1945), p. 345.

Comrade, – There seems to be no attempt by the E.C. [Executive Committee] to carry out a serious analysis of the situation and issue a Marxist thesis for discussion in the Party. [...]

Of democratic centralism practically everything has been liquidated, to leave us with the stifling and stultifying so-called democracy of social-democracy, in which the leadership is practically immutable and the membership expected to do as they are told. [...]

In recent months the leadership of the Party have [...] been leading the Party into the slough of social democracy.

We need truthfully and completely to return to a Marxist-Leninist policy and education, but it appears that the present leadership, or at least part of it, are either unwilling or incapable to pursue such a line.

W. Zak (London, N.W. 8)

World News and Views (17 November 1945), p. 346.

Notes

1 For these vicissitudes, see Kevin Morgan, *Against Fascism and War: Ruptures and Continuities in British Communist Politics, 1935–41* (Manchester: Manchester University Press, 1989) and Andrew Thorpe, *The British Communist Party and Moscow, 1920–43* (Manchester: Manchester University Press, 2000).

2 Kevin Morgan, *Harry Pollitt* (Manchester: Manchester University Press, 1993), pp. 105–6.

3 'Soviet Dramatic Peace Move to Halt Aggressor', and 'Soviet-German Talks Victory for Peace and Socialism', *Daily Worker* (23 August 1939). The pact was presented as a 'master stroke of Soviet peace policy'.

4 See Francis King and George Matthews (eds), *About Turn: The Communist Party and the Outbreak of the Second World War* (London: Lawrence & Wishart, 1990), Thorpe, *The British Communist Party and Moscow*, pp. 257–60 and Morgan, *Harry Pollitt*, pp. 107–14.

5 The faultline was the Soviet Union. The Left Book Club's decision to publish Leonard Woolf's *Barbarians at the Gate* (November 1939), with its criticisms of the Soviet Union, antagonised Communist club members; the decision to publish Hewlett Johnson's defence of the Soviet Union, *The Socialist Sixth of the World* (December 1939) incensed the club's non-Communists. Victor Gollancz sought to smooth the tensions in 'Show Down', *Left News* (January 1940), pp. 1415–20

6 Later that month Pollitt would write two brief articles for the *Daily Worker* (13 October 1939 and 23 November 1939) flagellating himself for his breach in discipline. See Morgan, *Harry Pollitt*, p. 112.

7 Willie Thompson, *The Good Old Cause: British Communism 1920–1991* (London: Pluto, 1992), p. 69.

8 Thorpe, *The British Communist Party and Moscow*, pp. 261–7.

9 See Ben Harker, 'Mediating the 1930s: Documentary and Politics in Theatre Union's *Last Edition* (1940)' in Alison Forsyth and Chris Megson (eds), *Get Real: Documentary Theatre Past and Present* (London: Palgrave, 2009), pp. 24–38.

10 Quotation from Dimitrov, *The Working Class Against Fascism* (London: Martin Lawrence, 1935), p. 9.

11 Morgan, *Harry Pollitt*, p. 131.

12 Thorpe, *The British Communist Party and Moscow*, p. 284.

13 William Rust, 'Labour and the Government', *Daily Worker* (27 February 1943).

14 'Harry Pollitt's Broadcast', *Daily Worker* (29 June 1945).

15 Morgan, *Harry Pollitt*, pp. 146–7.

16 James Hinton, 'Self-Help and Socialism: The Squatters' Movement of 1946', *History Workshop Journal*, 25 (spring 1988), pp. 100–27; Paul Burnham, 'The Squatters of 1946: A Local Study in a National Context', *Socialist History*, 25 (2004), pp. 20–46.

17 R. Palme Dutt, review of Pollitt's *How to Win the Peace*, *Daily Worker* (8 September 1944).

8

The national road and the British cultural tradition, 1947–56

The Communist Party's support for the post-war Labour government's domestic agenda was checked by misgivings over foreign matters. Through 1945 Communists were sharply critical of Labour's policy in Greece, which continued Churchill's opposition to the leftist resistance movement in preference for an autocratic monarchy; Communists also opposed the government's colonialist policy in Malaya, which again involved military conflict with Communists who had recently led anti-fascist resistance movements.[1] These flashpoints were soon eclipsed by broader tensions between the Soviet Union and its former wartime allies. By the final months of 1945 leading party theorist Rajani Palme Dutt could detect a 'Western Bloc' taking shape in opposition to the Soviet Union; Dutt saw in Labour's increasingly American-oriented foreign policy a strategy to retain British global influence in the midst of economic crisis.[2] This analysis appeared to be substantiated by the Anglo-American Loan Agreement of December 1945, the Truman Doctrine of March 1947 and the Marshall Plan three months later, measures collectively concerned with the stabilisation of European capitalism, the entrenchment of American hegemony and the containment of the Soviet Union, excluded from Marshall Aid.[3] The polarising logic of the Cold War found its equal in Stalin, who responded by shoring up his power in the Eastern Bloc through the imposition of Soviet-style dictatorships and in 1947 by the creation of a new nerve centre for an era of anti-American ideological struggle, the Communist Information Bureau (Cominform).

A new language of 'national roads to socialism' pervaded the Communist movement, extending the policy of nationally grounded Popular Fronts, and marking a further retreat from the revolutionary Leninism that, officially at least, had remained the fundamental creed of the international Communist movement throughout the 1930s. The causes for this shift were numerous: the election of post-war Popular Front governments across Europe (including France, Italy, Norway) appeared to demonstrate national Communist parties making headway through constitutional means; the so-called 'People's Democracies' in Eastern Europe were often cited to support the argument that socialism could be reached without revolution. Stalin was increasingly concerned with consolidating power within his Eastern European sphere of influence, and the Western Communist parties – most too remote from political power even to qualify for Cominform membership – seemed increasingly peripheral to his concerns.

In March 1946 Dimitrov formally explained that nations would reach socialism by different roads, depending on their 'historical, social and cultural circumstances'.[4] Harry Pollitt's pamphlet *Looking Ahead* (1947) echoed this analysis, invoking 'a British road to socialism' in terms which implied that the Leninist route of revolution and the dictatorship of the proletariat might be bypassed. These initially vague formulations were codified into a new programme, *The British Road to Socialism* (1951), which superseded *For Soviet Britain* (1935) with its now outmoded insistence that 'capitalism cannot be overthrown by Parliament' but only by 'workers' revolution'.[5] Prepared with input from Stalin but not the party membership, *The British Road to Socialism* was a striking synthesis of Cold War rhetoric – Britain was presented as a military base and 'satellite' of American imperialism – and a new confidence that the route to socialism lay in 'a People's Government on the basis of a parliament truly representative of the people'.[6] Optimistically launched to connect the party with these people, the new constitutional emphasis coincided with bruising electoral defeats, cruelly measuring the party's isolation.[7] The two Communist MPs, Willie Gallacher and Phil Piratin, lost their seats in the general election of 1950, drawing a permanent line under the party's parliamentary representation. In the general election the following year, the party contested just ten seats, losing its deposit in each.

The cultural front

During the war the British state had made unprecedented interventions into the country's cultural life when, under the Council for the Encouragement of Music and Art (CEMA) – the forerunner of the Arts Council – a wide variety of morale-boosting culture had been brought within reach of the broad population through a combination of local initiatives and touring productions.[18] Communists eagerly charted and participated in this 'cultural upsurge' and worked to stimulate and support 'a people's culture worthy of this great people's war'.[9] The Communist-dominated Workers' Music Association co-ordinated music activities;[10] the *Daily Worker* championed cultural advances in theatre and warned against the American domination of the film industry;[11] the Communist-dominated cultural journal *Our Time* became a key vector of the post-war cultural mood, reaching a monthly readership of 18,000 by 1945 under the judicious editorship of Edgell Rickword.[12]

The national post-war appetite for a cultural life that had traditionally been confined to a metropolitan elite was matched by an eagerness among Communists to debate the role and significance of national tradition and culture in political struggle. This new mood reached the floor of party Congress in 1945; two years later a motion was carried calling for Communists to 'support and encourage the great cultural awakening of the people at this time', and a National Cultural Committee (NCC) was established to co-ordinate cultural activity.[13] Chaired by Emile Burns with Sam Aaronovitch as a full-time secretary, the committee operated through ten sub-groups including those representing historians, scientists, musicians, film workers, artists and writers.[14]

At its best, this co-ordination served to legitimise and galvanise cultural work – often considered of secondary significance within party circles – and helped to lend momentum to a wide range of initiatives. The most effective functioned with relative autonomy from the NCC while drawing impetus from the *British Road to Socialism*'s overarching claim that the key to a socialist future lay in the resources of the people and the national past. In some cases, projects first initiated during the Popular Front period were revived and fleshed out. The Historians Group, for example, developed and deepened the recovery of radical national traditions initiated in A. L. Morton's *A People's History of England* (1938), through its journal *Past & Present* (launched 1952), its bulletin *Our History* (1953) and monographs and biographies written by members including Christopher Hill, Eric Hobsbawm and Dora Torr.[15] In a similar vein, Ewan MacColl and A. L. Lloyd drew upon the Popular Front period's emerging interest in the democratic resonances of folk song, and were prominent in laying the foundations of Britain's 1950s and 1960s folk revival.[16]

Success in these ventures lay in their sensitivity to the specificity of different historical experiences and cultural traditions, but the force-field of Cold War politics came to exert an increasingly distorting pressure on the party's cultural life. From the late 1940s onwards, the masthead for cultural priorities was the 'Battle of Ideas', which soon assumed variations on the title 'The American Threat to British Culture' for subsequent conferences and tie-in publications.[17] The central analysis was that American economic and military domination of Britain was reinforced by 'a Marshall Plan in the field of ideas', which Communists should resist and counter. Party intellectuals, ran the analysis, should expose the 'penetration' of American ideas and culture into British life, and its corrosive effects on 'our national dignity and independence'.[18] They should resist Americanisation by recovering and diffusing potent 'national' cultural traditions and icons – including Charles Dickens, Robert Burns and Geoffrey Chaucer – against the 'brain-softening' cultural invasion which functioned to impose an individualistic, capitalist ideology inimical to Britain's real national traditions and, ultimately, to the British road to socialism.[19]

If intellectuals initially, if cautiously, welcomed the party's cultural turn, the increasingly one-eyed application of this Cold War cultural policy antagonised many. Despite the new emphasis on the nation, party intellectuals were, as ever, under pressure to conform to Soviet-endorsed models, from those of the charlatan geneticist T. D. Lysenko – a favourite of Stalin's resisted by the party's Scientist Group – to the increasingly prescriptive doctrine of 'socialist realism', with its emphasis on cheerily accessible art wholly purged of 'bourgeois formalism'.[20] The Writers Group in particular suffered from the imposition of this less than nuanced aesthetic creed.[21] Two key Communist-dominated but independently run literary journals around which vibrant literary creativity and debate had clustered – *Our Time* and the richly cosmopolitan *Arena* – were co-opted into the dominant anti-American agenda and ruined in the process.[22]

Undaunted, in 1952 the NCC embarked upon a quixotic project to cultivate a nativist proletarian literature rooted in the experiences of Communists; the new journal *Daylight* lasted less than two years.

The paradox of the Communist Party structuring its policies around national independence when its own lodestar remained the Soviet Union was not lost on the party's critics.[23] As so often, events in the Soviet Union were the signal for re-orientation, this time when Stalin's death led to a less combative tone towards America, enabling the 'Battle of Ideas' to be scaled down. The post of full-time cultural secretary, which in 1947 had signalled the seriousness with which the party intended to prosecute the 'ideological struggle', was withdrawn in 1955. Many of the intellectuals who had loomed large on the frontline of the Cold War culture wars would depart the party over the next twelve months in the political crises that soon became synonymous with 1956.

8.1 Workers' music

Founded in 1936, the Communist-dominated WMA co-ordinated workers' involvement in many genres of music, and from 1939 boasted an in-house music label, the enduring Topic Records. This document from 1944 outlines current priorities.

[...] The rising spirits of our people have sought ever increased refreshment to renew them for battle and cultural activity thrives on the crest of their optimism. In spite of the mass of slushy music which commercial interests still think fit to feed the innocent, there are signs everywhere that response to healthy music is quickening. Composers generally, not only in the United States and the Soviet Union but here in this country are showing a more realistic attitude to current affairs. [...] Thus we find articles in most of the authoritative musical press – and not only by WMA contributors – which present musical problems in their correct social setting; we find more and more books being published along the same lines [...].

Thus we find composers of the calibre of Vaughan Williams writing not only new concert works which obviously reflect an earnest contemplation of current events but also turning their hands to the incidental music for documentary films close to the war effort. We find crowded audiences for factory concerts everywhere and music clubs resulting from this new contact with the workers. We find new choirs, new instrumental groups springing up around the places of production. We find old-established musical Summer schools coming down to earth and discussing music for youth clubs and jazz. Surely a damning answer to those who argue that the arts cannot flourish at times of stress! Whether all this would have been possible without State art endowment through such organisations as ENSA [Entertainment National Services Association] and CEMA is a nice point for sober reflection.

We find a great urge among our professional artists to pay tribute to the culture of the allied nations, giving concerts devoted to the latest American and Soviet compositions, and these allied nations reciprocating with concerts of contemporary British works. A grand example of a united front in art and of reconciliation between culture and politics!

In this picture of national art-consciousness our organisation has its corner. Working-class in its origin, it still sees its mission clearly as a guide to the greater labour movement, the trade unions and the co-operatives and a link between them and the community in general – between past achievements and present adventure; as a rallying ground for the musical needs of the people and a resolute opponent of vested interests [...]. Our members are playing a great part in the musical revival of our time. Lecturing, composing, researching, performing, writing, teaching, criticising – they are to be found now throughout the country, many in key positions, carrying through their work of national importance. [...]

Workers' Music Association, Draft Executive Committee's Report (January–June 1944), p. 1.

8.2 Cultural upsurge

Here 'Jack Knife', pseudonym of CPGB activist Jack Woddis, takes the temperature of the 'cultural upsurge'.

People's war – people's culture

[...] The present war, and especially the last two years, have awakened the minds of our people more than at any time in the last two decades. This new development also finds expression in the cultural field. Not only are Soviet novels read by an ever-increasing public, but the best classical novels. [...]

Turn to music, and we find the same development. Last year's Promenade concerts – a record. [...] And the situation today – London with at least six well-filled concerts a week. Hundreds of workers from Hendon's factories come each Sunday to the Orpheum's musical concerts. The BBC Listener Research Department reports symphony concert audiences have risen from 3,000,000 to 4,000,000. In towns and villages all over the country, the Philharmonic Orchestra plays to packed houses. Pianists and violinists under the CEMA scheme play the best classical and modern music to attentive factory workers in canteens. The Postal Officers' Engineering Union sponsors a symphony concert at the Albert Hall; and the ARP [Air Raid Precautions] Co-ordinating committee follows suit with a concert at Kingsway Hall.

In the field of painting 40,000 people visited the recent AIA [Artists International Association] Exhibition at Lewis' blitzed site in Oxford Street. On Easter Sunday 2,000 peoples passed through the National Art Gallery. For every two art exhibitions held before the war, there are now three. CEMA and the Institute for Adult Education are sending art shows all over the country. [...] There have been art shows to raise funds for the Soviet Union, art shows for China, art shows for painters who are fighting, art shows by children, art shows by Civil Defence Workers. Art exhibitions have been held in factories and air-raid shelters. [...]

The biggest task still lies ahead, namely, to produce a people's culture really worthy of this great people's war that will decide the fate of humanity.

Jack Knife, *World News and View* (29 May 1943), p. 176.

8.3 Roads to socialism

Like *How to Win the Peace* (1944) and *Answers to Questions* (1945), Pollitt's pamphlet *Looking Ahead* (1947) anticipated the constitutional emphasis soon fleshed out in the party's new programme, *The British Road to Socialism* (1951).

Roads to socialism in the world today

Marxists have never maintained that the road to Socialism in any country is neatly mapped out and time-tabled, that each county will pass to Socialism in the same way and at the same speed, with similar forms of State organisation, with similar methods of overcoming opposition. Communists have never said that the Russian Revolution of October, 1917, is a model which has exactly to be copied. [...]

The progress of democratic and Socialist forces throughout the world has opened out new possibilities of transition to Socialism by other paths than those followed by the Russian Revolution. The path, in any case, is necessarily different for each county [...].

During the war, 100 million people in Eastern Europe, in Poland and Czechoslovakia, Rumania, Bulgaria, Hungary, Yugoslavia and Albania, in a heroic struggle against Nazi Germany and fascist Italy and against their own reactionary cliques and governments, who worked as puppets of the anti-Communist Bloc, broke the power of the old ruling classes and laid the basis for the new popular democracies, the new States in which the overwhelming majority of the people, the workers, peasants, intellectuals, craftsmen and small traders, the people who do the useful work, play a decisive role, and the State apparatus is manned by their representatives, not representatives of big capitalists or landowners as it used to be. [...]

Thus, 1947 is different from 1917. In a number of countries where popular democracies have been established, a new road to Socialism has opened before the people. In these countries [...] it is possible to see how the people will move towards Socialism without further revolution, without the dictatorship of the proletariat, and how the transition will be far less painful for the people than it was in Russia. [...]

The strength of the progressive forces in the world makes the advance to Socialism easier in every country, but in the last analysis the character of the transition is determined by the unity and strength of the working class and democratic movements within each country. Socialism is not an article of export, and each people must move to Socialism in its own way.

In Britain

In Britain the capitalist control of the State is as yet substantially untouched. British economy is still overwhelmingly capitalist. [...]

Yet the Britain of today is not the Britain of 1939, or the Britain of 1919. The elections of July, 1945, showed a deep change in the outlook of the people, a deep desire to do away with the old conditions and build a new Britain ruled by the people. Thus there exist today new possibilities for the advance to Socialism in Britain also, new ways in which power can be removed from the hands of the capitalist class. The fulfilment of our programme at every stage raises question [sic] of class power. To carry through our programme means that important changes in the State machinery will be necessary. It will be necessary to develop new forms of democracy from the factory upwards, a new democratic development of local government. It will be necessary to purge from the State machine at every stage those elements who are working against the interests of the Labour movement and the people.

We should have no illusions that the capitalists will gracefully accept such changes. We know from experience in this and all countries that no ruling class ever allows power to slip from its influence without furious and prolonged resistance. Socialism will never be given on a plate. But in the measure to which the Labour movement is united, in the measure to which it presses forward energetically for the fulfilment of its programme, the development of a general economic plan, extended nationalisation, reduction of rent, interest and profit, democratisation of the Armed Forces, the Courts and the State, increased working-class and popular control of industry, new recruitment of personnel from the Labour movement for every part of the State machine – to that measure it will succeed in changing conditions in Britain. In that measure it will reduce the power of the capitalist class, increase the power and control of the workers and people, and carry Britain along a new British road to Socialism in which British democratic institutions will be preserved and strengthened, and which will not necessarily be the road the Russian workers and peasants were compelled to take in 1917. It would be stupid to think that it is possible to map out at this time every stage of this road, but the key is the unity and determination of the Labour movement, the refusal at any stage to withdraw before counter-attacks of the capitalists, the steadfast resistance to the colonisation of Britain by the American trusts.

Harry Pollitt, *Looking Ahead* (London: CPGB, 1947), pp. 87–92.

8.4 Battle of ideas

Woddis strikes the keynote of the 'Battle of Ideas'.

Battle of ideas

Another American export for Britain
In his speech at the recent Battle of Ideas Conference organised by the Communist Party, the well-known historian, A. L. Morton, pointed out that America has 'a Marshall Plan in the field of ideas as well as in the field of economic and politics'.

American imperialism is conducting an ideological drive alongside its general and economic campaign. This deliberate ideological drive is accompanied and assisted by the development of private monopoly control over the means of production of ideology – films, theatre, press, radio, publishing – through which the fake 'American Way of Life' is being boosted with a vengeance.

[...] With cynical disregard for the true traditions of America [...] the present-day rulers of America are seeking to corrupt the ideas and outlook of the people. They are developing a social and cultural atmosphere of brutality, vulgarity, obscurantism and immorality. Every backward instinct – chauvinism, anti-Semitism, race hatred, violent anti-Communist phobia – has been enlisted by the present day rulers of America for their war aims. And all who stand in their way, no matter how great their talents and abilities, are being ruthlessly purged from the films, radio, press, theatre, schools universities [sic].

In his famous speech at Waco, Texas, President Truman said that, 'in an economic as well as in a political sense, the United States can no longer find security within its own borders'. It is clear from the speeches of the Hollywood film kings, of Truman, Marshall and others, that ideologically, too, America will find 'security' outside her own borders. American imperialism needs to debauch the people of the rest of the world in addition to her own people.

How far this American ideological invasion has gone is not sufficiently realised in Britain. Economically, America already has a firm grip on the British film industry, and a growing grip on the British theatre, which she seeks to extend. The British film industry, both economically and ideologically, now stands on the threshold of a major crisis into which it has been manoeuvred by the joint efforts of the British film magnates and the servile Labour Government. It is worth noting that, in their efforts to beat down British resistance on this front, American film barons protested strongly about the 'nationalistic attitude' adopted by British film critics. On [sic] has only to compare some of the trash now appearing with the fine promise of war-time films to appreciate how deeply the rot has already penetrated. [...]

In the realm of fiction, too, the same danger is to be seen. Economically the vast increase in America book exports (from $5,200,000 in 1938 to $18,600,000 in 1946, and probably to a much higher figure since), is causing grave concern to British publishers. Of equal gravity is the growing American habit of purchasing British copyrights – and the future dangers of this are obvious. [...]

Our universities, too, are being invaded. An increasing number of professors, undoubtedly hand-picked, are streaming across the Atlantic to 'educate' British students on the Marshall Plan [...]. American diplomatic staffs in Britain now have cultural attaches who have the responsibility of assisting, in the ideological field, to rivet American domination on Britain. The ideas of American philosophers, who are working in the service of American imperialism to provide a 'philosophical' justification for American aggression, are being freely peddled in British academic circles. Even the comic strips in our daily newspapers are largely the products of America.

It is time to call a halt to this cultural invasion from America. Our national culture is one of the essential bases of our national dignity and independence. We cannot afford our cultural life to become dominated by the uncouth tycoons of Wall Street any more than we can allow them to dominate our economic life.

Jack Woddis, *World News and Views* (5 June 1948), p. 235.

8.5 Insidious media

This article identifies the corrupting effects of American and Americanised comics on young British minds.

Communism and liberty

Children in the battle of ideas

Based on a contribution to the Conference on 'Communism and Liberty'

Capitalist ideology has always before it the task of preventing the people from thinking, of giving them false ideas about society, and of turning them away from an understanding of the world around them. Of no section in society is this more true than of children, whose curiosity, lack of experience, and respect for the authoritative spoken and written word can be and are ruthlessly exploited. [...]

I want to stress here that some of the most potent and degrading influences on children are instilled by means of comics, including those manufactured for children and those meant for 'adults' that are also read by children. Here we see the hero, who is always right, coming out regularly on top, instilling the leader-principle: brutality and force, the supremacy of the white and a caricature of coloured peoples; and of course the pseudo-science with its dreams of fantasy turning children away from reality and the real wonders of life. [...]

And here we should discuss the specifically American character of this form of perverted amusement. The comic strips are becoming increasingly Americanised, and actual American comics are beginning to enter the English market. We have not yet felt the full impact of these flowers of American culture, but they are on their way [...]. The insidious medium of the American comic deals in brute force and direct sadism, disguised pornography, the unquestioned superiority of the capitalist way of life.

What is the effect of these influences? Nothing less than the numbing and deadening of all critical faculties of thinking and judging. In greater degree or less, the child is led away from the desire to want the decent things in life, or to do anything constructive. A listening, passive approach is encouraged.

[...] Thousands of parents are worried and anxious about their children. They realise that these influences are harmful, but they don't know what to do about them. We must give them the lead, and in showing how capitalism operates to debase children's minds, draw them into the fight against this poisonous propaganda – and so into the fight for Socialism.

P. G. M, *World News and Views* (12 November 1949), p. 552.

8.6 Hollywood's grip

Here Communist film-maker Ralph Bond outlines the damaging effects of the American film industry on 'the cultural interests of the nation'.

Film

In no field of artistic endeavour is American penetration so obvious as in the case of film. Neither is this a recent process. Hollywood captured the British film industry as long ago as 1915, and it has never loosened its grip since.

Of course, no serious endeavour had even been made to loosen the grip, either by the film trade itself or by Governments, be they Conservative, Liberal or Labour. The film trade is perfectly content with things as they are. The big money is in cinemas, and cinema profits have always been kept rolling by the endless supply of American films, obtainable at cheaper prices than British films. The Labour Government has done nothing to bring about that complete structural change of the industry which is essential before an independent British film production industry can have a hope of survival, let alone expansion.

The complete subordination of British films to Hollywood, brought about by the failure of the Government to take up the challenge, is symptomatic of wider political policies. An indication of the contempt which so-called progressive politicians have towards the cultural interests of the nation.

It is significant and encouraging that it is the workers in the industry who are seriously making the fight for the preservation of British films, and making it not purely on the grounds of employment, but on the wider issue that the country can no longer tolerate seventy per cent of its film entertainment being permanently imported from Hollywood.

The fight to save the British film industry, and the policy programme adopted by the Unions, deserves the widest possible aid. In the first place it is necessary to win the support of millions of Trade Unionists, to show them what is happening, to convince them that this question affects them too and not only the workers in the film industry. [...]

The Labour movement on the whole has been content to leave this enormous power of persuasion entirely in capitalist hands. Only a handful of Trade Unions have sponsored films on their own work and achievements, and most of the Co-operative film activity is restricted to advertising their products.

Think of the great themes concerning our Labour movement that would make wonderful films: the birth and progress of the Co-operatives; the story of the Tolpuddle Martyrs; the Peasants Revolt [sic]; and so on. If the Unions and the Co-operatives with their enormous resources would finance a few films like this we could break the commercial stranglehold of the monopolies, and challenge the dominance of Hollywood. There are other things that can be done. Progressive Film Societies like *New Era* can be developed all over the country. Only a relative handful of people have seen the fine films made by progressive groups in France, Italy, America and other capitalist countries. Only a very small number have seen the new films from the Soviet Union, China, Czechoslovakia, and the other People's Democracies. We should extend the showing of these films by all possible means, such as the direct exhibition in Trade Union branches, in factories, and by forming progressive film clubs.

On a small scale it should be possible to make some progressive films ourselves. [...]

Our task is not simply to agitate against the vicious and corrupt influence of so many Hollywood films. That is important, but side by side must go the fight to ensure that our people see the best works of film art from all countries, and above all to create an independent and healthy British film industry. [...]

By actively exerting ourselves on all these questions, and by winning the broadest support from the mass of the people, we shall be well on the road towards gaining a British film industry that will be worthy of the cultural and artistic heritage and traditions of our country.

Ralph Bond, 'Film', *Arena Special Issue: The USA Threat to British Culture*, II: 8 (June/July 1951), pp. 48–9.

8.7 Musical activism

Communist composer Alan Bush indicates the role that music should play in the struggle for 'peace, national independence and Socialism'.

Music in the fight for peace and socialism

[...] Songs have furthered the common struggles of the British people throughout their history. The peasants of 1381 had their songs, the Levellers and Diggers, the Luddites and Chartists theirs. It is hard to see how the point of view can be maintained that in our own day our own Party, leading the struggle for peace, national independence and Socialism, can dispense with a weapon which is traditional in human struggle. It is especially traditional in British musical life for amateur musicians to sing in an organised way; our choral societies are famous throughout the world. And in urging our comrades to enter this field of activity where practicable, I am only introducing to them a form of political work in accordance with musical history and our own British tradition.

In other countries of the world the Communist Parties all foster their own musical activity. No important meeting or Congress of the Party in any of the New Democracies or in Italy or Holland would take place without music. [...] Already in our Party, since the Communist Manifesto Centenary Pageant of 1948, we have developed some musical groups. These have sung at meetings and demonstrations, in halls and in Trafalgar Square. They have assisted in open-air meetings during the election and other campaigns. Our Youth Brigades did excellent work on such occasions. This activity is, however, only in its beginning; we want to make it more widespread and better in quality as well as in amount.

The problem of how best to do this is the subject of a Party Conference, 'Amateur Musicians in the Fight for Peace and Socialism', to take place on Sunday, October 8, National TU Club, 12 Great Newport Street, WC2 [...]. If you are in any way musically inclined as a singer, player or listener to jazz or straight music, I appeal to you to support this conference, which is designed to advance in quantity and musical quality our Party's musical activity, and thus to increase the Party's influence throughout the country.

Alan Bush, *World News and Views* (23 September 1950), p. 455.

8.8 British road to socialsm

Launched in 1951, revised in 1958, and substantially re-written in 1976, *The British Road to Socialism* was the central text of the Communist Party for twenty-five years.

Peace and friendship with all peoples
The Communist Party fights for lasting peace as the vital need of the British people. [...]

Despite the acute danger of war, the Communist Party declares that a third world war is neither necessary nor inevitable.

The Communist Party rejects the 'theory' of the inevitable war between the socialist and capitalist camps. On the contrary, it declares that the peaceful co-existence of socialism and capitalism is possible, on the basis of mutual respect for national rights and independence. Communist policy is for trade with all states on a mutual, honest basis, and co-operation with all States in the preservation of peace through the United Nations [...].

The Communist Party brands as a lie the charge that Communism is to be imposed by aggression and conquest, and declares that social transformation can only come through internal changes in accordance with the actual conditions in each country.

A lasting peace is the vital need for all peoples and a main aim of Communist policy. [...]

The future of the British people, their prosperity and welfare, and the victory of the aims of Socialism in Britain, are inseparably bound up with the united international struggle of the peoples of all countries for peace, freedom and national independence.

National independence of the British people and of all peoples of the British Empire

The Communist Party fights for the national independence and the true national interests of the British people and of all the peoples of the British Empire.

The subjection of Britain to American imperialism is a betrayal of the British people in the interests of big business and of those who are planning a new world war. In the economic sphere, Britain has been turned into a satellite of America [...]. American big business controls our financial policy, imposes trade restrictions and bans, openly dictates policy, as in the case of devaluation, and is extending the network of American financial penetration and control over British industry. In the military sphere, Britain has been turned into an American base, and the American army of occupation is growing. The new arms programme was decided on American instructions, and under the Atlantic Pact, Britain's armed forces have been placed under an American Supreme Commander. The British Empire, similarly, has been subjected to increasing American financial and military penetration.

For the first time in its history, our country has lost its independence and freedom of action in its foreign, economic and military policy to a foreign power – the United States of America. [...]

People's democracy – the path to socialism

Only by the establishment of Socialism can Britain's problems be finally solved and its people guaranteed a good life, lasting peace and steadily rising living standards. [...]

The working people of Britain in industry and agriculture form the immense majority of the population and constitute with their families fully two-thirds of the population. To these must be added the great bulk of the clerical and professional workers, the teachers, technicians and scientists, the working farmers, shopkeepers and small business men, whose interests are equally threatened by the big landowning, industrial and financial capitalists, and whose security and future prospects are closely bound up with those of the industrial working class.

Together these represent a mighty political force, fully capable of defeating the present exploiters and rulers of the British people and returning a majority to Parliament which represents the interests of all working people, and a Government determined to carry through, with the active political and industrial backing of the people, a policy that will open out a new and glorious future for Britain.

But at present this potentially mighty political force is split and divided, misled by the propaganda of the ruling class and the policy and outlook of the right-wing leaders of the Labour Party and the right-wing leaders of the trade unions and co-operative organisations, who in practice support the ruling class and carry on the Labour Government in the interests of capitalism.

Despite the democratic rights which have so far been won by the struggles of the people, the real power in Britain is still concentrated in the hands of the tiny section of rich property-owners. They control the land, large-scale industry, finance and trade; their representatives hold the commanding positions in the Civil Service, the Armed Forces, the Judiciary, the Diplomatic and Colonial Services; they also control the greater part of the newspapers and periodicals, the B.B.C., and the cinemas.

Democracy under present conditions is restricted for the majority of the people by the privilege and power of the wealthy few and their agents, and is being reduced by attacks on the rights of free speech and organisation, and on the right to strike. The democratic rights won by years of working-class struggle must be defended with the utmost strength against the attacks of the capitalists and warmongers and their agents. At the same time we declare that the so-called 'free world' is in fact the world of capitalism, in which the capitalist class exercises a disguised dictatorship over the working class. The Labour leaders' 'democratic socialism' has done nothing to change this.

The people cannot advance to Socialism, therefore, without real political power, which must be taken from the hands of the capitalist minority and firmly grasped by the majority of the people, led by the working class. Only by this means can democracy become a reality.

The enemies of Communism accuse the Communist Party of aiming to introduce Soviet Power in Britain and abolish Parliament. This is a slanderous misrepresentation of our policy. Experience has shown that in present conditions the advance to Socialism can be made just as well by a different road. For example, through People's Democracy, without establishing Soviet Power, as in the People's Democracies of Eastern Europe.

Britain will reach Socialism by her own road. Just as the Russian people realised political power by the Soviet road which was dictated by their historical conditions and background of Tsarist rule, and the working people in the People's Democracies and China won political power in their own way in their historical conditions, so the British Communists declare that the people of Britain can transform capitalist democracy into a real People's Democracy, transforming Parliament, the product of Britain's historic struggle for democracy, into the democratic instrument of the will of the vast majority of her people.

The path forward for the British people will be to establish a People's Government on the basis of a Parliament truly representative of the people. [...]

The essential condition for establishing such a people's power is the building up of a broad coalition or popular alliance of all sections of the working people: of the organised working class, of all workers by hand and brain, of professional people and technicians, of all lower and middle sections in the towns, and of the farmers in the countryside.

This broad popular alliance of all sections of the people determined to end the arbitrary power of the rich over the future of Britain, can be built only on the basis of a united working class as its decisive leading force – the class that is most concerned in the struggle for a new order of society. [...]

In order, therefore, to bring about a decisive change in Britain, the millions of workers in the trade unions, co-operatives and individual members' sections of the Labour Party will have to use their political and industrial strength to make it impossible for either the right-wing Labour leaders or the Tories to carry on their present pernicious policy. They will have to rouse all the working people and progressive sections for active struggle against the present policy of surrender to American political and economic interests, against the war preparations and the wars in Malaya and Korea, against the two years' conscription, the calling up of reservists, and the rearming of Germany and Japan. Such a struggle is also necessary to secure higher wages and salaries, more houses, schools and hospitals, the raising of benefits and pensions, and on all issues which affect the people. It is through this struggle that the unity of all workers by hand and brain, of professional people and farmers, can develop into a movement strong enough to defeat the rich and their defenders in the Labour Party and to ensure peace and a future for all working people. Because of this working class unity, the united action of all sections of the working-class movement – Labour, trade union, co-operative and Communist – is the vital need. Only by united action between all sections of the Labour Movement can the working class rally all its forces and all its allies for decisive action to win a Parliamentary majority and form a People's Government. [...]

That great broad popular alliance, led by the working class, firmly based on the factories, which has democratically placed the People's Government in power, will have the strength to deal with the attacks of the capitalist warmongers and their agents.

The Government will rely on the strength of the organised workers to ensure that the programme decided upon by Parliament is operated in practice, and that all attempts to resist or sabotage it are defeated; and the enemies of the working class brought to justice.

It would be wrong to believe that the big capitalists will voluntarily give up their property and their big profits in the interests of the British people.

It would be more correct to expect them to offer an active resistance to the decisions of the People's Government, and to fight for the retention of their privileges by all means in their power including force.

Therefore the British people and the People's Government should be ready decisively to rebuff such attempts.

The power of the working people, uniting all sections who recognise the need for social change and participate in carrying it through, as expressed and laid down through the elected Parliament, is alone capable of securing peace, high wages for working people, raw materials for British industry and markets for British goods, and creating the conditions for the establishment of Socialism in Britain. [...]

The British Road to Socialism: Programme Adopted by the Executive Committee of the Communist Party of Britain, January 1951 (CPGB: London, 1951).

8.8 Co-ordinating the cultural front

Sam Aaronovitch served as full-time NCC secretary between 1947 and 1955. Here he maps the committee's origins and priorities.

Culture and the people
By Sam Aaronovitch

A report on the work of the National Cultural Committee of the Communist Party
[...] The National Cultural Committee was set up, following the nineteenth Party Congress of February 1947, to give leadership to Marxist work in the arts and sciences, to enable the Communist Party to fight reactionary and anti-human ideas more effectively, and put forward progressive, humanist ideas in their place. It has the task of using all aspects of cultural activity as a weapon in the fight of the Party for peace, independence and Socialism. Working under its direction are a whole number of groups, covering many aspects of the arts, social and natural sciences.

In this fight, we are fortunate in the guidance of the Soviet Union. The great controversies on literature, music, biology, philosophy, medicine and linguistics, to mention a few of them, have resulted in major contributions not only to Soviet development *but to the battle of ideas on a world scale.* Socialist practice and ideas have put capitalist practice and ideas on the defensive throughout the world. [...]

The Executive Committee, in its resolution *On the Cultural Work of the Party* (published below), analyses the main weaknesses and main tasks of the Cultural Committee and the Groups. It is our task now to apply this resolution to all our work. [...]

The political importance of our work was never greater. We invite all readers to send us their suggestions and comments and to help in making the arts and sciences a weapon in the struggle of the people and for advance along the British road to Socialism.

The Cultural Work of the Party
Resolution adopted by the Executive Committee of the Communist Party, January 1952

The Executive Committee welcomes the work of the Cultural Committee and of the Party Groups working in the fields of science and the arts, and congratulates the comrades on the contributions made through conferences, books and other published materials.

The E.C. considers that the further development of this work requires:

(1) Systematic efforts by our professional workers to strengthen their Marxist outlook and fighting spirit, to apply this outlook to their special field; and to bring their work closer to the Party organisations, especially our Factory Branches, and to the needs of the Party's fight for peace, independence and Socialism.

(2) More public activity on current political issues and on issues directly concerning their professional fields; more initiative in polemics in every field, exposing the false ideas which serve the interests of the warmongers and the reactionaries, helping to build up a united movement for peace and social progress, of explaining the world outlook and the policy of Communism.

(3) A deeper study of the Party's programme, *The British Road to Socialism*, and continuous efforts to make it well known among their professional colleagues; as well as the preparation and publication of material to illustrate and develop aspects of the programme.

(4) The continuous study and popularisation of Soviet achievements in each field of the whole advance to Communism; and of cultural advances in the People's Democracies and People's China.

(5) The continuous fight for the extension of cultural facilities for the people.

(6) New efforts by our writers, artists and musicians to produce work relating to the British working class struggle, and based on the standpoint of Socialist Realism.

The Executive Committee calls on Districts and other Party Committees to help in the development of work in the cultural field, and to make the fullest use of our comrades in this field to strengthen and widen the whole work of the Party.

World News and Views (2 February 1952), p. 55.

8.10 Historians

Established in 1946, the Communist Party Historians' Group launched two publications in the early 1950s to stimulate and showcase radical historiography. A journal, the enduring *Past & Present*, first appeared in February 1952, and a monthly bulletin, *Our History* in October 1953. This is the editorial to the first issue of *Our History*.

A few words of introduction are perhaps needed for the first issue of *Our History*. This bulletin will appear monthly, and will normally include three short articles. We hope the subjects will be sufficiently varied to interest all readers. But they will have two things in common.

In the first place, they will all relate in some way or other to the historical development of the British people towards our socialist future; that is to say, they will be concerned with the kind of history that illuminates our own present struggles for a better life. This is intentionally broad, and no aspect of British history from which socialists can derive some new understanding or inspiration will be excluded.

In the second place, the articles will normally include unpublished material, or will attempt a new approach to the subject, and will therefore have some historical value in themselves.

This bulletin will be duplicated at present. But our ultimate aim is a printed magazine [...].

The articles this month can speak for themselves. The first gives a glimpse of our pioneer socialists participating in a form of social democracy which we lost with the abolition of the School Boards in 1902. The second article is a reminder that much of British capitalism was built up on the bodies of British children, just as it still lives on the bodies of children in the Empire. The third article throws light on the origins of class-collaboration in industry [...].

Our History, Number One (October 1953), p. 1.

Notes

1 Willie Thompson, *The Good Old Cause: British Communism, 1920–1991* (London: Pluto, 1992), pp. 75–6.

2 Rajani Palme Dutt, 'Notes of the Month', *Labour Monthly* (November 1945), p. 327.

3 John Callaghan, *Rajani Palme Dutt: A Study in British Stalinism* (London: Lawrence & Wishart, 1993), pp. 222–3.

4 Cited in Callaghan, *Rajani Palme Dutt*, p. 239.

5 *For Soviet Britain* (London: Marston, 1935), p. 6.

6 *The British Road to Socialism* (London: CPGB, 1951), pp. 9, 10, 14.

7 Kevin Morgan, *Harry Pollitt* (Manchester: Manchester University Press, 1993), p. 170.

8 Jack Lindsay, *British Achievement in Art and Music* (London: Pilot, 1945).

9 Jack Knife, 'People's War, People's Culture', *World News and Views* (29 May 1943), p. 176.

10 *A Policy for Music in Post War Britain* (London: WMA, 1945), p. 4.

11 John Ross, 'From Hollywood and Rank – Preserve Us', *Daily Worker* (24 November 1946); Beatrix Lehmann, 'Learning to Be an Actor', *Daily Worker* (10 June 1943).

12 Andy Croft, 'Writers, the Communist Party and the Battle of Ideas, 1945–50', *Socialist History*, 5 (1994), p. 5.

13 Noreen Branson, *History of the Communist Party of Great Britain 1941–1951* (London: Lawrence & Wishart, 1997), p. 170.

14 Croft, 'Writers', p. 12.

15 Dennis Dworkin, *Class Struggles* (Edinburgh: Pearson, 2007), p. 51 and Harvey J. Kaye, *The British Marxist Historians* (Oxford: Blackwell, 1984), pp. 1–21.

16 See Ben Harker, *Class Act: The Cultural and Political Life of Ewan MacColl* (London: Pluto, 2007), pp. 92–114.

17 The 'Battle of Ideas' conference was held in 1948; the Party Cultural Conference of 1951 was entitled 'The American Threat to British Culture' and proceedings were published in a special issue of *Arena: A Magazine of Modern Literature* (June–July 1951), which shared the same title.

18 Jack Woddis, 'Another American Export for Britain', *World News and Views* (5 June 1948), p. 235.

19 Sam Aaronovitch, 'Against the Yankee "Way of Life"', *World News and Views* (17 March 1953), p. 131.

20 John Callaghan, *Cold War, Crisis and Conflict: The CPGB 1951–1968* (London: Lawrence & Wishart, 2003), p. 94; originating in the mid-1930s, 'socialist realism' was re-circulated in Britain via A. A.

Zhadanov, *On Literature, Music and Philosophy* (London: Lawrence & Wishart, 1950).
21 Croft, 'Writers', pp. 6–10.
22 Andy Croft details the transformation of *Arena* and *Our Time* in 'Writers', pp. 14–16 and 'The Boys Round the Corner: The Story of Fore Publications' in Croft (ed.), *A Weapon in the Struggle: The Cultural History of the Communist Party* (London: Pluto, 1998), pp. 142–63.
23 Responses to *The British Road* are summarised in Callaghan, *Cold War*, pp. 177–8.

9

1956 and Communist crisis

In June 1948 Stalin denounced the independently minded Yugo-slavian leader Tito as a fascist spy, unleashing three years of purges, show trials and executions to eliminate 'counter-revolutionary' networks across Eastern Europe. Individual members of the CPGB, some of whom had visited Tito's Yugoslavia and been inspired by its post-war reconstruction, queried the denunciations and attempted to stimulate debate;[1] some quietly withdrew from the party, including the art historian Francis Klingender.[2] But the party leadership's knee-jerk loyalty to the Soviet Union was typical of the early Cold War period. Official publications backed the Soviet line, while Pollitt's own statements revealed a blind faith in Stalin's judgement.[3]

Following Stalin's death in 1953, however, a shift in Soviet priorities and outlook became apparent. Characteristic Soviet Cold War manoeuvring – the acquisition of the hydrogen bomb, the signing of the Warsaw Pact – was now combined with a wary diplomacy with Western powers couched in terms of 'peaceful coexistence'.[4] This cautious rapprochement coincided with the beginning of a critique of the Stalin years. 'De-Stalinisation' was implicit in Khrushchev's trip to Belgrade in 1955, during which allegations against Tito were set aside and the line on independent, national roads to socialism re-affirmed; this trend became explicit at the 20th Congress of the Soviet Communist Party. Held in Moscow between 17 and 24 February, the Congress was pervaded by an unfamiliar atmosphere: the usual iconography of Stalin was conspicuously absent; delegates openly referred to the 'cult of personality' surrounding Stalin. In a session closed to delegates from beyond the Soviet Union, Khrush-chev opened the Pandora's box of Stalinist terror. His speech graphi-cally detailed show trials generated by suspicions and sustained by confessions; gulags and mass deportations; the 'immense and limit-less power' exercised by Stalin and the ruthless state apparatus subordinate to his wishes.[5] Though none of the British delegates – Pollitt, Dutt and George Matthews – heard the speech, few at the Congress were oblivious to it.[6] The contents of Khrushchev's revelations quickly seeped through and beyond the Communist movement, first by word of mouth and soon by dissident leftist channels and the mainstream media; on 10 June the whole document was set before the British public in the *Observer*.[7]

Despite the seismic force of the revelations, the party leadership behaved as though the habitual combination of suppression, bluff denial, Soviet-philia and the call for discipline would contain the disbelief, shock and outrage felt by many party members. The strategy was to make minimal and guarded acknowledgements of the matter, congratulate itself for openness and self-criticism and declare the issue closed. Barely three weeks after Khrushchev's speech, *Daily Worker* editor J. R. Campbell announced that the 'cult of the individual' had been dealt with, that readers' correspondence was becoming 'repetitive', and that no more letters would be printed.[8] The party Congress held between 30 March and 2 April 1956 thwarted rather than ventilated the feelings of the membership. Pollitt's published statements did little to address the fundamental issues;[9] Dutt took a characteristically pro-Stalin hardline in his 'Notes of the Month', a position he reluctantly toned down after protests.[10] The pressure on the leadership to open a discussion was increased by ongoing revelations about the persecution of Jews under Stalin's regime: investigations led by party activists revealed that anti-Semitic practices in the Soviet Union were real and ongoing.[11]

Up to 2000 Communists left the party in the wake of Khrushchev's speech; others militated for an open discussion.[12] Frustrated in their attempts to trigger a debate in the official channels, Yorkshire-based activists E. P. Thompson and John Saville launched *The Reasoner: A Journal of Discussion* as a forum for Communists to debate the crisis. After the first issue the party's Yorkshire District Committee instructed that the journal should be closed; very shortly after the second, this became a demand from the Executive Committee. Unrepentant when called to the King Street party headquarters to explain themselves, Saville and Thompson planned one final issue, which was soon drawn into the vortex of a new crisis, the Hungarian uprising.

Khrushchev's revelations had winched up tensions in Eastern Europe, further legitimating discontent and galvanising popular

187

resistance to the regimes imposed by Stalin. Riots in Poland were followed by insurrection in Hungary in late October. The Soviet Union responded with military action on 24 October; a second military onslaught the following week restored Soviet control. The intervention was promptly endorsed by the *Daily Worker* as necessary to avert fascist counter-revolution, and the conflicting eyewitness reports dispatched by its correspondent Peter Fryer were suppressed.[13] The third issue of *The Reasoner* took a characteristically independent line: Saville and Thompson not only called for the party's Executive Committee to engage honestly with the Soviet military action, but also for party members to keep 'faith in Socialism' while 'dissociat[ing] themselves openly' from a leadership who failed to think for themselves.[14] The editors were formally suspended from party membership for three months, soon withdrawing from the party they had failed to open up for reform.

The leadership's defensive responses had once again brought into sharp focus parallels and connections between the autocratic structures and psychologies of Stalinism abroad and those within the CPGB at home. Approximately 5000 members left in response to the Hungarian crisis, while others stayed in for the time being, awaiting the Congress that the leadership had eventually scheduled for the spring of 1957. Initially conceived as a discussion forum, the Special Congress was empowered with decision-making authority in response to the strength of feeling registered in critical resolutions and correspondence.[15]

Held at Hammersmith Town Hall between 19 and 22 April 1957, this 25th Congress was to address not only the broader crisis but also a specially commissioned report on internal democracy; it was destined to prove a pivotal moment in the party's history. Sixty-six year old Harry Pollitt's health was poor; the party's top job was now taken by Johnny Gollan, a working-class Scott with impeccable party credentials stretching back over thirty years. But if the contrast between Pollitt's avuncular charisma and Gollan's anxious efficiency had already prompted grim jokes about a new cult of impersonality, the tenor of the Congress served to highlight not new directions but steadfast continuity with party tradition.[16] The familiar rhetoric of Gollan's address paid customary homage to the Soviet Union, warned against 'revisionism' at home and referred to the defeated forces of 'reaction' in Hungary.[17] The commission on inner-party democracy had reached few surprising conclusions (two thirds of its members were thoroughly institutionalised full-time party officials); a more critical 'Minority Report' had been rejected by the Executive. But if the leadership had proved characteristically adept in heading off any radical change in constitution or personnel – the so-called 'recommended list' of candidates for the Executive Committee had been endorsed by Congress – the most incisive and articulate voices in the Congress now came from those beyond the reach of the leadership.[18] In a moving speech, historian Christopher Hill encapsulated the insularity and self-deceit of recent Communist experience when accusing party members, himself included, of having lived in a 'snug little world of our own invention'.[19]

The leadership's hollow victories of the Party Congress provoked a further 2000 resignations, bringing the total to 9000 of the party membership and half of the YCL.[20] The latest round included many the party could ill afford to lose, including prominent trade unionists Alex Moffat and Lawrence Daly of the National Union of Mineworkers (NUM); Daly's Fife Socialist League, formed in 1957, would soon successfully challenge the CPGB for council seats.[21] The *Daily Worker*, which had flagrantly subordinated accurate reportage to the party line was also greatly damaged: sales dropped by 20 per cent in 1956, and longstanding members of the staff, including reporter Peter Fryer, features editor Malcolm MacEwen and the cartoonist James Friell ('Gabriel'), left the party and its newspaper.[22]

In his address to the Congress, Gollan had warned would-be deserters, especially those intellectuals repeatedly chastised for their corrosive criticisms, that there is 'no such thing as Marxism without the Communist Party'.[23] Some intellectuals proved vociferously loyal to the party line, including literary critic Arnold Kettle and composer Alan Bush;[24] many others, including novelist Jack Lindsay, folklorist A. L. Lloyd and historian Eric Hobsbawm, said less in public but remained committed to practising their Marxism within the party. But around half of the party's intellectuals, including key figures recruited during the Popular Front period such as Randall Swingler and Edgell Rickword, did resign; many defied Gollan by remaining Marxists. Saville and Thomson re-launched *The Reasoner* as *The New Reasoner: A Quarterly of Socialist Humanism* in 1957. Like another new journal, *Universities & Left Review*, with which it would soon merge to form *New Left Review*, these publications helped to shape a 'New Left', a loose movement, in which former Communists loomed large, concerned with developing an ethical, democratic socialism in late 1950s Britain. The party's status as Britain's powerhouse of Marxist thought was now being contested by this energetic and more youthful anti-Stalinist left sharply attuned to contemporary cultural trends and shifts in the nation's class composition; the Trotskyism to which Peter Fryer was initially drawn would also become a renewed threat in the decade after 1956 (the enduring Trotskyite journal *International Socialism* joined the field of British Marxist theory in 1958). While the party would recover ground in the trade unions and replace members within six years, it would never restore the intellectual and cultural authority it lost in 1956.

9.1 Khrushchev's speech

Khrushchev's 'secret speech', delivered to a closed session of the CPSU's 20th Congress on the evening of 25 February 1956, was finally published in Britain by the *Observer* on 10 June.

[...] It was precisely during this period [1935–1938] that the practice of mass repression through the government apparatus was born, first against the enemies of Leninism – Trotskyites, Zinovievites, Bukharinites, long since politically defeated by the party – and subsequently also against many honest Communists, against those party cadres who had borne the heavy load of the Civil War and the first and most difficult years of industrialization and collectivization, who had fought actively against the Trotskyites and the rightists for the Leninist Party line.

[...] In the main, and in actuality, the only proof of guilt used, against all norms of current legal science, was the 'confession' of the accused himself; and, as subsequent probing proved, 'confessions' were acquired through physical pressures against the accused.

This led to glaring violations of revolutionary legality and to the fact that many entirely innocent individuals – who in the past had defended the party line – became victims.

We must assert that in regard to those persons who in their time had opposed the party line, there were often no sufficiently serious reasons for their annihilation. The formula, 'enemy of the people', was specifically introduced for the purpose of physically annihilating such individuals. [...]

[...] It is clear that here Stalin showed in a whole series of cases his intolerance, his brutality and his abuse of power. Instead of proving his political correctness and mobilizing the masses, he often chose the path of repression and physical annihilation, not only against actual enemies, but also against individuals who had not committed any crimes against the party and the Soviet Government.

[...] This terror was actually directed not at the remnants of the defeated exploiting classes but against the honest workers of the Party and of the Soviet state; against them were made lying, slanderous and absurd accusations concerning 'two-facedness', 'espionage', 'sabotage', preparation of fictitious 'plots', etc.

[...] The wilfulness of Stalin showed itself not only in decisions concerning the internal life of the country but also in the international relations of the Soviet Union.

The July Plenum of the Central Committee studied in detail the reasons for the development of conflict with Yugoslavia. It was a shameful role which Stalin played here. The 'Yugoslav affair' contained no problems which could not have been solved through Party discussions among comrades. There was no significant basis for the development of this 'affair.' [...]

I recall the first days when the conflict between the Soviet Union and Yugoslavia began to be blown up artificially. Once, when I came from Kiev to Moscow, I was invited to visit Stalin, who, pointing to the copy of a letter recently sent to Tito, asked me, 'Have you read this?'

Not waiting for my reply, he answered, 'I will shake my little finger – and there will be no more Tito. He will fall'.

We have paid dearly for this 'shaking of the little finger'. This statement reflected Stalin's mania for greatness. [...]

Observer (10 June 1956).

9.2 Mounting crisis

Though not published until June, news of the 'secret speech' was widespread, generating concern among party members. Pollitt addressed the question in the *Daily Worker* on 24 March; here he repeats his reassurance in the party's weekly.

The 20th Congress of the CPSU – and the role of Stalin

[...] Although we attended the twentieth Congress of the CPSU, no foreign guests attended the Closed Session of the Congress which discussed the new assessment of the role of Stalin.

It should be remembered that the Communist International was dissolved in 1942 and no connection between our Party and other Parties have existed since that time. The Communist Information Bureau was established in 1947; we have never been members of it or attended any of its meetings. [...]

[...] Under [Stalin's] leadership, Trotsky and Bukharin were defeated, the basis for industrialism and collective agriculture was established, and his drive for carrying through the first Five Year Plan prepared the ground for the future successes of the Soviet Union in peace and in war.

After the defeat of the internal enemies at the Seventeenth Party Congress in 1934, Stalin more and more began to turn away from principles of collective leadership, and his personal methods created a position where the security organs could misuse their powers and increasingly place themselves above the Party and the State.

A series of purgings and wrongful arrests took place, 'confessions' of guilt were made under pressure; the Party rules were violated and members of the Central Committee who were arrested were denied the right to place their case before the meetings of the Central Committee. [...]

For all these reasons it would be wrong to underestimate the damage that has been done, and the seriousness of the task of overcoming it.

When Stalin placed himself above the CPSU, the Soviet Government and the people, it was inevitable that future investigations would reveal what the consequences of such a policy were to be. That is what we are now seeing as a result of the examination into the last twenty years of Stalin's personal rule. [...]

[A]t each stage in the last twenty years of Stalin's life the carrying through of the correct general line by the Party and the people was accompanied by mistakes, abuses and injustices arising from Stalin's increasing dependence on the security forces instead of on the Party and the people. [...]

All this was necessarily associated with Stalin's personal methods. [...] His error was to place himself, stage by stage, above the rest of the leadership of the CPSU, gradually substituting personal power for collective leadership. [...]

In connection with Yugoslavia, it is now evident that whatever criticisms were made of the political line of the Yugoslav Party in 1948, these could have been discussed in a fraternal way without the break that was made; and that in the following period, the position was greatly aggravated by the unfounded accusations against the Yugoslav Communist leaders on the basis of material fabricated by [Soviet Security chief] Beria and his associates.

[...] We, in the Executive Committee of the British Communist Party, were misled by evidence that is now stated to have been fabricated, and we now withdraw our previous attacks on Tito and Yugoslavia, including the statement made by myself at the London membership meeting in 1948, and James Klugmann's book *From Trotsky to Tito*.

[...] Whatever the mistakes made and the abuses associated with Stalin's personal methods, however, the great historic achievement of the Soviet people and the CPSU is that they have proved, for all the world to see, the superiority of the socialist system over the capitalist system. Despite the faults, weaknesses and mistakes, all the basic Marxist principles have been proven correct, and confirmed again and again, above all in the indestructible socialist system of the world today.

There is no doubt that the new estimation of the role of Stalin has come as a shock to the members of every Communist Party in the world, precisely because of what Stalin has stood for and his outstanding contribution to the building of socialism in the Soviet Union – the base for all the further advances of socialism in the world. [...]

Harry Pollitt, *World News* (21 April 1956), pp. 246–8.

9.3 The great debate

Dutt tried to minimise the impact of the Khrushchev revelations by emphasising the economic achievements of the Soviet Union and the growth of the anti-imperialist struggle. Here he also delivers a version of the slogan 'you can't make omelettes without breaking eggs'.

[...] What are the essential themes of the Great Debate? Not about Stalin. That there should be spots on the sun would only startle an inveterate Mithra-worshipper. Not about the now recognised abuses of the security organs in a period of heroic ordeal and achievement of the Soviet Union. To imagine that a great revolution can develop without a million cross-currents, hardships, injustices and excesses would be a delusion fit only for ivory-tower dwellers in fairyland who have still to learn that the thorny path of human advance moves forward, not only through unexampled heroism, but also with accompanying baseness, with tears and blood. The Great Debate that has opened is about larger issues, which spring from the swiftly moving new world situation, and which were spotlighted by the Twentieth Congress of the Communist Party of the Soviet Union. Three above all. First, the future of mankind in the nuclear age, of East–West relations, of peace and peaceful co-existence. Second, the future of the labour movement to meet the challenge of new conditions. Third, the future of the transition to socialism, for the completion of national and social liberation throughout the world [...]

'The Great Debate', *Labour Monthly* (May 1956), p. 194.

9.4 Clash of ideas

Hull University lecturer and CPGB historians' group member John Saville considered the party's 24th Congress (30 March–2 April 1956) a 'fiasco'; he threatened to resign unless the leadership opened a genuine debate about the content of Khrushchev's speech. Here he makes the case in the pages of *World News*.

Problems of the Communist Party
What are the main problems facing the British Communist Party?

(1) The Twentieth Congress of the CPSU revealed that there had been many miscarriages of justice and many crimes committed that went far beyond what can be explained by that convenient term 'historical inevitability'. Associated with these crimes were certain major political mistakes, especially in the realm of foreign policy. The present Russian leadership has suggested that the main, indeed the only, reason for these mistakes was the assumption of personal power by Stalin.

(2) These revelations meant that many of the policies of the CPSU which we had supported were wrong. In International politics Yugoslavia is the obvious example. More important, we were shown as having vigorously denied that arbitrary arrests, deportations and executions, could occur in a socialist democracy. It is important to remember that, as a Party (whatever individuals may have said in private), we did deny such things and we argued that, in all respects, socialist democracy, as it has established itself in the Soviet Union, was superior to bourgeois democracy. In most other matters (the exceptions are trifling) we followed the line of the CPSU. [...]

(4) Where does the division of opinion arise? Why are we faced with a number of comrades seriously questioning whether they can remain within our ranks? The division has arisen because the leadership, or a majority of the leadership, are apparently not willing to recognise that here is a major problem for us. They are not willing, that is, to admit that we shall stand discredited before the Labour movement unless we honestly and frankly state where we went wrong and that we will ensure, as far as we can, that similar errors are not made in the future. This is not an academic issue, as some pretend. It is our political honesty as a political party that is at stake [...]

(5) There are many fundamental problems of theory and practice which require the most thorough and widespread discussion. I would mention only three. Firstly and to my mind the most important, the question of our attitude to the Soviet Union in the future; secondly, the political forms within which transition to socialism will take place; thirdly, the preservation and active extension, both now and in the future, of inner-Party democracy.

(6) I believe that the tradition of controversy within the Party has become much weaker in recent years. Of late, we have become much more conformist. At the present time questioning is more widespread than it has been for well over a decade, and only the widest debate will re-establish confidence. [...] [I]t is the responsibility of our Party leadership actively to encourage the development of political unity out of the present clash of ideas.

Yours fraternally,
John Saville
(Hull)

World News (19 May 1956), p. 314.

9.5–9.6 Truth and falsehood

E. P. Thompson was an extra-mural tutor in Leeds and an active member of the Yorkshire District Committee. In this article for *World News*, he follows up John Saville's attempt to open debate through the official channels.

9.5: Winter wheat in Omsk

John Saville (*World News* 19.5.56) has referred to the weakening tradition of controversy in the Communist Party. This is true. How often has the routine of the unanimous vote, the common front against the class enemy, the search for the 'correct formulation', inhibited the development of sharp controversy? [...]

Our party must create the conditions for the re-birth of controversy in our press and throughout our organisation. We might recall Marx's demand for 'ruthlessness – the first condition of criticism'. Or some words of Milton: 'Let truth and falsehood grapple [...]'. Certainly we must bear this in mind when building socialism. [...]

It should be clear now to all that conscious struggle for moral principle in our political work is a vital part of our political relations with the people. The British people do not understand and will not trust a Monolith without a moral tongue. It is also clear that the best of formulations can conceal shame and unreason: that we must still read Shakespeare as well as Marx. [...]

When I speak of our democratic climate I mean that the British people will not trust a party that regards its democratic liberties as an optional or extra item. [...]

195

Bourgeois democracy, as we know, is a liar and a cheat. But it is libel on our proudest history to say that all our liberties are illusions, the 'fig leaf of absolutism'. It is a libel upon the British working class to suggest that they would exchange these liberties for a higher standard of life. [...]

These questions are not academic. So long as our attitude towards these liberties is in doubt, we may win from the workers their *industrial* support, but not their *political* confidence. How many comrades secretly believe that only slump or catastrophe will win the British working class to our side? Is socialism such a savage medicine as this, that the people will turn to it only at the point of death? Let us shatter this caricature of our case: and as a necessary condition for winning clarity, and as a proof to the people we have no fear of the free clash of ideas, let us drop this fetish of the Monolith and get some real controversy in our midst.

Edward Thompson, *World News* (30 June 1956), pp. 408–9.

Here, printed back-to-back with Thompson's piece, Assistant General Secretary and Executive Committee member George Matthews responds.

9.6: A caricature of our party

In his legitimate desire to stimulate controversy, Edward Thompson has presented a picture of our Party which most members will feel to be caricature. [...] I suspect that what Comrade Thompson is really getting at, though he does not say it openly, is that our past attitude to the Soviet Union has shown a lack of moral principle – that our Party knew that wrong and criminal things were happening and deliberately refused to condemn them.

If this is his view, he is utterly and completely mistaken. It is now obvious that we made serious errors in our estimate of certain aspects of the position in the Soviet Union. But these errors were not due to lack of principle, but to lack of information, or to wrong information. Comrade Thompson can legitimately argue that we should have made more effort to get accurate information: but he is not entitled to imply that our Party was unprincipled, dishonest and immoral. [...]

I agree with Comrade Thompson that we need to do more to learn from and popularise the democratic traditions of the British working people. But in view of the general tone of his article, perhaps a warning against a type of narrow nationalism which can be anti-international would not be out of place. [...]

Nor should our recognition of the merits of the great Englishmen from whom he quotes blind us to the fact that in their time they could not see the way forward so clearly as Marx was later to see it; they were not, and could not be, scientific socialists. [...]

George Matthews, *World News* (30 June 1956), pp. 409–10.

9.7 Hungarian crisis

Here the CPGB Executive Committee asserts the party line on the Hungarian uprising, justifying the Soviet Union's military intervention.

Hungary
The following statement was issued last night by the executive committee of the Communist Party.

The Hungarian events have reached a climax, in which the class issues now stand out clearly after days of confusion. [...]

The choice for the Soviet troops was clear; whether to help the Hungarian Communists and Socialists fighting to prevent a return to fascism, or to stand by and watch Hungarian and Western reaction crush the Hungarian people; whether to help preserve the achievements of Socialism in Hungary, or allow imperialism once again to take over in Hungary and use it as a base against the Socialist countries.

The Soviet Union, in responding to the appeal made to them to help defend Socialism in Hungary, is also helping to defend peace and the interests of the world working class.

The people of Hungary have suffered heavy blows in recent days, and the working class and progressive movement there in particular has lost many of its best members in the recent tragic events.

The Communists, Socialists and working people of Hungary will have many difficulties to face in the coming period.

But the Socialist System is being saved. The restoration of fascism is being prevented. This is the basis on which they can go forward to correct the errors of the past and strengthen Socialism in Hungary.

The Executive Committee of the Communist Party considers that the new Hungarian Government and the action of the Soviet forces in Hungary should be supported by Communists and Socialists everywhere, and expresses to the Hungarian working people its solidarity with them in the fight against counter-revolution and reaction.

Daily Worker (5 November 1956), p. 1.

9.8 *The Reasoner*

Frustrated in their attempts to initiate discussion in the official party channels, Saville and Thompson launched *The Reasoner: A Journal of Discussion* as a forum for Communists to debate the crisis. Their editorial to the third and final issue, written amidst the Suez crisis and the Soviet suppression of the Hungarian uprising, concludes with a declaration of their intent; this would trigger their suspension from the party.

Editorial
This final edition of *The Reasoner* was planned several weeks ago: most of it was typed and duplicated before the events of the past fortnight in Poland and Hungary.

Three days before publication, Eden launched his brutal aggression against Egypt. Every one of our readers will be fully occupied in organising protests and demonstrations of every kind, to end this war and to bring down the Government. Our first thought was to withdraw or postpone this number while the emergency lasts.

But even while we considered, Soviet forces surrounded Budapest and, as we write these lines, we hear the tragic news of the attack on the city.

Even the urgency of the Egyptian crisis cannot disguise the fact that the events of Budapest represent a crucial turning-point for our Party. [...]

The intervention of Soviet troops in Hungary must be condemned by all Communists. The working people and students of Budapest were demonstrating against an oppressive regime which gave them no adequate democratic channels for expressing their popular will. The fact that former fascists and those working for the restoration of Capitalism joined the revolutionaries does not alter this central issue. The criminal blunder of unleashing Security Police and Soviet forces against these crowds provoked the mass of the people to take up arms, in the name of independence, liberty and justice against an oppression that was operated in the name of Communism. [...]

In this crisis, when the Hungarian people needed our solidarity, the British Communist Party has failed them. We cannot wait until the 21st Congress of the CPSU, when no doubt the attack on Budapest will be registered as another 'mistake'. The international communist movement, and also the World Peace Movement, must exert its full moral influence to effect the immediate withdrawal of Soviet troops from Hungary: at the same time demanding the neutralisation of Hungary and resisting all Western attempts to turn the situation to their military and political advantage.

The E.C. of the British Party must at once:

1. Dissociate itself publicly from the action of the Soviet Union in Hungary.
2. Demand the immediate withdrawal of Soviet troops.
3. Proclaim full and unequivocal solidarity with the Polish Workers Party.
4. Call District Congresses of our Party immediately and a National Congress in the New Year.

If these demands are not met, we urge all those who, like ourselves, will dissociate themselves completely from the leadership of the British Communist Party, not to lose faith in Socialism, and to find ways of keeping together. We promise our readers that we will consult with others about the early formation of a new Socialist journal.

In attacking Budapest the Soviet Union has struck a blow at the moral authority of the international working class movement. Only the political demands outlined above will give the right to Communists to play a part in ending British aggression in Egypt, and in restraining those Western generals and politicians who will see the present situation in Eastern Europe as an opportunity to unleash a new war.

Sunday 4 November, 1956.

The Reasoner, Final Number (November 1956), pp. 1–2.

9.9 Peter Fryer

Daily Worker reporter Peter Fryer had uncritically reproduced the official line in his reports of Stalinist show trials of 'Titoist' Hungarian Laszlo Rajk back in September 1949; he deeply regretted it as soon as he realised the truth. Nonetheless, *Daily Worker* editor Johnnie Campbell sent him back to Hungary to report on the uprising in October 1956. Fryer's unblinking eye-witness accounts, of which this is the third, were suppressed by the paper. He resigned from the *Daily Worker*, explained why to the *Daily Express*, and quickly produced *Hungarian Tragedy*, a book analysing what he'd seen. Unrepentant about his public criticisms of the party leadership, he was formally expelled in 1957.

Vienna. November 11
I have just come out of Budapest, where for six days I have watched Hungary's newborn freedom destroyed by Soviet troops.

Vast areas of the city – the working-class areas above all – are virtually in ruins. For four days and nights Budapest was under continuous bombardment. [...] To anyone who loves equally the Socialist Soviet Union and the Hungarian people it was heart-breaking. [...]

In public buildings and private homes, in hotels and ruined shops, the people fought the invaders street by street, step by step, inch by inch. The blazing energy of those eleven days of liberty burned itself out in one last glorious flame. Hungry, sleepless, homeless, the Freedom Fighters battled with pitifully feeble equipment against a crushingly superior weight of Soviet arms. [...]

Bread queues were fired on by Soviet tanks, and as late as Thursday I myself saw a man of about seventy lying dead outside a bread shop, the loaf he had just bought still in his hand. Someone had half-covered his body with the red, white and green flag. Soviet troops looted the Astoria Hotel as far as the first story, even taking the clothes from the porters' rest room [...]. On the other hand, five Hungarian bullets broke five windows at the British Legation. These are things that happen in the heat of battle, and it should be said that the Soviet troops are now making efforts to fraternise with the people. Some of the rank-and-file Soviet troops have been telling people in the last few days that they had no idea they had come to Hungary. They thought they were in Berlin, fighting German fascists.

Peter Fryer, unpublished dispatch for *Daily Worker*; printed in Peter Fryer, *Hungarian Tragedy* (London: Dobson, 1956), pp. 83–6.

9.10 Anti-Semitism in the Soviet Union

In October 1956 a delegation from the British Communist Party visited the Soviet Union to explore the situation faced by Soviet Jews under Stalin and subsequently. Communists involved included *Daily Worker* editor J. R. Campbell, historian A. L. Morton and mathematician Hyman Levy. This is from their report.

Jews in the Soviet Union
The Soviet Union was the first country to take official cognisance of anti-Semitism and to make it illegal. In doing so it not only recognised the role which hatred of the Jews had played in the class struggle throughout the ages, but it won the admiration and the affection of millions of Jews throughout the world to whom the existence or repudiation of anti-Semitism had become the acid test of an enlightened society.

[...] For some years prior to the death of Stalin rumours began to spread that all was not well in this field, and that well-known Jewish writers and intellectuals had disappeared. Then came the revelations of the Twentieth Congress and later (4.4.56) specific charges in the *Folkzstyme*, a Polish Jewish workers' paper, that could not be ignored, for these charges were consistent with the kind of accusations which Khrushchev had levelled against Stalin, Beria and the security police.

The charges specifically name a number of Jewish writers, artists and intellectuals as having been tortured and physically destroyed, especially during the period 1948–52 [...]. The charges implied also that deliberate efforts had been made to repress all expressions of Jewish culture; that the Moscow Jewish State Theatre had been shut down; that Jewish papers had ceased publication and the Yiddish Publishing House had been closed.

Naturally these charges created consternation and bewilderment in the ranks of Jewish Communists in all countries, so that it became a matter of urgency and of importance to expose their truth or falsehood. Moreover, these again in their minds became an acid test of the extent, if any, to which the Soviet Union had moved away from the path of socialism. Accordingly one member of the delegation, Comrade Levy, was given the specific task to examine this problem and to report on it. [...]

The first piece of concrete information came from a visit to the Lenin State Library. This is an enormous and very modernised institution second in size only to the Congress Library in Washington. [...]

It turned out that there is nothing in Yiddish later than 1948, when publication of Yiddish papers and journals must therefore have ceased.

The Soviet Encyclopedia, which in its 1932 edition devoted about 160 columns to Jews, reduces this in the 1952 edition to four columns. The biographies of many eminent Jews had been removed. Marx was no longer referred to as a Jew. [...]

Then came the discovery from private conversations by Comrade Levy with Jews that the years 1948–52 were known among them as 'The Black Years', the period during which many Jews were dismissed from their post, Jewish poets and writers were arrested and charged with treason and executed; Yiddish disappeared from the street and the market place, the population closed up together, becoming tense and nervy, and young Jews who might otherwise have merged with the general population and have forgotten they were Jews awoke to a new sense of unity in distress. This situation, we were assured, was shared by other national minorities besides Jews; but let it be said that this fear did not emanate from any general feeling of antagonism from among the Russian population but from official or quasi-official sources: from the security police in fact. Many sections of the Soviet working class went out of their way to show sympathy and support for harassed Jewry.

Conversations with the relatives of cultural workers who had been liquidated seemed to suggest that the procedure was invariable. Those arrested and charged in secret were prominent political or cultural workers. Shortly after his arrest the immediate relatives of the arrested man would be deported to some distant place and there set to work and often at low wages. Finally the husband would be shot, perhaps after torture, to try to force him to confess or to incriminate others. In this way practically the whole of the Jewish Anti-Fascist Committee was liquidated, and the proce-dure was carried through by the security police under the direct authority of Beria, with the agreement of Stalin himself, who had apparently become convinced of Beria's genuineness in seeking out the class enemy. [...] It was not until after the Twentieth Congress revelations that steps were taken to bring back the families of the murdered men, to reinstate them in their homes, and to recompense them in some measure for the suffering through which they had passed.

It is unnecessary to give chapter and verse as proof of these crimes. They are known, admitted and accepted as fact in the Soviet Union today, and no attempt is made to deny them. [...]

In the face of this, and a great deal of other evidence, it seems impossible to deny two conclusions:

1. That prior to the death of Stalin and certainly from the termination of the war, a deliberate policy was being pursued by a powerful element in Soviet life to exacerbate feeling between nationalities, and especially against certain smaller nationalities, and that this developed in an extreme form which led to the physical extermination of some of the best brains of Soviet life.
2. That since the death of Stalin, tremendous efforts are being made to make amends for this terrible state of affairs, and to prevent it ever happening again.

[...]

Crimes and distortions of this type cannot have been the work of one man. It must have been the case that sectors of the administrative personnel must have been aware what was taking place and must have taken the steps necessary to implement it. This argues a certain level of degeneration in this sector; a certain measure of indifference to human values which does violence to those of us, brought up in the bourgeois capitalist society, who have given our support to the socialist cause. Rightly or wrongly, we have expected something vastly different from this. [...]

World News (12 January 1957), pp. 20–3.

9.11 New left

True to their word, outside the party John Saville and E. P. Thompson launched a journal, *The New Reasoner*, which provided a forum for an emerging 'new left'. In this article from the first issue, Thompson produces a critique Stalinism, presenting an ethically oriented 'socialist humanism' as an alternative.

Socialist humanism: part one

[...]

Stalinism as an ideology

'Stalinism' is, in a true sense, an ideology; that is, a form of false consciousness, deriving from a partial, partisan, view of reality; and, at a certain stage, establishing a *system* of false or partially false concepts with a mode of thought which – in the Marxist sense – is idealist. 'Instead of commencing with facts, social reality, Stalinist theory starts with the idea, the text, the axiom: facts, institutions, people, must be brought to conform to the idea'.
[...]

Thus we must view Stalinism as an ideology – a constellation of partisan attitudes and false, or partially false, ideas; and the Stalinist today acts or writes in certain ways, not because he is a fool or a hypocrite, but because he is the prisoner of false ideas. But this is not to suggest that Stalinism arose just because Stalin and his associates had certain wrong ideas. Stalinism is the ideology of a revolutionary elite which, within a particular historical context, degenerated into a bureaucracy. In understanding the central position of the Russian bureaucracy, first in developing and now in perpetuating, this ideology, we have a great deal to learn, from the analyses of Trotsky and even more from the flexible and undogmatic approach of [Trotskyite intellectual] Isaac Deutscher and others. Stalinism struck root within a particular social context, drawing nourishment from attitudes and ideas prevalent among the working-class and peasantry – exploited and culturally deprived classes; it was strengthened by Russian backwardness and by the hostility and active aggression of capitalist powers; out of these conditions there arose the bureaucracy which adapted the ideology to its own purposes and is interested in perpetuating it; and it is clear enough now to most people that the advance of world socialism is being blockaded by this bureaucracy, which controls the means by which it is attempting to prevent – not a new ideology – but a true consciousness from emerging. In Russia the struggle against Stalinism is at one and the same time a struggle against the bureaucracy, finding expression in the various pressures for de-centralisation, economic democracy, political liberty, which are becoming evident. But –

important as this – we must not allow the particular forms which this revolt is taking in Russia and in Eastern Europe, to obscure the general character of the theoretical confrontation which is now taking place throughout the world communist movement. Stalinism did not develop just because certain economic and social conditions existed, but because these conditions provided a fertile climate within which false ideas took root, and these false ideas became in their turn a part of the social conditions. Stalinism has now outlived the social context within which it arose, and this helps us to understand the character of the present revolt against it.

This is – quite simply – a revolt against the ideology, the false consciousness of the elite-into-bureaucracy, and a struggle to attain towards a true ('honest') self-consciousness; as such it is expressed in the revolt against dogmatism and the anti-intellectualism which feeds it. Second, it is a revolt against inhumanity – the equivalent of dogmatism in human relationships and moral conduct – against administrative, bureaucratic and twisted attitudes towards human beings. In both senses it represents a return to man: from abstractions and scholastic formulations to real men: from deceptions and myths to honest history: and so the positive content of this revolt may be described as 'socialist humanism'. It is humanist because it places once again real men and women at the centre of socialist theory and aspiration, instead of the resounding abstractions – the Party, Marxism-Leninism-Stalinism, the Two Camps, the Vanguard of the Working-Class – so dear to Stalinism. It is socialist because it re-affirms the revolutionary perspectives of Communism, faith in the revolutionary potentialities not only of the Human Race or of the Dictatorship of the Proletariat but of real men and women. [...]

E. P. Thompson, *The New Reasoner*, 1 (Summer 1957), pp. 107–9.

Notes

1 Harry McShane recalls Pollitt's responses to questioning over Yugoslavia in McShane, *No Mean Fighter* (London: Pluto, 1978), p. 245.
2 Grant Pooke, *Francis Klingender 1907–1955: A Marxist Art Historian Out of Time* (London: Marx Memorial Library, 2008), pp. 176–7.
3 Harry Pollitt, 'On the Situation in the Yugoslav Communist Party', *World News and Views* (17 July 1948), pp. 295–301; James Klugmann, 'Tito in the Service of Imperialism', *Communist Review* (July 1950), pp. 217–23; James Klugmann, 'Lessons of the Prague Trials', *Communist Review* (March 1953), pp. 79–86.
4 John Callaghan, *Cold War, Crisis and Conflict: The CPGB 1951–1968* (London: Lawrence & Wishart, 2003), p. 61.

5 Ibid., p. 65.
6 See Francis Beckett, *Enemy Within: The Rise and Fall of the British Communist Party* (London: Merlin, 1995), pp. 124–41; Willie Thompson, *The Good Old Cause: British Communism, 1920–1991* (London: Pluto, 1992), pp. 90–113; Kevin Morgan, *Harry Pollitt* (Manchester: Manchester University Press, 1993), pp. 171–84; for the recollections of the key players, see the *Socialist Register* (1976).
7 Reuters rapidly made known the fact that Khrushchev had addressed the closed session. John Rettie, 'How Khrushchev Leaked His Secret Speech to the World', *History Workshop Journal*, 62, 1 (2006), pp. 187–93.
8 *Daily Worker* (12 March 1956).
9 Harry Pollitt, 'The Role of Stalin', *Daily Worker* (24 March 1956); 'The 20th Congress of the CPSU – and the Role of Stalin', *World News* (21 April 1956 and 5 May 1956).
10 Dutt, 'The Great Debate', *Labour Monthly* (May 1956), p. 194; Dutt, 'Notes of the Month' (June 1956), pp. 250–1.
11 Callaghan gives a full account, *Cold War*, pp. 66–8. The delegation reported on 'Jews in the Soviet Union', *World News* (12 January 1957), pp. 20–2.
12 Notably John Saville and E. P. Thompson. Saville, 'Problems of the Communist Party', *World News* (19 May 1956), p. 314; E. P. Thompson, 'Winter Wheat in Omsk', *World News* (30 June 1956), pp. 408–9. The latter was instantly rebutted by George Matthews, 'A Caricature of Our Party', pp. 409–10.
13 'Stand by Them', editorial in *Daily Worker* (25 October 1956); 'Eternal Vigilance', editorial in *Daily Worker* (26 October 1956). For Fryer, see Beckett, *Enemy*, pp. 130–4.
14 The Executive Committee justified its actions in *World News* (17 November 1956).
15 *World News* (1 December 1956).
16 Andy Croft, *Comrade Heart: A Life of Randall Swingler* (Manchester and New York: Manchester University Press, 2003), p. 227.
17 Contributions are gathered in CP/CENT/CONG/10/06.
18 Callaghan, *Cold War*, p. 76.
19 Thompson, *Good Old Cause*, p. 110.
20 Callaghan, *Cold War*, pp. 76–7.
21 Thompson, *Good Old Cause*, p. 101.
22 Malcolm MacEwen, 'The Day the Party Had to Stop', *Socialist Register* (1976), and MacEwen, *The Greening of a Red* (London: Pluto, 1991), pp. 179–99; for an inside view of the *Daily Worker* and 1956, see Alison Macleod, *The Death of Uncle Joe* (London: Merlin, 1997).
23 Thompson, *Good Old Cause*, p. 109.
24 Callaghan, *Cold War*, pp. 74–5.

10
Communists and trade unions since 1945

Communists always regarded trade union work as an essential aspect of what they did. By 1929 they had abandoned the strategy of organising the National Minority Movement as a way of building influence within the unions in compliance with Third Period emphases on separate Communist organisations and divorce from non-Communist left-wingers. This briefly inspired attempts to establish 'red' unions, more durable enthusiasm for unofficial strike actions and greater confrontation with non-Communist trade union officialdom. There were many reasons for regarding the unions as a vehicle for Communist influence. Organised labour wielded power, trade union members could be expected to be above the average in class consciousness and industrial conflict presented opportunities to use that power and enhance that consciousness. Communists were diligent trade unionists who could command the respect of their workmates simply by virtue of their industry, conscientiousness, negotiating ability and organisational skills. Where they could, Communists sought to inject political leadership into their trade union work. But even in unions that they dominated, such as the Electrical Trades Union (ETU), they recognised that the non-Communist majority set definite limits to what they could normally achieve.

After 1945 the CPGB pursued a dual strategy in the unions of championing wage militancy and the promotion of Communists into leadership positions. Wage militancy promised to bring the unions into conflict with the state as well as the employers because successive governments were concerned that excessive wages were the cause of Britain's falling competitiveness in international markets and the main cause of inflation. Capturing the leadership of unions affiliated to the Labour Party held out the prospect of using their block votes to dominate the Labour Party annual conference and its policy-making bodies.[1] The years 1945–91 were punctuated by successive attempts to control wages by both voluntary and statutory measures and eventually both Labour and Conservative governments proposed legislation to curb trade union powers. Between 1968 and 1974 strikes multiplied in scale and often acquired a political edge, notably when a national miners' strike provoked a Conservative government to call an early election on the question of 'who governs?', an election which it lost. The Communist Party was prominent in many industrial conflicts and contributed to the development of the Alternative Economic Strategy, which became the dominant programme of economic reforms championed by the Labour left in the 1970s. It entered this period of tumult with party members holding prominent positions in the NUM, the Union of Construction, Allied Trades and Technicians (UCATT), the National Union of Teachers, the Amalgamated Union of Engineering Workers – Technical, Administrative and Supervisory Staffs and the Amalgamated Engineering Union (AEU); it counted Lawrence Daly (NUM), Hugh Scanlon (AEU), Jack Jones (Transport and General Workers Union, TGWU), Ray Buckton (Associated Society of Locomotive Engineers and Firemen), Alan Sapper (UCATT) and Ken Cameron (Fire Brigades Union) as 'broad left's', that is potential allies. The model case Marxist–Labour alliance in the unions was the NUM, led by former Communists such as Lawrence Daly and Arthur Scargill; Communists such as Mick McGahey, Dai Francis, Jack Dunn, Arthur True and Sammy Moore; and Labour leftists such as Emlyn Williams. The party also boasted an array of militants at the forefront of industrial conflict. At the 30th Party Congress in 1967 John Gollan boasted that 'dozens' of them had led the recent wave of strikes.[2]

The early 1970s continued the trend, notably in the occupation of Upper Clyde Shipbuilders in 1971, when party members Jimmy Reid and Jimmy Airlie succeeded in politicising the threatened closure of the yard by campaigning for the 'right to work'. Then there were the opportunities presented by the hastily introduced Industrial Relations Act. The TUC organised mass demonstrations in January and February 1971; in March a special congress rejected the Act's requirement that unions register with a new registrar. Five dockers – three of whom were Communists – were imprisoned under the Act for unofficial strike action. Bert Ramelson, the party's national industrial organiser, now lobbied for a general strike and succeeded in organising solidarity actions for the imprisoned dockers on Fleet Street, as well as within the building trade and engineering. The following year more days were lost in strike activity than in any since the General Strike. The first national miners' strike since 1926 was notable for its 'flying pickets' and the enthusiastic support of other workers in closing down the power stations. By the end of 1973 the three-day week was instituted to cope with more power cuts and a second national miners' strike, which led to the 'Who Governs?' election already mentioned. After four years, and five states of emergency, Edward Heath's Conservative government was at its end.

Ramelson was not alone in claiming that the party's industrial strength had never been greater – hostile observers made the same point – and the Communist congresses of 1971 and 1973 encouraged the perception, as they had in 1967 and 1969, that the party was pulling the strings. The party could not disguise the fact, however, that the one thing it always stressed as essential to its plans had not materialised: membership growth. The current wave of trade union growth and increasing militancy had coincided with a fall in Communist membership from 33,734 in 1965 to 28,378 in 1974. Internal critics of the wage militancy policy seized upon this fact. What was worse, from the point of view of the party's industrial militants, its factory cells were also in steep decline. With the emergence of the Social Contract in 1974, the party's erstwhile broad left allies – now supporting a Labour government – no longer looked so useful. Scanlon and Jones led a retreat from wage militancy, which the Communists refused to follow. Clinging to the policy of wage militancy the party entered a prolonged crisis in 1974 as its postwar political-industrial strategy crumbled in every detail. But by this time the first doubts were being aired publicly by Communists who questioned whether wage militancy was having the desired effect of strengthening the party's claims to working-class leadership.

Although Communists were prominent in the conflicts of 1968–74, many of them having positions on trade union executives as well as at rank-and-file, shop steward level, such prominence only briefly concealed the extent to which the party suffered from a long-term failure to recruit within the unions. The Cold War had been a factor in this failure, but so had the crisis of 1956 when the party lost a third of its members and the world was forcefully reminded of the murderous Stalin dictatorship and the dictatorial character of his successors. Communist efficiency in organising trade union ballots for leadership positions was exposed in court as ballot-rigging in the case of the ETU during 1961, after years of damaging accusations and counter-accusations were given prominence in the press. Left-wing trade unionists might be repelled by all of this, but by the late 1950s they might also calculate that they did not need to belong to the CP to rise to positions of prominence. The party also had left-wing rivals in the unions, especially in the 1960s, and the sheer scale of wage militancy by the middle of that decade was evidence itself that militancy did not depend on, or indeed promote, Communist leadership.

10.1 Full employment in a capitalist economy

The Communists confidently predicted a return to mass un-employment after the Second World War and continued to do so throughout the 1950s. As in this first document the threat of unem-ployment always served as part of the rationale for wage militancy.[3]

[...] Full employment, as we have seen, has never been achieved under normal peacetime conditions in a capitalist system; neither in the age of free competition in the nineteenth century, nor even less in the monopoly capitalism of the twentieth century. The Socialist economy of the U.S.S.R. is so far the only example of a modern industrial society which has fully and freely developed all productive forces without crises and unemployment.

The Marxist analysis of the contradictions of capitalism makes its clear why this system, built on private property in the means of production, is unable to achieve and to maintain full employment permanently. This system, left to its own devices, can only produce permanent mass unemploy-ment on a growing scale.

The fight for full employment – one of the most important aims of the Labour Movement – is therefore a part of the fight of the working class and all progressive people against the domination of capitalist monopolies, for the control of the economic life of the country by the people in the interest of the people.

The fight for full employment has to be waged on many fronts, the most important of which are:

The fight for an increase in the living standards of the people (in the main, the real earnings of the workers) which must not lag behind the growing productivity of labour. The workers will be able and willing to increase production per man hour only when they are assured that rising production will result in improved conditions and not in growing unemployment.

The fight for a speedy and uncompromising implementation of Labour's nationalisation programme in such a way that the power of capitalist monopolies is broken and the control of the key economic positions in industry and finance passes into the hands of a government and its democratic institutions which really serve the interests of the working people.

The fight for a radical change of Britain's foreign policy and her international trade policy: instead of an imperialist colonial policy and a policy of subservience to American big business, the fight for a policy of international co-operation for expanding world production and world trade, based on friendly agreements with the U.S.S.R. and all truly democratic and progressive nations.

Finally, whether the world market will expand in the next few years or not depends not on economic policy alone, but on politics. A policy of peace and reconstruction, of consistent eradication of all vestiges of Fascism, of assistance to those countries which were devastated by the war or neglected by centuries of colonial rule, will be essential if the promises of an expanding world economy are to be realised. Strict adherence to and a determined fight for the principles of the United Nations Organisation and for lasting and real friendship with the Soviet Union are the essence of such a policy.

J. Winternitz, *The Problem of Full Employment: A Marxist Analysis in Four Lessons* (Lawrence & Wishart 1947), pp. 31–2.

10.2 British economic problems

Communists expected to find evidence of economic problems arising from Britain's imperial position, as well as evidence of recessionary tendencies in the world capitalist economy.

[…] The central feature of the capitalist world economic situation at the end of 1957 is the decline of the American economy. The US economy ceased to expand in 1955 and levelled off in 1956 but this year there has been an actual decline. The industrial index, which reached 147 … had fallen to 144 by September of this year and is expected to show a further fall.

[…] The fall in demand by US industry has led to a weakening of the world commodity markets with the result that the purchasing power of the primary producers has declined […]

[...] One of the effects of the capitalist world economic crisis is to add to the pressures leading to the disintegration of the British Empire. The policy of the British imperialists has been to maintain the Empire as a supplier of raw materials; as a privileged market for British industrial goods, and as a field for profitable capital investment. To this end Tory Governments have declared it as their prime objective to be able to secure large surpluses each year for investment overseas and to this end the British people have been denied an improvement in the standard of living.

[...] The recession in America and particularly the decline in raw material prices may well stimulate the tendency towards disintegration of the Empire. In addition, the under-developed countries see the danger of their position as primary producers and they naturally see industrialisation as part of their struggle for independence [...]

[...] The establishment of the European Common Market places a fresh strain on Britain's links with the Empire.

In this situation ... the Empire is less able to provide the same profits as formerly. British monopoly capitalism turns to a tougher policy at home with the workers seen as the main source for funds for accumulation [...]

[...] the Macmillan Government has undertaken an offensive against the British working class [...]

Taking their cue from the US Government, the Macmillan Government has strenuously endeavoured to scare the British people by talking about the dangers of inflation ... The Tories seem to frighten the more faint-hearted leaders of the Labour Movement so that the fight for wage increases will be diminished.

[...] Our first task, therefore, is to convince the British people that their main economic danger at the end of 1957 is not one of inflation but one of depression ... Hence we must fight in the Labour Movement against any defeatist talk of freezing wages so as to stabilise prices [...]

'The Trade Cycle in Post-War Britain', 4 December 1957, report of the Economic Committee, CP/CENT/ECON/4/12.

10.3 A militant wages policy

Some socialists took the view that economic planning had to be applied to incomes if it was to be effective overall.[4] But the dominant view inside the trade unions favoured free collective bargaining. This was also the position of the Communists.

Wages policy is a major subject for discussion at the coming Trades Union Congress ... expressed in resolutions which:

Oppose the Government White Paper on Incomes Policy, and presumably the National Incomes Commission.

[...] There are, however, two resolutions which defend the principles of an incomes policy ...

The General Council is asked 'to work out a positive statement for the general guidance of the trade union movement on ... economic planning, including the planning of incomes and role of collective bargaining' (Inland Revenue Staff Federation). This resolution also asserts 'the need for some planning of personal incomes, to bring about greater equality and promote more rapid economic growth'.

[...] [the second resolution wants] ... 'a positive plan to eradicate the anomalies of the current wage and profit scramble ... to ensure a just, adequate and progressively better return for labour, skill, applied knowledge and enterprise' (Chemical Workers Union).

[...] The Government wages policy is designed to bring the utmost pressure on the unions to prevent wages and earnings from rising.

[...] In 1960 the Organisation for European Economic Co-operation ... carried out an investigation which came to the conclusion ... that the only way to prevent price rises was for every Government to have a wages policy ... It is this document which provides the theoretical basis for the policy now adopted by the Tory Government.

[...] [the National Incomes Commission] would be a permanent organisation for attacking the unions.

[...] [it] is an impudent attempt to blame the unions for the post-war inflation.

[...] In the last analysis wage differences under capitalism are based on the strategic position of the industry concerned, and on the strength and militancy of the unions operating in it. There is no substitute for militancy with the unremitting pressure which it involves. It is the duty of the unions to make this point abundantly clear.

[...] With regard to low paid industries and occupations the General Council mobilising the Trades Councils should help the unions operating in these spheres in a great recruiting campaign ... It must as a matter of extreme urgency consult with unions organising women on how they suggest the demand for equal pay for equal work should be implemented.

'A Militant Wages Policy: The Alternative to NIC', 21 August 1962, pp. 1–13, CP/CENT/IND/10/08.

10.4 The inflationary problem and political leadership

Bill Warren was one of the first Communists to question the party's militant wages policy. This is an early attempt of his to explain to other Communists why British governments were increasingly concerned about the persistence of inflation. Such views were not yet published in the party press as they ran counter to its wage militancy strategy and accepted the thesis that excessive wage demands damaged Britain's international competitiveness.

In the post-World War 2 era, with the expectation by the working classes of the industrialised world of a better life, with the immense strengthening of the socialist world and with the dependence of the economies of the politically awakened underdeveloped world on the prosperity of the developed world, the political fears of the ruling class of a repetition of the mass unemployment of the 1930s have dictated a policy of maintaining full employment.

The policy of full employment has in turn given rise indirectly to the policy of inflation restraint, since full employment on the one hand strengthens the trade unions in their efforts to raise money wages and on the other hand implies a sufficient level of demand relative to capacity to permit the resultant rise in labour costs to be passed on to prices, so that inflation becomes a semi-permanent feature of the full employment economy.

The necessity for a policy against inflation arises neither from the alleged inefficiencies of an inflationary economy (which are probably less than those of a deflationary economy) nor from the dangers of a 'breakdown of the monetary system or "confidence" in the currency etc.' (none of these have [sic] ever happened historically except after wars and revolutions) [...]

The ruling classes of most capitalist nations oppose inflation for two reasons:

(i)   because failure *relative to other countries* to hold down prices affects international competitiveness and thus the relative power balance;

(ii) because rising prices, even when money wages are rising *faster*, have the double effect of drawing attention to the exploitation of the working and middle classes on the one hand, and of suggesting the limitations of trade union action alone to raise real wages on the other [...]

(iii) The necessity to maintain full employment causes inflation to become a more or less permanent feature of economic life.

(iv) Inflation undermines the position of the ruling class, politically vis-à-vis its own working class, and economically vis-à-vis its international rivals, by threatening the balance of trade, via the decline in British competitiveness, and by threatening the use of sterling as a world currency.

(v) The attempt to restrain inflation endangers the policy of full employment so that a continuous political problem is faced by the ruling class, vacillating between the drawbacks of inflation and the political consequences of even mild unemployment.

(vi) The attempt to restrain inflation accentuates in the medium and long run the problems it is dealing with in the short run, i.e. the problems of rising prices and balance of payments deficits. This is because the anti-inflationary policies pursued above all hinder the productivity increase on which economic health depends.

'The Economic Policies of Post-war Tory and Labour Governments Till November 1964', by William McCallum (Bill Warren), CP/CENT/ECON/6.

10.5 Being Frank

Frank Watters was born in 1920 in the mining village of Shotts in Scotland. He worked as a miner and Communist Party organiser in Scotland until 1953 when he was asked by the party to move to the Yorkshire coalfield as a full-time organiser. Yorkshire was seen as the key to the political balance in the NUM and the NUM was important in the Labour Party. But, as Watters explains, it was difficult in the 1950s for the Communists to find allies.

[…] the Korean War had a big impact, especially with the *Amethyst* incident, when a Chinese gunboat fired on a British warship. The Party was under great strain, and we talked about the possibility of going underground.

[…] I was asked by the Party to go into the Yorkshire coalfield in 1953 in order to help create a broad left-wing to oppose the right-wing in the area NUM. The NUM had become a bastion of right-wing theory and practice, and the Yorkshire area was a powerful right-wing area […]

[…] In 1953 there was a good deal of militancy in the coalfield … Wages weren't fully related to the amount of coal produced … The militancy revolved around this struggle at the point of production over pay. There were tremendous 'bushfire' strikes in 1954. It was the highest number of strikes in the post-war period in Yorkshire […]

[…] The Party was organised in a mixture of residential and pit branches based upon villages, with the main object of winning the coalfield for left

214

political and industrial positions. Because of the importance of Yorkshire, the CP there was helped by national figures such as [Arthur] Horner, [Abe] Moffat, [Willie] Gallacher, and Pollitt, though we also used local talent, especially Jock Kane and Sammy Taylor. At the age of sixteen or seventeen, Arthur Scargill was on the platform in the Barnsley Public Hall with Harry Pollitt. We would have large coalfield meetings and pub meetings. The Industrial Department of the Communist Party gave help to all sections, but responsibility for how we applied general policy was in the hands of individual industrial organisers. They had to do it that way, they didn't know very much about what was happening in the coalfield.

I was asked to go into the coalfield to construct a broad, not exclusively Communist, left and to reverse the serious right-wing position there. But there really wasn't an effective Labour left until after 1960. For a long time there was nothing between very right-wing Labour and the Communist Party. But I worked with anyone I could find [...] even people who were against the Communist Party. In 1953 a significant breakthrough was made with the appointment of Eddie Collins as Compensation Agent. Eddie was an old, uncorrupted militant, whose loyalty and devotion to the miners won my fullest admiration. We developed a bond of friendship and trust in each other. He passed on knowledge and information and greatly helped my work. And I was able to keep a nucleus of my contacts informed.

If we seemed sectarian, it was the historical period we got caught up in. There was no Labour left to ally with until Bevan, and Bevanites never recognised the importance of trade unionism. But the Party conducted the battle in the Yorkshire coalfield for Bevan to be nominated and supported as Labour Party Treasurer. The only panel that ever invited Bevan to speak at a rally was the Doncaster Panel, under the influence of the Communist Party [...]

[...] Developments in Yorkshire undoubtedly played a major role in laying the basis for the emergence of a national left leadership. The development of an organised national left was sealed by the unanimous decision on the left to support Lawrence Daly for General Secretary. By this time all those left-wingers who had contested against [Alwin] Machen for the Presidency were either too old or dead. People like Hughes, [E. P.] Thompson, [John] Saville and members of the Tribune Group helped in formulating progressive policies. The campaign for votes for Daly generated a left organisation. In Yorkshire the apparatus built around the Taylor and Kane campaigns were tremendous aids. The CP in Yorkshire had built an infrastructure which included the Communist Party and the non-Communist left. With the election of Daly, Joe Whelan in Nottinghamshire, Emlyn Williams in South Wales, a national organised left became a natural development. And in Scotland, McGahey ushered in a new era of younger leadership. McGahey played a big part in the Daly election. The left in the National Executive Committee became stronger and more united. This helped to lay the basis for 1972. By then, there was a strong militant rank-and-file feeling and a

215

leadership that took notice of the rank-and-file. These were ideal conditions for struggle; a strong rank-and-file movement with official backing that could pressure the right wing leaders [...]

Source: an interview with Frank Watters conducted by Peggy Kahn and published in the *Bulletin of the Society for Labour History*, 43 (autumn 1981), pp. 54–67.

10.6 Taking stock in the unions

In the winter of 1964 the party reconsidered its working methods within the trade unions in the light of the damage done to its position within the ETU by the ballot-rigging scandal. As this in-house discussion of Communist shop stewards reveals, the majority view favoured more open alliances with Labour left-wingers. This is the origin of the broad left strategy which remained in force throughout the strike wave of 1968–74 and into the 1980s. The discussion is revealing of the semi-conspiratorial methods the party had been using up to 1964, including the use of advisory committees, which linked the party's industrial department to the leading Communist militants in certain industries. These were supposed to take decisions on a range of industrial issues but were overwhelmingly preoccupied with the organisation of election campaigns within unions to ensure the maximum impact for the CPGB and its allies.

Discussion of CP organisation in the trade unions in November–December 1964, after the ETU ballot-rigging trial

L. W. Dawson (ETU shop steward in Fleet Street)
[...] [Len Dawson said he had] been giving a lot of thought to the question of [CP] industrial work in the light of our experience in the ETU ... as in this period I have been involved in the leadership as far as the ETU is concerned.

The fact that the existence of advisory committees was denied in court has ... restricted the personnel in number and content for security reasons ... in the two years that I have sat on this committee, although we paid a certain amount of lip service to the need to discuss and shape industrial policy in the union ... we were so wrapped up in discussions on the election of union officers that it would have needed a weekend on every occasion that we met rather then an evening.

[...] There is little doubt that prior to 1961 the party machine in the union broadly speaking classified the left in the union into four groups: (1) Those in the Party on the inside and trusted with all the under-cover work that went on; (2) The rest of the Party who were loyal to the Party and thought everything was above board; (3) Those members of the Labour Party and the left who were prepared to follow instructions and were treated with contempt for doing so, and (4) All those who opposed the old leadership, who were bastards no matter for what reason they were in opposition.

[Dawson favoured more open work but expected] [...] objections to this course from comrades who ... think that the capture of a trade union leadership will transform the political situation.

Reg Beech
[...] When I personally tried to intervene in the matter of rigged ballots the only effect was to arouse personal suspicions. In fact, I have had the argument put to me – urging me as a then branch secretary – to agree to fiddling a ballot on the alleged Marxist argument that the TU environment must be changed in order to create socialist union thinking [...]

The method used of having secret meetings to discuss policy – advisories – creates suspicion amongst our fellow workers and members, even those who support our policies.

F. W. Griffiths
The situation we find ourselves in is not all black ... looking back I find that whatever should have happened *theoretically* I ceased to (1) recruit to the Party; (2) Do serious political work (Communist work) as soon as I became involved in running the ETU; never mind that it was at a very lowly level.

[...] I am against taking office under cover ... we should disband secret advisory committees [...]

R. Bonner, National Union of Railwaymen
Our salvation lies in forging unity on a lasting basis.

L. Dawson, ETU
It is because we are so secret in our deliberations that the atmosphere is created whereby our enemies can make use of them in organs such as the *Daily Express*.

Furthermore, it might be asked if the Advisories are such good things in themselves ... sometimes 90% of the time being used to discuss elections and only 10% to discuss policy.

Bill Smart, Amalgamated Union of Building Trade Workers
[...] we have reached the stage where we can come right out into the open [...]

[...] In Building we must have nearly 2,000 comrades in the industry (including ETU and AEU and other unions in the building line). You would think this would lead to effective District Advisory Committees but there are none.

E. Rechnitz, TGWU
This kind of thing indicates that there are two Communist Parties – members of one work in ward branches and members of the other work in industry.
W. Ferrie, National Union of Vehicle Builders
[...] In the Midlands ... there is no industrial organiser ... The situation today demands a complete reappraisal of every aspect of our industrial work.

A. F. Papworth, TGWU
Against widening – most dangerous thing for the Party to do or to make public the question of Advisory Committees.
[...] It is unwise to have open meetings – better if anything to tighten up to do work properly.

Dick Woolf, DATA
[...] we came out in the open ... The majority on EC now is a mixture of Party and progressives.
We still meet as an advisory group but ... when we have had our conference we have called a meeting of anybody of the progressive section of our union, to talk about our policy and discuss who ought to be elected.

JRC (John R. Campbell)
The old leadership of the ETU gave the appearance of being manipulated by King Street but, in my view, they manipulated King Street.
[...] to have some broad relationships of a permanent character with the left forces ... we have got to play the game with the left forces. When Ernie Roberts gets a smaller vote than Reg Birch ... it creates the impression that communists were not so interested ... when Ernie Roberts was being elected [...]
[...] As far as elections are concerned a certain degree of secrecy is necessary.
[...] The most important thing is there is a big gap in generations and we must take positive steps to bring in new party members or we will find ourselves without any cadres because we have neglected their training.

Untitled document: CP/CENT/IND/12/8.

10.7 Factory cells

Throughout the post-war decades the party attached enormous importance to factory branches but was unable to arrest their decline; this document refers to one of many attempts to do so. It refers in passing to a perennial dispute within the party according to which work in general elections and local elections wasted resources that would be better spent in industrial work.

Communists and the factories

The speech of Frank Stanley, chairman of the Communist Party, to the Communist Party's factory branch conference held in London, June 11th–12th, 1966.

This is one of the most important conferences the Party has held for many years.

What we want to get out of it is a new turn to the factories at a time when the political situation makes the factories the central point for generating the political change that is so badly needed and a big field for the renewed growth of the Party and the YCL.

[...] This conference takes place as a result of the decision of our 29th National Congress. That put the aim of creating a mass movement of such scope and power as to win decisive changes in policy in Britain – and to get this by resolute work for the unity in action of all the left forces.

[...] The Government's attack on the seamen in the interests of its incomes policy, is a clear indication of the lengths to which it is prepared to go, and shows the need for decisive counter-action.

[...] The factories are the key centre of the class struggle.

Most of our factory organisations that have gone out of existence during the period since the last factory branch conference have been due to pit closures, redundancy and closing down of factories and completion of building jobs. Only a few have been due directly to political reasons or organisational neglect.

Some have disappeared because they were small branches of three, four, or five, and when a couple of members retire or leave, the organisation goes out of existence.

But it should be noted that even in industries which are contracting, new factory branches can be set up, because in many cases hand in hand with redundancy and rationalisation has gone the concentration of production into larger units.

At the same time other industries have grown. The labour force, in the engineering and electrical industries for example, went up by 275,000, construction by 235,000, and paper, print and publishing by 53,000 [...]

Electoral work

Some members argue that we have counter-posed electoral work to factory work. This is an oversimplified answer that does not get us very far. We have to advance more and more on the electoral front at the same time as we develop our existing factory branches and set up new ones [...]

[...] Why is Communist work in the factories of such importance in the coming period?

The factories are the key points in the struggle against the Government's incomes policy – now the main immediate issue confronting all trade unionists. The factories are decisive for generating *mass action* on all the major issues – whether wages and hours, Vietnam, war and peace, anti-trade union legislation. The factories can be decisive in influencing the trade union movement in a left progressive direction. In addition, the factories – where we work alongside active Labour Party members, Labour councillors, and prospective Labour MPs – is one of [sic] the main places where we can develop left unity on the one hand and get the growth of the Party on the other.

It is in the factories that class understanding is strongest and the workers most conscious of their common class interests.

It is on the job that the power and influence of the workers can be most rapidly and effectively organised and brought into action.

[...] The question of wages, hours of work, redundancy and so on – once regarded as exclusively economic questions and coming only within the purview of the trade union movement – are now more than ever highly political, because the Government has chosen to make its incomes policy a challenge to all trade unionists, using, as in the case of the seamen, all the powers of state.

Whereas before within the uneven development of trade union organisation, some sections, some factories, some industries, could, because of superior organisation and sometimes other factors, play a leading role and secure significant advances before other sections, a powerful combination of forces now exists of employers, Government, and some trade union leaders, and is attempting to end this situation. A united, concerted factory movement is now vital to meet this challenge [...]

The Communist Party organises branches in the factories because the factory workers are the most decisive political sections of the population. While trade union organisation is important for the workers, political organisation is even more important – that is why we must have Party branches in the factories.

The Communist Party is a party of class struggle. The factories are the key points of the class struggle where it proceeds day in and day out.

The factories bring hundreds of thousands of workers together under the same roof. This makes it possible for us to work in an organised fashion with greater advantages than when the individual workers are scattered to their homes all over the place. The factories are the most fruitful field for consistent Communist work.

CP/CENT/ORG/2/1.

10.8 Incomes policy

Bert Ramelson was the CPGBs Industrial Organiser from 1965 until 1977, a period of mounting wage militancy and an enormous strike wave – especially in 1968–74. It was also a time of repeated attempts by successive governments to curb trade union powers. Throughout this period Ramelson stood for wage militancy and the defence of free collective bargaining. CPGB literature supplied shop stewards with arguments and alternatives to official policy and in this pamphlet Ramelson outlines an early version of the Alternative Economic Strategy which – repeatedly modified – became the focus of left-wing thinking in the Labour Party in the 1970s and up to its general election defeat in 1983.

On July 20th, 1966, Harold Wilson launched in his crisis speech in the House of Commons, the most vicious attack on the working people since the MacDonald Government's onslaught in 1931. He simultaneously announced a series of measures aimed at a steep increase in the cost of living [...] and demanded a wages standstill, which in such circumstances can only mean a slashing of real wages and earnings. In addition he proposed drastic cuts in public expenditure by the Government, local authorities and nationalised industries. All this makes it absolutely certain that ever-growing queues will again be lining up at the labour exchanges.

The Prices and Incomes Standstill White Paper spelt out what it means.

[...] With breathtaking effrontery the Government justifies the standstill by declaring 'the country needs a breathing space of twelve months, in which productivity can catch up with the excessive increases in incomes which have been taking place'.

By the taxation and other measures announced, production in general will be reduced and productivity in particular. So that this 'breathing space' far from 'catching up' will at best stagnate and could actually reduce output. In that case, the 'norm' could remain at zero for a long time after the standstill.

The Government pretends to freeze prices. But in fact, unlike wages, it provides for many exceptions. Prices can and will rise because of higher import prices, extra taxation and, where rents are frozen, rates will go up to enable local authorities to balance their housing accounts.

[...] Here is an attack on wages and salaries unprecedented in its scope, and is deliberately aimed at artificially creating a recession – characterised by cuts in production, reduction in real earnings and rising unemployment – the logical consequence of attempting over the years to solve Britain's economic problems through incomes policy.

[...] The incomes policy has two main features. First to keep wage rates *and earnings* below what is attainable by the trade unions as a result of their present organised strength in negotiations with the employers. Secondly, to secure state intervention in one form or another to ensure that wage rates and earnings are in conformity with a norm.

This norm is to be pre-determined by the state and operated regardless of the merits of any claim or the strength of the trade unions. It is related to output. If that goes down, so will the norm. Indeed, there is pressure to reduce it now, and even a suggestion to reduce it to zero, a fancy term for wage freeze.

The theory of the incomes policy

It is no accident that the incomes policy has become the pet theory of most capitalist economists. There was a time when the very thought of the state interfering with the free play of the market as the only possible way of determining wages and salaries was unthinkable. But times have changed.

What is the essence of the change?

In the past the reserve army of labour, the unemployed, was a built-in feature of the capitalist system. The commodity labour power was more or less permanently a glut on the market. In these circumstances where supply of labour was in excess of demand, the employer as the buyer of the commodity was able to use the conditions of the market to his advantage in bargaining ... with the workers selling their labour power. So the employers' rallying cry was 'No state interference with the free play of the market in determining wages'.

[...] But for the past two decades in a number of advanced capitalist countries, and particularly in Britain, there has existed a situation unique in capitalist history. Since 1946, except for brief periods, there has been a general shortage of labour and a chronic shortage of skilled labour.

For the first time in the history of capitalist society this has led to the position where the seller of the commodity labour power (the trade unions) has the advantage in bargaining with the buyer (the employers). This situation provides the best setting for working class advances on the economic front, within the confines of capitalism [...]

Incomes policy – needed to halt inflation
Undoubtedly this is the most widely used argument. It takes note of the indisputable fact that in Britain during the postwar years there has been a generally mild inflationary tendency. In other words, prices have tended to rise. But this tendency has been gradual, nothing like the frightening run-away inflation of the twenties, but well below an annual 4 per cent on the average.

[...] In our view there are four factors which mainly give rise to inflation, and none of them is directly related to wages.

One is the huge arms expenditure, unprecedentedly high [...]

A second factor is the change in the composition of the labour force. There has been a considerable increase in the proportion of 'workers in non-productive enterprises, e.g. advertising, salesmen, banking, the services'.

This is a new feature of capitalism, and again means that workers not producing goods for sale, nevertheless use their wages to chase after consumer goods.

Then the high degree of monopoly development in the postwar years means that the prices of an ever-growing number of goods are permanently held at high monopoly price levels.

The fourth factor is the deflationary budgets of all postwar governments, Tory and Labour alike, which have been brought in to reduce demand on the home market by cutting our spending. Every budget has resulted in raising prices in some form or another. As a result of this deliberate increase in the cost of living the wage and salary earners have been compelled to use their organised strength, to maintain their real earnings by compensatory wage and salary increases [...]

[...] And there is an alternative policy, based on true economic facts. We put it forward here.

It is not a policy which will solve all the problems facing capitalist Britain. That calls for full socialist measures. Only when production for private profit is abolished and the country owned by the people and fully developed for the benefit of all will economic crises be ended.

But this policy will above all help to solve the balance of payments crisis, lift the economy from stagnation, and create favourable conditions for carrying on the struggle for a socialist Britain.

Overseas Military Spending. The Government should end its East of Suez policy and its support for the U.S. war in Vietnam, it should close down all bases overseas and bring the troops home. This in itself would save over £300 million a year in foreign exchange.

[...] **End Private Investment Overseas.** The Government must put a stop to private investment abroad. This would also save about the same amount in foreign exchange. Wilson has ignored this major factor in our payments deficit in his July budget. This money should be used to modernise backward sections of industry at home, for this is the real cause of our disadvantages in competing with other countries.

Keep Up Demand. Total and absolute opposition to any wage freeze; resolute determination to compel the implementation of all agreements entered into [...]

Prices. The Government should introduce a national price stop. It should stabilise the price of food, using subsidies where necessary, and cut purchase tax on all except luxury goods.

Foreign Trade. All barriers to trade with the socialist countries should be removed. Selective export subsidies and export credit facilities, should be introduced. The Government should use its powers to impose selective, physical import controls, so that such expanded foreign trade would not lead to excessive import increases which would endanger the balance of payments position.

Extend Public Ownership. In order to plan investment, which is the key to planning the development of the whole economy, the Government must step by step take over the big monopolies. This will enable a real national plan to be made, very different from the present so-called plan.

[...] **Pay Off our Debts.** The Government should stop trying to maintain the £ sterling as a world currency. This is the only way to stop foreign speculation against the £ [...]

The policy outlined above is what Britain needs to expand the economy.

It is supported by millions of people in the labour movement. It is advocated by Communists and left Labour people.

If all who agree unite to campaign for it then Britain can make a turn to the left and open the way for real socialist change.

Bert Ramelson, *Incomes Policy: The Great Wage Freeze Trick* (London: CPGB, 1966), pp. 3–21.

10.9 The Communists' answer to Wilson's smear

The Prime Minister, Harold Wilson, told the House of Commons on 20 June 1966 that the strike of the National Union of Seamen was the work of the Communist Party operating through 'a select few' on the union's Executive Council.

[...] If as a Party and as individuals we have helped the seamen in their just struggle, then we are proud. In doing so we were only fulfilling our elementary duty as a working class party [...]

Mr Wilson named Mr Jack Coward, Mr Roger Woods and Mr Gordon Norris, along with Mr Bert Ramelson and Mr Dennis Goodwin as being responsible for the alleged pressure on the NUS Executive [...]

[...] Mr Wilson said we were not only concerned to extend the strike for the seamen but to torpedo his incomes policy.

Our attitude to the incomes policy is well known – we are against it ... [but] It is an absolute lie ... to suggest that communists are concerned with injuring the British economy ... for what it is worth we prefer to see the capitalist economy operating as near as possible to full employment [...]

John Gollan's statement at the Communist Party Press Conference, 28 June 1966, CP/CENT/STAT/2/3.

10.10 Leading the strikes

A recurring complaint within the CPGB was that the party wasted its energy and resources fighting local and general elections. The leadership always refuted that argument. But when John Gollan did so at the 30th Congress in 1967 – associating the anti-electoral argument with the Surrey District and its leading spokesman Sid French – he paid tribute to the work of Communist industrial militants and probably reinforced the conviction of many of those present that Communist advance depended on the organisation's position within the trade unions.

[...] Look at the people who have come to this rostrum, yesterday and today. Jack Henry, Lou Lewis, Cyril Morton, Dave Bowman, Arthur Harper and others. And others who have not spoken here – Dick Etheridge, Jack Dash, Johnny Tocher, and dozens of others.

I say this is a veritable roll-call of militants and fighters of which this Party should be proud.

How can anyone talk of lack of attention to the industrial struggle [...]

[...] Politics is about power and we are playing at being Communists unless we persist in battle to win through to the Councils and to Parliament [...]

[...] Important policy decisions have been made. We should now step up the struggle on wages, Vietnam, the coal industry and win the alternative policy ... Let us ... develop the progressive alliance in the Trade Union Movement which is the key to changing the whole position of the Labour Movement [...]

John Gollan, closing speech in reply to the resolution on left unity in action for an alternative policy, 30th Congress 1967, CP/CENT/CONG/16/07.

10.11 Workers' control

Workers' control was an increasingly popular idea among trade unionists, many of whom had been influenced by the work of the Nottingham-based Institute for Workers' Control set up in 1968 by rival Marxists such as Tony Topham and Ken Coates. Ramelson wanted to ensure that the interest in worker participation in plant management was not allowed to soften or obscure the class struggle in industry which CPGB policies were supposed to be promoting.

Industrial democracy has in recent years become a lively topic for discussion. The debate is not confined, as is sometimes thought, to fringe extremist groups.

The TUC devoted considerable space in its evidence to this subject and the Royal Commission itself found it necessary to refer in its Report to this theme.

The Labour Party set up a working party which produced a Report dealing with industrial democracy ... to be submitted to this year's Labour Party Conference [...]

[...] we must begin by making a clear distinction between what is possible before the working class take power and after.

[...] precisely because basic conflict between management and workers disappears, the extent of industrial democracy in a socialist state is considerably more extensive than is conceivable in a capitalist state [...]

[...] Nevertheless there is no substitute for a vigilant trade union even under socialism [...]

But even under socialism there are limits to the workers' rights in running the plant [...]

[...] Pricing, allocation of investment funds, decisions on whether a particular plant or industry should expand or contract, I think must remain a function of the state [...]

Before Power
A serious examination ... must start with the recognition that there is an irreconcilable conflict between the employers and the workers [...]

[...] And because the capitalist state ... pursues policies advantageous to the employing class, the conflict of interests is extended as between the state and the working class. This basic conflict will therefore exist not only in the private sector of industry but also in the nationalised industries [...]

[...] In such circumstances to talk about workers' control is to spread confusion and weaken the struggle [...]

[...] The right to strike is the be all and end all of industrial trade union struggle ... Thus the fight to preserve the right to strike [is] ... at the very heart of the struggle to extend industrial democracy [...]

Workers' representation in nationalised industry
[...] representation ... is ancillary to trade union struggle to consolidate the inroads made and to encroach still further on managerial functions [...]

[...] under no circumstances should the workers feel themselves committed by decisions accepted by their elected members – any more than they feel themselves bound by the decisions of a Labour Government that are contrary to their interests.

In private industry workers' directors would, in my view, be a red herring [...]

Bert Ramelson, 'Workers' Control? Possibilities and Limitations', *Marxism Today* (October 1968), pp. 296–303.

10.12 Productivity deals

The Communists' opposition to all forms of state intervention in industrial relations was ultimately justified by the belief that 'the wages struggle' would lead to enhanced political understanding on the part of workers and the emergence of a positive socialist alternative. Collisions with state policy in the field of 'industrial relations' were supposed to be especially congenial to this outcome.

The Government's latest While Paper *Productivity, Prices and Incomes Policy* (Cmd. 4237) is but the latest in a mounting campaign, unprecedented in scope, to sell 'productivity' agreements to low wage and salary earners in this country.

[...] The effect of this campaign has been considerable. Barbara Castle boasts in her latest White Paper that 'over 6 million workers have been involved in over 3,500 productivity agreements' [...]

[...] The productivity agreement is the latest and most sophisticated technique devised by the ruling class to implement its main objective on the wages front – 'incomes policy'; that is, to limit wage and salary increases to a portion of the results of increased efforts on the part of the workers; or to use an old-fashioned, but nonetheless true description of what is involved, to increase the rate of exploitation.

Its purpose is to *replace* traditional bargaining based on a true reflection of the balance of strength at any given time between the organised workers and employers [...]

[...] to do away with traditional collective bargaining on a national, firm or plant basis. The aim is to deny workers the right to use their collective strength to demand and achieve increases through struggle [...]

Shop stewards
Central to the employers' objective is to use productivity agreements to destroy the shop stewards movement and workshop organisation. The aim is to convert the shop stewards from being the key lay trade union officials leading the daily class struggle at the place of work, into staff men with the major task of monitoring the successful operation of the productivity agreements.

[...] Only the combined struggle for increased wages and earnings, and shorter working time, can ensure that advances in technology and science do not result in a catastrophe for the workers in terms of mass unemployment, speed-up, and increased strain for those remaining in work. It alone can guarantee that increased productivity resulting from technological advances benefits the workers, whether by hand or brain, and their families, who constitute the overwhelming majority of the population [...]

[...] Militant struggle from below far from creating difficulties for the official leaderships of unions is positive assistance to those trade union leaders who are actively fighting to advance the interest of their members. Such militancy and actions by the membership strengthens the bargaining position of the official negotiators. Without such militancy and action, the left wing members on the Union Executives and the General Council of the T.U.C. could never have shifted the Executives of Unions and the General Council itself to conduct the campaign which compelled the Government to withdraw *In Place of Strife*.

Bert Ramelson, *Productivity Agreements: An Exposure of the Latest and Greatest Swindle on the Wages Front* (London: CPGB, January 1970), pp. 3–23.

10.13 Kill the bill

Opposition to the Conservative government's legislative proposals in 1970 on industrial relations was widely based in the trade unions and promised a wave of political strikes, which the CPGB was keen to promote.

The Industrial Relations Bill 1970 is the most vicious piece of politically motivated class legislation since the Combination Acts ... It has been framed by big business for big business. It has no parallel in any capitalist country in the world other than in those Fascist countries like Spain and Greece, where there is no attempt at any pretence that trade unions are allowed to exist [...]

The Bill is not only an attack on the trade unions and militant trade unionists. As will be shown later, it is aimed equally to deprive the British people of some of their basic inalienable democratic rights such as freedom of speech and expression, and the right to demonstrate and organise in support of their views and opinions [...]

All existing trade union rights scrapped

What has not been sufficiently publicised so far is that all existing trade union legislation is repealed, starting with the Trade Union Acts of 1871 and 1875, and the Trades Disputes Act of 1906, right through to the Trades Disputes Act introduced by the Labour Government in 1965 to partially restore trade union rights encroached upon by the Courts [...]

The new Bill replaces all existing legislation wrenched out of the ruling class in thousands of class battles over the past centuries, many of which were proudly recorded in the TUC Centenary publications only two years ago. All the rights won in these battles, which have now become part of custom and practice, as important as the laws themselves, are to be erased as if they never existed [...]

[...] What is at stake is not a wage claim but the very existence of a trade union movement capable of using its strength to advance its members' interests [...]

Industrial action needed

The defeat of this Bill won't be achieved by argument or holding indoor rallies or even 'lunch hour' factory gate meetings [...]

The rank and file movement must combine the development of actions with the maximum pressure on the General Council and the National Executives telling them the time is short, that it is high time to go over to action.

229

The TUC should be recalled earlier than in March ... to plan national industrial action before it is too late.

[...] The only power that is irresistible is the full force of determined and working class action and that involves industrial action. If the entire trade union movement, united and determined, were to make it clear that it was prepared to use its full power, no Government, whatever its political complexion, could stand out against it [...]

Bert Ramelson, *Carr's Bill and How to Kill It* (London: CPGB, 1970), pp. 3–24.

10.14 British capitalism since the war

In this two-part piece the author rejects standard CPGB explanations for British capitalism's relative decline – including the stop-go argument, under-investment and the export of capital. Instead he focuses on the relative strengths of the principal class forces. His arguments amount to a repudiation of the CPGB's approach inside British trade unionism because they point to the failure to supply a political leadership and show that the initiative in Britain has passed to the political right. The fact that these views are published in the party's theoretical journal is an indication of wider dissatisfaction with the party's industrial strategy. It is now 1976 and the biggest strike wave since the early 1920s has done nothing to increase Communist influence in the unions or the Labour Party.

[...] the working class in Britain has been in a structurally stronger position to defend its interests as an economic class than the working class in the other major advanced capitalist states; [...] the ability and willingness of the British ruling class ... to renovate the ... British economy ... were powerfully inhibited by their commitment to preserving the legacy of Britain's imperial past.

[...] if we consider the post-war period as a whole, British capitalism's record is one of insular success and international failure [...]

[...] by far the greatest discrepancy between Britain and other countries lies in the *productivity* of UK investments in plant and equipment [...]

[...] in the new conditions of full employment and strong union organisation management was forced to acquiesce in shop-floor bargaining over wages and other issues which partially eroded their control over the labour process [...]

[...] Opposition, actual or anticipated, to technical innovation and work reorganisation which threatened job security and control, restricted the scope for a successful investment and productivity drive. The same defensive strength blocked any major redistribution of incomes against the working class to help shift resources into investments and exports [...]

[...] From the early 1960s onwards the advanced sections of the ruling class's political and ideological leadership came to appreciate that new departures were needed to avert the maturing crisis [...]

[...] In the labour process management must assert ascendancy through a thoroughgoing reform of the collective bargaining system ... On the wages front the prevailing anarchy unleashed by a regime of permanent full employment combined with administered company pricing, had to be suppressed by means of an incomes policy.

[...] given the underlying strength of the working class ... the whole process of re-adjustment was particularly intractable and fraught with political risks ... The upshot was ... a decade of class deadlock and economic stagnation.

[...] the rate of inflation continued to accelerate to a peak of 27 per cent in the summer of 1975 ... the long decline of British capitalism had reached its nadir.

What above all characterised the decade from 1966 to 1975 was that the ruling class was unable decisively to impose a new strategic course on the working class, whilst the working class in turn failed to advance beyond the bounds of corporate defencism ... The central stumbling block here was, to put it crudely, that whereas the ruling class wanted to plan wages whilst leaving the rest of the economy substantially unplanned, the left advocated planning virtually everything except wages [...]

[...] the very magnitude of the crisis of 1974–75 ... has been turned to good effect. Popular fright at the inflationary menace has been a major factor behind ... the union's acceptance of the general principle of a social contract [...]

[...] the post-war commitment to full employment has now been so severely compromised in the interests of combating inflation that ... Unemployment has clearly become an instrument of policy rather than a target [...]

[...] what is now envisaged is the maintenance of a permanently higher reserve army of unemployed both to buttress pay policy and to raise productivity in the labour process ... keeping labour costs low relative to Britain's competitors ... redistributing income in favour of profits and restoring domestic capitalist confidence ... breaking the resistance to ... modernising investment in plant and equipment [...]

It is not inconceivable that this strategy will in its own terms succeed, and that British capitalism will enter the 1980s leaner and fitter than at any time this century [...]

Dave Purdy, 'British Capitalism Since the War, Part Two: Decline and Prospects', *Marxism Today* (October 1976), pp. 310–18.

10.15 The social contract

Critics of the party's industrial politics may have been able to get their views published in party publications by the mid-1970s but they were yet unable to change the party's stance. Ramelson remained steadfast in his advocacy of wage militancy, free collective bargaining and a version of the Alternative Economic Strategy, which was still gaining ground in the Labour Party

It is doubtful whether the TUC ever took a more disastrous decision than it did in September 1975 in endorsing the 'Social Contract'.

It was an unprecedented decision. The TUC agreed, for the first time in its history, to collaborate with the Government and employers to *cut* real wages, and to police the implementation of the cuts.

The Social Contract was presented as the latest wonder drug that would restore the ailing economy to radiant health and open the road to limitless prosperity in the future.

It was presented as an overall bargain or agreement, and hence a contract between the TUC on the one hand and the Labour government on the other.

For a short period of only one year, August 1975 to August 1976, the TUC would undertake that £6 should be the *maximum* wage increase negotiated; that any fringe benefits (pensions, working hours, holidays, etc.) should be offset against the £6, and that there should be only one settlement within 12 months.

The government undertook to pursue policies aimed to reduce unemployment to 700,000 by 1978, and to increase Government expenditure on the social services, with special emphasis on housing, child benefit scheme, pensions and health.

Despite the government's failure to fulfil any one of these undertakings, the TUC agreed to an extension of the Social Contract for yet another year, to August 1977.

[...] It was never true that the main cause of inflation in the capitalist world was wages, and that the cause of Britain's higher than average inflation rate was high wage settlements forced on the employers in a free-for-all jungle – the phrase often used to describe free collective bargaining.

We argued that the inflation which infected the whole capitalist world was the expression of the general crisis of capitalism.

We itemised a series of specific causes whose cumulative and irreversible effect was a persistent inflation – varying from time to time, and country to country, only in its rate [...].

There is no economic and political strategy capable of permanently eliminating unemployment, inflation, and recurring stagnation so long as capitalism remains the system under which we live.

We believe that the resistance of the working class to the effects of capitalism on their lives – and in the course of it the deepening of their political consciousness through struggle and a growing awareness that there is no permanent solution within the framework of capitalism – will lead many millions into the struggle to replace capitalism by a socialist planned society [...]

This, however, does not mean that nothing can be done now to alleviate the lot of our people, to reduce unemployment, stabilise prices and restore and expand the social services.

There is an alternative strategy which could do all that in a relatively short time, while capitalism still exists, but only if there is a government, backed by the organised Labour movement, which recognises that such a programme will meet with the resistance and sabotage of big business, and is ready to accept that challenge.

In the course of the heightening struggles to implement such a policy, the people's political consciousness will deepen and more far-reaching demands will be made that will take us in the direction of socialism.

Bert Ramelson, *Bury the Social Contract: The Case for an Alternative Policy* (London: CPGB, March 1977), pp. 1–21.

Notes

1 See J. Callaghan, 'Industrial Militancy, 1948–79: The Failure of the British Road to Socialism?', *Twentieth Century British History*, 15, 4 (2004), pp. 388–410; and Callaghan, 'The Plan to Capture the Labour Party and its Paradoxical Results', *Journal of Contemporary History*, 40, 4 (October 2005), pp. 707–27.

2 J. Gollan, 'Speech on Left Unity', 30th congress CPGB, CP/CENT/ CONG/16/01.

3 J. Callaghan, *Cold War, Crisis, and Conflict: The CPGB 1951–68* (London: Lawrence & Wishart, 2003), pp. 157–9.

4 Ian Mikardo took this view in his contribution to R. H. S. Crossman (ed.), *New Fabian Essays* (London: New Turnstile Press, 1952).

11

The 'new social movements'

In the twenty years following 1956, tensions emerged within the Communist Party, which would eventually lead to its dissolution.[1] Differences cut across many debates and constituencies, but a recurrent issue was the degree to which identities and strategies rooted in class and industrial struggle should remain at the core of the party's purpose and vision. Many would remain attached to these traditional concerns. More modernising minds would argue that industrial militancy alone did not automatically create radical political consciousness, and that oppression was not reducible to capitalism but was also manifested in sexism, racism and homophobia. Communists, modernisers argued, should find common ground with the 'new social movements' that resisted such oppression, embracing a more decentred sense of where power could be resisted, from 'cultural politics' to the practices and assumptions shaping 'private' life.[2]

Faultlines emerged with challenges to the party's ageing and male-centred authority from Communist youth and women, whose radicalised perspectives in the 1960s and 1970s reflected broader economic, social and political shifts. The party had traditionally represented the issues facing youth and women in its organisational structures.[3] Since 1921 the YCL had provided an apprenticeship to party life; though in the 1920s the YCL was central to the Third Period putsch of the rising Stalinist vanguard, the YCL was usually safely subordinate to the parent party, with whom its interests were considered to be identical.[4] The same was true of the sections created to reflect women's issues: despite a strategic embrace of feminist perspectives during the coalitionist emphasis of the Popular Front years, gender issues were usually conceived as subordinate to those of class.[5] Within this framework the party had adopted progressive positions on many issues including contraception and equal pay, but the overarching analysis was that patriarchy was commensurate with capitalism and would wither away in Communist future, a claim frequently justified through upbeat descriptions of Soviet women's lives.[6]

1956 provided a brief premonition of the trouble ahead. An independently minded YCL conference resolution criticising the Soviet repression in Hungary won widespread support, and was only rejected after intervention from the party's new General Secretary, John Gollan.[7] Like a father slightly anxious about a child on the threshold of teenage-hood, in this period Gollan would often insist that the YCL had been well behaved in the past.[8] In the following years the YCL would break with this tradition, marking its distance from the party leadership over issues including CND (which it embraced with none of the parent party's ambivalence), 1960s pop music (in which YCLers detected the vibrant creative energies of working-class youth), Czech resistance to Soviet oppression in 'Prague Spring' (supported by the YCL without any equivocation) and in an eagerness to debate counter-cultural issues such as the decriminalisation of drugs.[9] As Geoff Andews argues in his *Endgames and New Times: The Final Years of British Communism 1964–1991* (2004), many of the critical positions first formulated and developed in the YCL – around issues such as the need for pluralist, democratic politics in the model of European Communist parties, and the importance of culture as a location of political power and resistance – would soon loom large in debates about the party's future identity and direction.[10]

The 1970s emergence of the Women's Liberation Movement brought additional pressure on the party leadership. In synch with the movement's formative energies, a critical party sub-group called the Smith Group (soon renamed the Party group) took shape in 1970.[11] Sharply attuned to the intellectual and political currents circulating around the so-called 'new social movements' (feminism, anti-racism, students), the group took issue with those patriarchal assumptions that allegedly blemished the party's internal culture and stymied its ability to conceive truly radical policy on gender issues. An alternative motion to the 1971 Congress soon followed, contesting the CPGB's quietism over the 'complex of social, psychological and sexual oppressions' within and beyond the party.[12] This line of critique was further developed through a dissident monthly journal *Red Rag* – the very title implied a lumbering, bovine leadership in need of goading – published in transgression of party rules and including contributions from non-CP members.[13]

The outbreak of such forceful feminist critique from a new generation within the ranks of the CP at least indicated the party's ability to attract new women members; some saw in the CPGB of the late 1960s an organisation genuinely open to the process of turning away from a Soviet-facing and patriarchal past.[14] The party had less success in developing its membership among Black, Asian and other ethnic communities, despite a long and in many ways distinguished record of campaigning against colonialism and racism.[15] The party was effective in supporting Black and Asian workers on the familiar terrain of industrial conflict, notably in the Grunwick dispute of 1976 in which Asian women came to the forefront of class struggle. But it was less assured when speaking to the concerns of the broader community and addressing cultural differences and more dispersed and casual forms of discrimination and oppression.[16] Embedded in the culture it also sought to challenge, it was not insulated from racist reflexes – some party members supported immigration quotas – and paternalistic and patronising attitudes sometimes surfaced.[17] Though it established designated West Indian, West African and Indian branches in the 1950s, membership of these soon fell away and few remaining Black members achieved prominence within the party.[18] In the words of disillusioned Black activist Trevor Carter, the party's habitual mindset was incapable of analysis that 'recognised that racial oppression cannot just be neatly packaged up in subordination to class oppression'.[19]

Emerging divisions within the party around these and other issues were sharpened through the 1970s; the 1974 collapse of Edward Heath's Conservative government and the return of a minority Labour administration brought questions of Communist political identity, allegiance and long-term strategy to the fore.[20] The emerging critique of the party's so-called 'economism' – the assumption that material realities straightforwardly determined consciousness, and that economic crisis and industrial confrontation led dependably to significant working-class political radicalisation – increasingly drew upon a revitalised Communist intellectual culture most evident in the Communist University of London (CUL), established in 1969.[21] The CUL became a key forum for leftist debate in the 1970s;[22] the writings of Italian Communist Antonio Gramsci, whose substantial *Prison Notebooks* first appeared in English in 1971, were also increasingly important to those challenging the party's fundamental assumptions and priorities.[23] Especially relevant was Gramsci's analysis of how ruling powers established and maintained 'hegemony' through a combination of coercion and consent, of how subordinate groups and their 'organic intellectuals' resisted and countered this hegemony, and of how culture formed a key site of ideological domination and resistance.[24] Significant early interventions from Gramscian perspectives criticised the narrowly industrial economism of the left, arguing instead for a broader field of political contestation that would mobilise not only the working class, but the resources of the new social movements.[25] Martin Jaques, who was elected onto the party's Executive Comittee in 1967, drew on Gramsci's work to re-conceptualise the relationship between intellectuals and radical political movements, and to emphasise the importance of culture in building and sustaining radical oppositional consciousness; here his work anticipated the party's successful 1977 counter-hegemonic alternative to royalist pomp, the People's Jubilee festival.[26]

The British Road to Socialism remained the central text of the CPGB; its mid-1970s updating occurred at a moment when the differences that now fissured the party were widening. The draft document was co-written by Martin Jacques, for whom the CPGB's willingness to criticise the 1968 Soviet invasion of Czechoslovakia was a positive and formative political moment, and party veteran George Matthews, a hardliner of the 1956 crisis shaped by an altogether different history.[27] The process magnified competing visions for Communism in Britain. For the modernisers, the coalition-building strategies variously pursued by the Italian, French and Spanish Communist parties in the mid-1970s furnished a political model; a fully theorised democratic strategy was advocated to settle the longstanding tension within Communism between constitutional and insurrectionist visions. The revised draft of *The British Road to Socialism* duly referred to the need to construct a 'broad democratic alliance';[28] in a separate statement the party formally jettisoned its commitment to the 'dictatorship of the proletariat' that had, in truth, been more rhetorical than real for many years.[29] The new text of the programme also registered the existence of diverse modes of oppression, the importance of the new social movements and the principle of multi-party democracy under socialism. But pulled between the impulses of modernisers – for whom democratic alliances should contain a socialist future in embryonic form – and a more traditional emphasis on the ongoing leadership provided by the organised working class, the document remained out-of-focus on the key issues. The exact outlines of the 'broad democratic alliance' were unclear, as was the question of how the newer elements would integrate, or be integrated into, the party's traditional class-based constituency and concerns.[30]

For some, the revised *British Road to Socialism* was a step too far. Surrey district official Sid French regarded the document as an unacceptable renunciation of Leninist principles, and departed to form the New Communist Party, taking approximately 700 members with him.[31] For many modernisers, the document was too timid, marred by lingering attachments to former positions;[32] some would leave a party that seemed unable to make the necessary re-alignments.[33] The decade to follow would see the party's significance as a national political force decline in rough proportion to the energy-sapping acrimony of its internal feuds, as modernisers came to dominate the Executive Committee, while a more traditionalist grouping won control of the *Morning Star* (formerly the *Daily Worker*).[34]

11.1 No colour bar

In 1955 the CPGB distributed 100,000 copies of a leaflet spelling out a charter of rights for 'coloured workers in Britain'. The document below is an extract from the tie-in pamphlet, which sold 10,000 copies and fleshed out the leaflet's arguments.

[...] The attitude of the Communist Party is clear. It has always declared that the interests of British workers are identical with those of the colonial people. It welcomes the arrival of coloured immigrants and says they should be brought into trade unions and other organisations of the Labour movement without delay.

A statement issued by the Communist Party in February 1955 says:

> The motto 'United We Stand, Divided We Fall' has inspired the British trade unions for over a century. It is equally true today for British and coloured workers. They have a common interest in waging a united fight against a common enemy – the Tory imperialists and the big monopoly firms who exploit them.

It is therefore in our joint interests to wage a determined fight for a Charter of Rights for coloured workers in Britain.

Here are the four points of the Charter:

1. No form of colour discrimination by employers, landlords, publicans, hotel proprietors, or in any aspect of social, educational and cultural activity. Any racial discrimination to be made a penal offence.
2. Opposition to all Government restrictions and discrimination against coloured workers entering Britain.
3. Equality of treatment in access to employment, wages and conditions; coloured workers to receive the rate for the job (including equal facilities for apprenticeship and vocational training) and the maintenance of full rights to social security benefits.
4. Full encouragement to coloured workers to join their appropriate trade unions on equal conditions of entry with British workers, and to exercise their trade union and political rights. [...]

Phil Bolsover, *No Colour Bar for Britain* (London: CPGB, 1955), pp. 11–12.

11.2 Youth

A leading figure in the 1960s YCL, George Bridges went on to become a modernising voice in the 1970s CPGB. Here he spells out the significance and potential of emerging youth movements.

British youth in revolt

Marxists, from Marx onwards, have always made the observation that one of the greatest weaknesses of the British working-class movement is its relative contempt for theory. When one marries to this historic attitude, a similar neglect for youth and the youth movement, it should come as no surprise that material of a theoretical nature on the youth movement is scarce indeed.

This, unfortunately, seems to be particularly true of the Communist Party and Marxists associated with it. Against the background of the 'youth revolt' – a British reflection of an international phenomenon – this weakness seriously hampers our work amongst the new generation. [...]

Historically, youth has always been to the forefront of struggle and revolution. This seems to come from objective and subjective circumstances of their position in society and their attitudes to life. Youth has opportunity, energy, militancy and rebelliousness. Coming fresh to the field of ideas it is obviously more open to new and revolutionary ideas, less fully formed in its ideas. It is a less 'stable' part of society, has less to lose in a sense, a lifetime to change, and is therefore less conservative.

Against this historic dynamic of youth and revolution, the present phenomenon, which dates approximately from the late 1950s, has a special significance. This is because the traditional role and features of youth are posed against a historical context of a world in crisis, a world of speedy and revolutionary change where imperialism as a world system is giving way to the movements of national liberation and socialism. The economic breakthrough of the socialist camp was symbolised to the imperialist world by the flight in space of Gagarin, a Soviet Young Communist, in 1961. British imperialism has its own particular crisis within this dramatised to the British people by the Suez fiasco of 1956. [...]

Since 1964, new forces have come into play, although generally there has been an overall advance in this mood, embracing more young people, more sections of youth on a more conscious, more political level. The moral, anti-Tory mood of the early 'sixties began to take on a more revolutionary mood as faith in social democracy evaporated in the face of Labour government's betrayal of youth's aspirations. The slogans of 'No to the Bomb' became 'No to Imperialist Aggression'. The slogans of 'Peace in Vietnam' became 'Solidarity with the Vietnamese People'. [...]

The 100,000 youth [sic] who demonstrated in solidarity with Vietnam in October 1968 representing a generation which rejected US imperialism *consciously*. [...]

All this is tremendously positive and hopeful and must be welcomed by Communists and Marxists as a first step in moulding a generation able and willing to assume at some time the mantle of revolutionary leadership.

Nevertheless there are some special problems which could become decisive negative features. [...]

Youth's main political action has been on the broad moral, international, peace and democratic issues, rather than the economic, domestic questions [...]. Youth tends to come into activity from *outside* the Labour movement, direct on to a political demonstration or student sit-in.

This has led to positive features. Youth are free from reformist illusions. [...] But it can also have many negative features. The rejection of social democracy and right-wing domination of the Labour movement can be a stepping stone to rejection of the Labour movement itself. [...]

It is not far from these positions to the development of ultra-left movements. [...]

One of the more sophisticated forms of Cold War Ideology [...] is the popularisation of the 'anti-Communism of the Left' among the youth movement. This portrays Communist Parties, in Britain and abroad, as being no longer revolutionary, but corrupt, part of the power structure, old-fashioned, authoritarian, etc. [...]

Historically, also, we have to remember that 1956 was not only the year of Suez, but of the disclosures about the Stalin era and the intervention in Hungary. This not only brought about a certain disorientation amongst Communists, but left a deep scar in the public image of the Communist movement (which subsequent divisions and the events in Czechoslovakia have done nothing to remove). In addition, our Party is relatively small, is not always seen, as perhaps are other mass Parties in the west as a really effective political force. [...]

As Communists we need to ask ourselves how we can make a far more effective appeal. This must involve ideological work, allocation of resources, forms of activity, propaganda and organisation adequate to the job. [...]

But the rewards can be high if we can achieve the job of bringing youth with all its energy, power, and militancy into the job of winning our working class for united struggle for socialist change.

George Bridges, *Marxism Today* (August 1969), pp. 252–6.

11.3–11.4 Women and the family

These two documents form a dialogue about gender and family between Rosemary Small, the party's National Women's Organiser, and Maria Loftus, whose more sophisticated and radical perspective showcases the intellectual energy of the early Women's Liberation Movement.

11.3: Marxism and the family

[...] *Changes in family situation*
[...] Capitalism dehumanises all human relationships, and because of the nature of class society and private property vested in male supremacy, the dehumanisation is at its worst in man–woman relationships. But it is a tribute to the family structure that, despite all this and even under capitalism, the family remains, at worst, some sort of bulwark to cling on to, at best, a source of support and security, warmth and happiness. The qualities of strong feeling, of love and tenderness which the majority of us experience within the family, are evidence that the tensions associated with the family are a product of the social structure and not based on the natures of men and women. [...]

The family and socialism

To say this is not to imply that under a different social structure the family will remain unchanged, but to say what form such changes would take is difficult. [...] What we may legitimately do, however, if we agree that the form of the family arises out of the structure of society, is to look at the features of the society we expect to build and draw some conclusions from that. There are two main features of Socialist society which seem to me of vital importance in their effect on the family.

One is the equality of women, particularly in the economic field. The enactment of laws on equal pay, equal education and training, equality of job opportunity, has an obvious effect on the status of all women, but will be of particular importance to wives and mothers, making it more possible for them to participate in social production at a level commensurate with their abilities and on a more equal footing with their husbands. [...] In a work-based society, the valuation put on work is crucial; when women's contribution is valued at something like its true worth, then the whole valuation of women by society begins to change more rapidly. [...]

The other feature is that of the extension of the family through the social services. Many of the tensions of present-day family life arise from the necessity for 24-hour-a-day responsibility for home and children, most of which is borne by the wife and mother [...]. When there is a network of facilities providing for every need (day nurseries, nursery schools, after-school centres and school holiday facilities) much of the pressure on the individual family and particularly on the mother is relieved. [...]

But the true freedom of the family and its members cannot be achieved on an individual basis, because the basic question involved – the freeing of the family, particularly the women, from the major chores and responsibilities – are not private questions but dependent on the organisation of society. In Engels' words, 'private housekeeping is transformed into a social industry. The care and education of the children becomes a public affair'. This will undoubtedly transform the situation of the family and its members; whether it will radically change the form of the family is a matter for discussion. [...]

Rosemary Small, *Marxism Today* (December 1972), pp. 360–5.

11.4: Marxism and the family

Up to the present moment Marxist theory has failed to cover adequately either the family and its function in modern capitalist society or the oppression of women, both of which need to be seen as dialectically related. The emergence of an autonomous Women's Liberation Movement has been the stimulus for questioning and challenging the existing Marxist theory, or absence of it. Family study and other theoretical groups in Women's

Liberation, using the principles of historical materialism, have been almost alone in creatively developing analysis of these vital areas of our social and economic existence. [...]

When analysing the family it is essential to see it as a very complex institution, the result of the interplay of economic, superstructural, and ideological forces in our present mode of production. However, Rosemary Small's article appeared to be marked by a tendency to separate the economic aspects of existence from social institutions and ideologies. She has grossly underestimated the family as an institutional site for particular forms of social consciousness, an institution which is itself (partially) determined and cemented by ideological pressures. This is not to say, however, that in the last analysis the family is not an effect of the economic structure of present day capitalist society. [...]

Control of sexuality

A necessity emerges for those who own the means of production to control the producers of people such that their sexual relations reproduce the social relations that sanction their dominant position. As the family is the site for the reproduction of labour power it is necessary that families in their turn be produced and also that female sexuality be defined in certain ways to facilitate this. Institutions such as the church and the school engender the need for security to be discovered in heterosexual relationships with one person at a time. Marriage, a vital ingredient for the family, is the normal site for sexual relations. [...]

Though it is necessary for women's sexual activity to be controlled, a similar inhibition on men is not vital. In ideology we find female sexuality defined as being qualitatively different from that of the male, i.e., passive. To maintain the production of the labour force, woman's sexuality is defined in terms of her future capacity for motherhood and men's pleasure. The production of children does not necessarily require either that she initiate sexual activity or has pleasure or satisfaction in copulation. Hence an important aspect of the Women's Liberation Movement has been to challenge, and attempt to redefine the existing concept of women's sexuality. [...]

Family in socialist society

[...] Rosemary Small suggests that in order to formulate blueprints for the family we should be looking at the features of the socialist society we expect to build. This ideology maintains that the family provides warm, loving, secure relationships etc. In fact it tends to produce people suited to capitalist relations of production, people who are insular and cannot transcend narrow family ties and who display distrust, unconcern, and indifference to others outside [...]. Even more important is the vast section of the population it excludes. Far from encouraging solidarity which is necessary for combination and comradeship in struggle it would seem to encourage divisions, which invariably serve the maintenance of class rule. To transcend this under socialism the family would have to change in such a fundamental way that it would no longer be recognised as 'the family'.

Maria Loftus, *Marxism Today* (April 1973), pp. 124–7.

11.5 Socialist feminism

Red Rag was a monthly socialist-feminist journal set up by party members who worked closely with non-party members, including Sheila Rowbotham. The editorial team, which included prominent party feminist activist Beatrix Campbell, defied the party rule that journals established by members should be approved by the Executive Committee. This editorial 'declaration of intent' is from the first issue.

Declaration of intent
Red Rag is a magazine of liberation and in particular women's liberation.

We stand for revolutionary change in society, for ending capitalism and establishing socialism.

We challenge whatever and whoever denies the right of women to be free – from economic inequality and from the tyranny of the role forced upon them in our society.

Our aim is to help build an alliance between women liberators and the working-class movement. [...]

The organised labour movement – that is the trade unions, co-ops and the left political parties – is the decisive force in this country for social progress and for socialism. Its wholehearted and active support is essential for the success of the women's liberation movement.

It is argued by some that there is no need for a women's liberation movement, that any issues of concern can be dealt with by the movement in general.

But 'in general' we've been getting trodden on for a very long time!

We will offer in *Red Rag* our Marxist explanation of why women are oppressed and how the oppression can be fought and overcome. [...]

We will explain the immense benefits of a socialist society for working people. We shall also explain the necessity, now and under socialism, of a

continuing struggle to root out all those old ideas, habits and prejudices which stand in the way of total liberation.
We are in no mood, however, to wait for socialism to bring us liberation. We are interested in liberation now and in wrenching from capitalist society every advance we can get. [...]

Red Rag, Number One, (1972), p. 2.

11.6 Culture in the struggle

A modernising CPGB intellectual, Martin Jacques would co-write the draft of *The British Road to Socialism* in 1976 and edit *Marxism Today* from 1977. Here, writing in characteristically Gramscian tones, he identifies the importance of culture in the shaping of social and political consciousness.

Culture, class struggle and the Communist Party
Martin Jacques' report to the EC May 8/9
Culture and cultural activity are an integral part of every person's life. The sport people play or follow, the TV programmes they watch, the clothes they wear, the books they read, the music they listen to or make, the films they enjoy, the education they receive: these are some of the things we mean by culture [...] everybody engages in cultural activity. [...]
And culture cannot be seen as separate from class struggle, as a neutral island within class society. On the contrary, culture is an important, indeed an increasingly important, area of class conflict. Just as class conflict takes place at work so it also finds expression in leisure. [...] One of the most important developments of recent years has been the radicalisation of young sections of young cultural workers, of young intellectuals. As a result of the changing composition of the labour force and the related expansion of education and culture, these intellectual strata have greatly increased in number and are now, in both their backgrounds and economic and social situation, much closer to the industrial working class than was previously the case. [...]
The party can play a unique role in the cultural sphere. Firstly, as a revolutionary party we recognise that class struggle is not confined to economic struggle – or even the economic and political spheres – but is also ideological and cultural. Secondly, our party embraces both the working class and other sections, including, in particular, these new cultural strata. As a

consequence, we have the unique possibility to bring together industrial and cultural workers both within and outside the party, and, on this basis, provide cultural leadership both in broad campaigning and in the life and activity of the party itself. [...]

Comment (29 May 1976), pp. 163–5.

11.7–11.9 Revising *The British Road to Socialism*

The process of updating *The British Road to Socialism* in 1976–77 began with George Matthews and Martin Jacques co-writing a draft. This was circulated to members who provided extensive feedback in the pages of the party's fortnightly journal *Comment*. Documents 11.7 and 11.8 are sample responses to the draft.

11.7: Sid French would leave the CPGB in 1977 over the revised *British Road to Socialism*, taking with him 700 members to form the New Communist Party. This document, from the Surrey District where French was a party official, represents the views of his circle.

Whilst claiming to be based on scientific socialism, the draft *British Road to Socialism* revises Marxism-Leninism by dropping the concept of the dictatorship of the proletariat. In fact it ignores the need for the working class to take state power unto itself and to crush the resistance of the displaced exploiters and to win to its side the majority of people for the creative task of building Marxism in Britain.

Marx, Engels and Lenin understood the need for the working-class winning allies and the inter-connection of the struggle for democracy with the struggle for socialism, but they stressed that socialism could only be realised in *all* circumstances through the dictatorship of the proletariat. This position is adhered to by the vast majority of the Communist Parties today.

By contrast, the draft claims that state power is to be exercised by the working class and its allies. The capitalist state is to be superseded from the outset by the state of the broad alliance. What a brilliant example of scientific socialism 'democratically' reduced to petty bourgeois liberalism.

The theory of gradualism permeates the draft document. The possibility of a revolutionary situation arising from the interplay of deepening capitalist economic and political crisis isn't considered. The only perspective advanced is socialism via a series of left governments and the gradual transformation of the economy and the state machine. In spite of various escape clauses, the balance of the document suggests the primary role of Parliament. The mass struggle is presented as interrelated but secondary – another fundamental mistake. [...]

That Parliament should be used as part of the overall struggle for socialism is not in dispute, nor is the possibility of a peaceful road being achieved. A peaceful road is infinitely preferable to a violent road and must be striven for, but any road should project the concept of coercion to force through the change. The draft is too short on coercion and too free with liberalism. [...]

If one is dropping the revolutionary process, there is no need for a revolutionary party. [...]

If this draft is endorsed by Congress, the party remains Communist in name only. In actuality it becomes a left social democratic party with a left social democratic programme. There is no way forward for the party or the working class to be found in this document. It must be rejected.

Surrey District Committee

Comment (30 April 1977), p. 146.

11.8: Moderniser Jon Bloomfield, District Secretary in the West Midlands and formerly National Student Organiser, responds to the draft.

For well over a century capitalism has been breeding its own grave-diggers. Yet the graves remain to be dug. How does the new draft equip us for the task?

There are two debates going on. One is exceptionally sterile, concerning those who have forgotten the lessons of Dimitrov and the Popular Front period. Hostility to the Labour Party left, elitism and contempt for the mass of people are sure-fire political cul-de-sacs. [...]

It is essential that the real debate, the constructive disagreements, come out clearly. These seem to me to lie between the present leadership and what can best be termed a revolutionary, democratic current in the party. These positions agree on three central issues. Firstly, that it is the masses who make history and that numerical and political majorities have to be won for revolutionary advance. Secondly, that revolutionary advance will be a process, which is not to suggest it will be smooth but does mean we don't see revolution coming in a similar way to Russia in 1917. Thirdly, that political parties and mass organisations other then the CP will play prominent parts in the process and will continue to do so afterwards. These areas of agreement mark out a major cleavage from ultra-left views of revolution, whether Stalinist, Trotskyist or Maoist.

But major differences exist. I want to spotlight four.

(1) *How the ruling class rules.* Our leadership fails to grasp the real roots and strength of ruling class hegemony. Consent to capitalist rule arises largely spontaneously from real material circumstances. To see ideology as 'false consciousness' leads to the view that it is a conspiracy played by the ruling class on the working class [...]. This view breeds illusions as to how capitalist ideology can be overcome and fails to appreciate the significance of all forms of struggle. The women's movement is especially important in this respect.

Related to this is a constant exaggeration of the political situation. Only if we distinguish between militancy and political understanding can we explain why the fierce class battles of the early 1970s didn't bring an upsurge in left politics and why we now face a resurgence of the right. [...]

(2) *Economism.* These weaknesses link in with the frequent economism of our party. Too often we see *political* change coming *through* the trade union movement. [...]

(3) *Operative democracy.* Capitalism breeds passivity and apathy: our strategy must encourage popular initiatives at work and in the localities, to show that working people can run their own lives. Hence the importance of industrial democracy. The encouragement of all mass organisations – trade unions, women's groups, tenants' residents' associations – and the creation of new ones are central threads of our strategy for operative, active democracy, for power in the hands of the people. These are the organisations which can show the constructive capacity of the people. For its success a left government will be heavily dependent on their support and capacity for popular mobilisation – a point ignored by the draft's over-constitutional emphasis.

(4) *Parties.* This strategy requires an enhanced role for politics and parties, above all the Labour left and ourselves. Yet the success of our strategy hinges on a well-educated, active party which acts as a political force in its own right in *all* fields. There are signs of change, e.g. local pamphlets, CUL, Marxist festivals, People's Jubilee, but the bulk of our work is still done through other organisations. Too often our independent identity is submerged. Unless we give a clear political message to our branches and advisories we will remain a ginger-group and our programme stays unrealisable.

To sum up. If we follow Surrey and co. we'll dig our own graves. If we follow the present leadership and draft we're likely to stay in our existing sticky clay. That line must be enriched by new thinking and practices if we're to strike it rich.

Jon Bloomfield, Birmingham

Comment (9 July 1977), p. 239.

11.9: The revised *British Road to Socialism* was adopted at the party's 35th National Congress in November 1977. The extracts below were the most contentious sections.

How capitalist rule is maintained

[...] [P]olitical power is not just a matter of the elected government, but of all the institutions of the state. Ruling class ideas and interests are deeply entrenched in all these institutions – the civil service, the police, the armed forces, the judiciary, the Foreign Office, etc. Through them, as well as through its economic strength, the ruling class exercises a degree of coercion to maintain its rule.

However, in Britain today it relies primarily on the fact that millions of people believe that the capitalist system is the natural way to organise society, that the present political system is truly democratic, and that there is no realistic or better alternative. Every new generation is influenced to accept this. The family and school often perpetuate and reinforce capitalist ideas among children, while among adolescents and adults the media and social and cultural activities increasingly assume importance. Most of those in charge of the main informational, social, educational and cultural institutions of capitalist society accept its outlook and its values, and play an important part in securing acceptance of capitalist rule. [...]

Thus persuasion, politics and coercion are all utilised by the ruling class to maintain its rule. Though it is prepared to use coercion and violence, unless prevented by overwhelming working class and popular strength, it mainly relies on achieving a social consensus and class collaboration through its ideological control and influence, its alliances, and the effect of right-wing ideas in the labour movement.

To challenge capitalist rule the working class and its organisations need not only to defend and improve the living conditions of the people through economic struggle, but to overcome capitalist ideas and build alliances also in the fields of politics, ideology and culture. For all these areas are the arena of struggle between reactionary and progressive ideas, between the capitalist and socialist forces in society. It is a struggle which must develop in new ways and through new, as well as existing, forms of organisation, so that the people develop confidence in their own ability to run society. [...]

Social forces and movements

The basic force for change in our society is the class struggle between workers and capitalists. However, capitalism not only exploits people at work, it impinges on every aspect of their lives. Thus they react to it, and often struggle against its effects, in their communities, in their leisure activities, as men and women, black or white, young or old, Scottish, Welsh, Irish or English. So movements and groups develop which may not belong to a major class (for example, students) or embrace people from different class strata (for example, black, national, women's, youth, environmental, peace and solidarity movements). Hence the broad democratic alliance needs to be not only an expression of class forces, but of other important forces in society which emerge out of areas of oppression not always directly connected with the relations of production. [...]

Alliance – not isolation

It is clear, however, that if these movements and their struggles proceed in isolation from each other, they can do no more than challenge the position of the ruling class on a series of different issues, and not its overall domination. If they are isolated from the labour movement, not only will they themselves suffer from the lack of its support, but the working class will be unable to fulfil its role of the leading force in society.

The labour movement needs alliances with these other democratic movements because, in supporting their aims and aspirations, it becomes increasingly aware that class oppression, and the struggle against it, extend far beyond the workplace, and embrace strata beyond the working class. Such alliances are needed to bring the political weight of the overwhelming majority of the population to bear on the minority ruling class. They can lead to a greater awareness of the forces that oppress all workers, and also strengthen working class unity. It is therefore through such support and association that the labour movement becomes more conscious of its own national role as the leading force in society, and better able to fulfil that role, both now and under socialism. [...]

The work of the left is vital in building the broad democratic alliance. Left unity needs to be promoted both in the practical development of activity and in the battle of ideas. There are those who will be united by an understanding of the need for fundamental change, and those who will become involved only on specific issues. Communists and the labour left have a special role to play in developing broad left unity and in helping to build the alliances, of which only the most politically conscious sections of the new forces will see the need, between different sections of the working class and different social and political movements.

The Communist Party, as the organised Marxist political party, has a key and decisive responsibility. Throughout its history it has been active on many of the questions around which the movements detailed above have been campaigning – the fights against racialism and fascism, for women's rights, peace and national liberation, Scottish and Welsh parliaments, education, housing and other social issues. Just as it works to overcome sectional divisions within the working class movement and unite it for the struggle against capitalism, so can it help the labour movement and the other social forces to see the need for alliance between them, to the benefit of all. [...]

The 'new social movements'

The British Road to Socialism: Programme of the Communist Party, 5th edn (London: CPGB, 1978), pp. 8–10, 29–34.

Notes

1 For this period, see Francis Beckett, *Enemy Within: The Rise and Fall of the British Communist Party* (1995; London; Merlin, 1998), Willie Thompson, *The Good Old Cause: British Communism 1920–1991* (London: Pluto, 1992) and Geoff Andrews, *Endgames and New Times: The Final Years of British Communism 1964–1991* (London: Lawrence & Wishart, 2004).

2 The modernisers' position is spelt out in Jon Bloomfield, 'Crossed Lines: Communists in Search of an Identity', *Marxism Today* (April 1984), pp. 25–9 and Dave Cook, 'No Private Drama', *Marxism Today* (February 1985), pp. 25–9.

3 For the YCL, see Mike Waite, 'The Young Communist League and Youth Culture', *Socialist History*, 6 (1994), pp. 3–16 and 'Sex 'n' Drugs 'n' Rock 'n' Roll (and Communism)' in Geoff Andrews, Nina Fishman and Kevin Morgan (eds), *Opening the Books: Essays on the Social and Cultural History of the British Communist Party* (London: Pluto, 1995), pp. 195–210. For Women, see Sue Bruley, 'Women Against War and Fascism: Communism, Feminism and the People's Front', in Jim Fyrth (ed.), *Britain, Fascism and the Popular Front* (London: Lawrence & Wishart, 1985), pp. 131–57 and 'Women and Communism: A Case Study of the Lancashire Weavers in the Depression', also in Andrews, Fishman and Morgan, *Opening the Books*, pp. 44–64.

4 Waite, 'Sex 'n' Drugs', p. 210; Thompson, *Good Old Cause*, p. 45; see also Kevin Morgan, Gidon Cohen and Andrew Flinn (eds), *Communists and British Society 1920–1991* (London: Rives Oram Press, 2007), pp. 236–8.

5 Bruley, 'Women Against War', pp. 131–57

6 Noreen Branson, *History of the Communist Party of Great Britain, 1941–1951* (London: Lawrence & Wishart, 1997), pp. 45–9; Isabel Brown, 'Give Women a Square Deal', *Daily Worker* (4 February 1943); Tamara Rust, 'Soviet Marriage', *Daily Worker* (30 August 1940).

7 John Callaghan, *Cold War, Crisis and Conflict: The CPGB 1951–68* (London: Lawrence & Wishart, 2003), pp. 70–1.

8 Waite, 'Sex 'n' Drugs', p. 211.

9 Andrews, *Endgames*, pp. 32–9.

10 Ibid., pp. 39–40.

11 Ibid., p. 63.

12 Ibid., p. 65.

13 Morgan, Cohen and Flinn, *Communists and British Society*, p. 181; Andrews, *Endgames*, pp. 66–9.

14 Andrews quotes one feminist drawn by the party's willingness to engage openly with the process of 'changing from a traditional male dominated gender-blind left party'. *Endgames*, p. 62.

15 Back in 1952 the CPGB congress had been ahead of many on the left in recognising the day-to-day oppression faced by immigrant communities in Britain, and in calling for legislation to criminalise discrimination; Communists regularly confronted racism within the Trade Union movement, and came to function as an independent and critical voice opposing the often racist thinking that pervaded British political culture in the 1950s and 1960s. Callaghan, *Cold War*, p. 105, p. 107, pp. 110–13.

16 Andrews, *Endgames*, p. 159; see also Jack Dromey and G. Taylor, *Grunwick: The Workers' Story* (London: Lawrence & Wishart, 1978).

17 Callaghan, *Cold War*, p. 109.

18 Andrews, *Endgames*, p. 30; Hakim Adi, 'West Africans and the Communist Party in the 1950s', Andrews, Fishman and Morgan, *Opening the Books*, pp. 160–76.

19 Cited in Andrews, *Endgames*, p. 45 note 56; Carter's analysis is presented in his book *Shattering Illusions* (London: Lawrence & Wishart, 1986).

20 Thompson, *Good Old Cause*, p. 161.

21 Ibid., p. 164; Andrews, *Endgames*, p. 147.

22 For the CUL, see Andrews, *Endgames*, p. 59.

23 See David Forgacs, 'Gramsci and Marxism in Britain', *New Left Review*, 176 (July–August 1989), pp. 70–88.

24 Antonio Gramsci, *Selections from Prison Notebooks*, edited and translated by Quintin Hoare and Geoffrey Nowell Smith (London: Lawrence & Wishart, 1971).

25 Significant works here included Bill Warren and Mike Prior, *Advanced Capitalism and Backward Socialism* (Leicester: Spokesman, 1975); see Andrews, *Endgames*, pp. 146–7.

26 Martin Jacques, 'The Role of Intellectuals Today', *Marxism Today* (October 1971); 'Culture, Class Struggle and the Communist Party', *Comment* (29 May 1976), pp. 163–5; for the People's Jubilee, see Andrews, *Endgames*, p. 151.

27 For the significance of 1968 to younger CPGB activists, see Andrews, *Endgames*, p. 54.

128 The resonances of this phrase, as opposed to the alternative, 'broad popular alliance', are unpicked by Thompson, *Good Old Cause*, p. 171.

29 The CPGB issued a 'Statement on Dictatorship of the Proletariat' in November 1976. Andrews, *Endgames*, p. 163.

30 For accounts of the process of rewriting the document, see Andrews, *Endgames*, pp. 163–6 and Forgacs, 'Gramsci and Marxism in Britain', pp. 70–88.

31 Andrews, *Endgames*, p. 164; Morgan, Cohen and Flinn, *Communists and British Society*, p. 120.

32 Gramscian style criticisms around the document's residual economism, insularity and gender politics were aired in the pages of *Comment* in the year following the 1977 Congress. Andrews, *Endgames*, pp. 164–6.

33 As Andrews explains, Purdy and Prior were highly critical of the document. They produced a further critique, *Out of the Ghetto* (1979), and soon left the party. Andrews, *Endgames*, p. 169.

34 The opposing positions would be variously labelled as 'traditionalist' or 'economist' on one hand, and 'Gramscian' or 'Eurocommunist' on the other, terms which in reality homogenised differences within the groups and simplified the trajectories through which the various positions had been reached. As the divisions deepened, for instance, 'traditionalists' would run the spectrum from hard-line Leninists gathered around the journal *Straight Left* to the more moderate advocates of a Communist Party firmly rooted in traditions of working-class struggle, who won control of the *Morning Star*.

12

Things fall apart

The rapid decline of the CPGB in the 1980s has to be placed in the longer-term context of its shrinking membership since 1964, when the membership figure stood at 34,281. Working long term against the party was the reputation of the Communist regimes for totalitarian violence and cruelty, persistent authoritarianism, an inability to reform democratically and, finally, an economic inefficiency that left them lagging behind technological developments and living standards in the advanced capitalist countries. In addition, the party found itself no longer the de facto monopoly owner of Marxism in Britain as numerous rival far left organisations came to prominence in the 1960s (all of them sworn enemies of the 'Stalinism' that they saw in the CP) and a quasi-Marxist Labour left developed in the 1970s and early 1980s. As we registered in the previous chapter of this book, the concurrent growth of identity politics and other forms of radicalism, such as environmentalism, posed as many problems as opportunities for the party and certainly assisted the factionalism that had become conspicuous in the organisation by the mid-1970s.

At the eleventh hour the process of creeping disintegration was sharply accelerated by the fall of the Stalinist regimes in Eastern Europe, the rise of anti-Communist Boris Yeltsin in Russia and damaging revelations that the Soviet Union had supplied the British party with funds well into the 1970s. Some talked about the redundancy of a 'communist' political identity in this transformed context; others talked about not throwing the baby out with the bathwater.[1] But as even George Matthews admitted, the baby was small and the voluminous bathwater by now very dirty.[2] What remained of the Communist Party, now with fewer than five thousand members, elected to dissolve itself at the 43rd Congress in November 1991.

One of the few successes of these twilight years was *Marxism*

Today. Under Martin Jacques' editorship between 1977 and 1991, the party's twenty-year-old monthly journal was re-branded as a magazine committed to creative Marxism and the renewal of the left; circulation trebled.[3] Financially supported by the party, though increasingly detached – Jacques later explained that though the journal had come from the CP, it was 'never of it' – the editorial board and contributors were drawn from beyond the party.[4] Key articles conceptualised the current crisis facing the left; in different ways Eric Hobsbawm's 'The Forward March of Labour Halted' (September 1978) and Stuart Hall's 'The Great Moving Right Show' (January 1979) diagnosed a labour movement whose habitual ways of seeing bore little relation to current realities of Britain on the eve of Thatcherism.[5] But if the magazine proved highly effective in stimulating a Marxist-inflected reading of 'post-Fordism', Thatcherism's destructive energies and the postmodern dimensions of contemporary culture, it also served to widen the gap between the party's intelligentsia and its traditional values and shrunken industrial base.[6] In this sense, the iconoclastic strain of Marxism associated with *Marxism Today*, which resulted in an influential 'Manifesto for New Times' in the magazine's final years, quickened the disintegration of the party that had, for seventy-one years, conceived of itself as the political embodiment of Marxism in Britain.[7]

It was perhaps the contrast between the growth of militancy and the shrinking of the CPGB that made the clash of ideas within the party so destructive by the mid-1970s. The years 1968–74 had proved to be an exceptional period of industrial conflict on a scale not seen since 1915–22. The Labour Party swung to the left in a manner not seen since the 1930s as Tony Benn and his allies came to the fore.[8] The appearance of 'Eurocommunism', particularly in Italy and Spain, briefly held out the prospect of a successful adaptation of Communism to the political conditions of modern, democratic societies. All of this stirred the Communist Party in Britain but made no difference to its continued decline. Instead an accelerating loss of members fuelled increasingly public disputes within the party. Despite the mighty industrial conflicts, the economic crisis, the revived interest in Marxism after 1968, the rise of the Alternative Economic Strategy, the growth of the Labour left in the 1970s, and the bitter disputes that divided the Labour Party – all previously imagined as the ingredients of Communist advance – the party's role was reduced to critical commentary from the sidelines.[9]

The Labour Party's defeat in the general election of May 1979 only served to exacerbate these conflicts. The CPGB's industrial militants, trade union and Labour allies could point to the electorate's rejection of the Social Contract, the feeble moderation that had lost Labour the election, and the militant 'conviction politics' that had won it for Thatcher's Conservatives. Membership of British trade unions in 1979 had never been higher, the proportion of the workforce covered by collective bargaining was at an all-time peak. Labour's defeat had strengthened the Labour left which was able to force through constitutional changes at a special conference in January 1981, designed to augment the role of the mass party in the determination of Labour policy, the election of its leader and the accountability of its MPs. The AES had become Labour policy, the party's centre and right were in disarray and sections of the leadership were ready to desert Labour altogether, so convinced were they of the left's dominance in the party.[10] Against all of this was the evidence from opinion polls that public majorities were exasperated by strikes, convinced that the unions wielded too much power and had turned against standard Labour policies on public ownership, welfare expenditure and taxation. Strong Labour identifiers within the electorate were falling in number, large sections of the population that formed parts of its 'natural' constituency had defected to the Conservatives in 1979. Tony Benn's wing of the party wanted to correct all of this and inject life into the UK economy by means of a massive increase in public expenditure, public ownership and centralised planning – the sort of thing the CPGB had long championed as an interim programme on the way to socialism. A version of this programme was presented to the electorate in 1983 – in Labour's manifesto *New Hope for Britain*. It was roundly rejected, Labour's vote falling to its lowest share of the electorate since 1918, with the party recording its worst parliamentary return since 1935.

The Communist Party's modernisers found themselves on the same side as Labour politicians who wanted to win back the lost voters by throwing out the policies associated with the Bennite left. They saw the CPGB's problems as part of a broader canvas of socialist crisis. How to explain the success of the Thatcherite turn against the 'social democratic consensus' of the 1950s and 1960s became the main quest of the Communist revisionists. The more they looked, the more they found. In the course of the 1980s *Marxism Today* became the platform for arguments that linked the success of Thatcherism to profound socio-economic and cultural changes working against the labour movement. By the mid-1980s such reasoning pitched them against defenders of the old faith whether in the form of the *Morning Star*, the Bennite left, the leadership of the 1984–85 miners' strike or the advocates of confrontation with the Conservative government within the local authorities.

By the end of the decade the changes forcing this new revisionism were often said to be global in scope, reinforcing the intellectual trend against national Keynesian economic management and the common sense of the social democratic consensus. In many ways the most telling evidence of socialist crisis came from the Communist bloc itself, a perception not altered when Mikhail Gorbachev became General Secretary of the CPSU in 1985.[11] Gorbachev's reforms briefly held out the prospect of socialist renewal. Instead they rapidly lead to the collapse of the Communist system in the Soviet Union and Eastern Europe. The 1980s will thus be remembered as the decade when socialism collapsed across all fronts – intellectual, organisational and institutional. In the Communist Party's experience of this collapse, dying faith in the Soviet Union had long since informed the revisionist thrust of the party's would-be modernisers.[12]

12.1 Problems of socialism

Twenty years after Khrushchev's secret speech John Gollan, the party's General Secretary for the whole of that period, used the occasion to consider the nature of Soviet socialism. Gollan was on the brink of retirement and in some ways his thinking was an attempt to come to terms with a history that had dominated his life. The fact that it opened a debate in the party is remarkable. It was evidence that a range of often contradictory views about the Soviet Union now coexisted uneasily within the organisation. But if the leadership thought that a public debate would 'clear the air', it was wrong; it simply brought these differences out into the open.

[...] The fact that the socialist system emerged victoriously from the supreme test of the Second World War put an end to all imperialist hopes of destroying it.

[...] this victory showed that the basic socialist foundations of the Soviet Union were unshaken, despite the crimes in the period of Stalin's leadership [...]

[...] The two decades since the Congress have demonstrated the superiority of the socialist economic system over the capitalist system [...]

This contrast – continuing crisis of capitalism in its imperialist phase and of advancing socialism – is the central issue of world development.

[...] Current bourgeois argument is that the Soviet system, the one-party state, the dictatorship of the proletariat, is by definition undemocratic ... This line of argument ignores the issue which is at the heart of any political system, namely, which class exercises political power and what economic system prevails [...]

[...] The start of the problem of the Cult would appear to be that Stalin, and the leadership of the party associated with him, took political decisions at critical moments in complete variance with Lenin's approach [...]

[...] In one generation the Soviet Union had achieved the social transformation to an industrial society which took three generations of UK and US history ... The growth of Stalin's popularity and authority was therefore understandable.

[...] Stalin's conception of the monolithic party ... became increasingly identified with conformism [...]

It was in this period 1923 to 1930 that the party, partly through circumstances, but also because of Stalin's rigid thought on the party, became excessively centralised, and discussion on fresh developments was curtailed.

[...] My argument ... is that the basis was laid in these years for the further bitter period. In the battle against the opposition the party became increasingly centralised ... with increased power being given to the security organs.

[...] Yet this was a period of enormous socialist advance and social change [...]

[...] Why this tragedy occurred is a complex and difficult question to explain, as the facts, which only the Soviet comrades can supply, are not available [...]

John Gollan, 'Socialist Democracy – Some Problems: The 20th Congress of the Communist Party of the Soviet Union in Retrospect', *Marxism Today* (January 1976), pp. 4–30.

12.2 The Soviet enigma

Members of the party respond to Gollan's article, revealing a variety of positions. The dominant position, however, rejected the authoritarian elements in the Leninist tradition. This was also revealed in the updated *British Road to Socialism* of 1976–77. Factions opposed to this revisionism began to organise, especially after 1979 when they produced *The Leninist* and *Straight Left*. The Communist Party of Britain, claiming 1500 members, was formed in April 1988 from elements of this opposition.[196]

Pat Devine
[...] the article represents no advance in analysis and suffers from the shortcomings which have characterised the position of the Party on the Soviet Union ... ever since the 20th Congress. Stalinism is attributed, in effect, to the cult of the individual, which was itself made possible by departures from Leninist norms [...]

[...] the defects appear as aberrations, unrelated to the more deep-seated features of Soviet society [...]

Jon Dyson
[...] a one-sided and idealised account of Lenin's approach is given, ignoring the lengths he was prepared to go to preserve the Bolshevik government [...]

[...] The danger flows from the confusion over the use of force by the socialist state with unjustified mass repressions and terror [...]

[...] As Marxists we do not reject in principle the use of force – even against sections of our own class or our allies [...]

Eric W. Edwards
[...] It seems that ... some parties in order to impress non-traditional elements in their own countries and widen their recruitment area (as well as show a more 'democratic' image) have set themselves the task of setting up the Soviet Union as an international 'Aunt Sally' ... it appears that there are those amongst the ranks who seem to think that democracy is a thing in itself, a desirable aim ... socialism is itself a democratic system that is superior to that of bourgeois democracy [...]

Paul Fauvet
[...] At the moment it is obvious that the British working class does *not* trust the Communist Party; and this is due not simply to some sort of conspiracy in the mass media, but also to the fact that for many years –

whether consciously or not – our Party lied to the workers. It lied about the Soviet Union; it swallowed the fabrications of the show trials of the 30s, reproduced the absurd allegations against Tito, and regurgitated all the nonsense that Stalin and his dreary acolytes proclaimed as absolute truth in every field [...]

[...] The road to communism is seen almost exclusively in terms of economic advance, the achievements of Soviet industry, and so on [...]

[...] The formulations of Gollan and of the CPSU seem to posit an abso-lute divorce between the political structures of the Soviet Union (which are admitted to have been grossly damaged) and its socialist economic base (alleged to have remained untouched). The forces of production are thus seen as guaranteeing socialism regardless of what happened in the political and ideological spheres.

We have long passed the stage where platitudes about the Soviet Union's 'basic socialist foundations' could substitute for serious materialist analysis [...]

Martin Milligan
Some contributors to this discussion have suggested that it constitutes a violation of the principle of non-interference in the affairs of other Commu-nist parties [...]

[...] When ... clearly against the will of the majority of the Czecho-slovak peoples and Party, Soviet and other Warsaw Pact troops invaded their country to bring about changes in their government and the direction of their Party, that clearly *was* a violation of the principles of non-interfer-ence ... and it was one which gives us good cause to consider carefully the question of democracy inside the USSR, since it seems clear that the Czecho-slovak Communist Party in 1968 was trying to build in their country a kind of socialism we aim to build in Britain [...]

J. Papard
[...] The miracles achieved during Stalin's period of leadership against such overwhelming odds surely testify that J. V. Stalin, despite his faults, was an outstanding comrade and proletarian leader; a true Marxist-Leninist giant [...]

Colin Sweet
[...] it reads like a restatement of the debate of 1957 with an updating post-script added to it ... One mammoth article of 27 pages by Comrade Gollan, and almost nothing new to say [...]

[...] again the restatement without any change of the 1957 insistence of the leadership that they did not know of the violations of socialist legality. Why insist on such a point? It drains away all credibility for the Party in the eyes of the non-Communist left, and it must emphasise the gap between the Party Executive, who approved the statement, and the membership who cannot in all seriousness believe it [...]

'Discussion on "Socialist Democracy – Some Problems"', supplement to *Marxism Today* (December 1976), pp. 1–32.

12.3 The forward march of labour

As the best known historian in the party, Eric Hobsbawm was bound to attract attention when he gave the Marx Memorial Lecture of 1978. In fact his argument that the main indicators suggested a long-term weakness and even decline in the labour movement provoked a debate which divided left-wing opinion inside and outside of the CPGB, not least because of his criticisms of the wage militancy of the 1970s.

[...] we have, over this century, growing proletarianisation combined with the relative decline, within the wage-earning population, of the manual workers in the literal sense of the word.

This is a very general phenomenon in the industrial countries. However, in Britain the decline is particularly striking for a special historical reason. A hundred years ago the sector of white-collar work in the widest sense employed only a tiny number of wage-earners; probably relatively less than in other countries with a substantial bureaucracy, public and private [...] By 1976 about 45 per cent of the occupied population could be classified as non-manual.

[...] for the first seventy years or so of the last century, Marx and Engels would have been neither very surprised nor very disappointed by the tendencies of development in the British working class ... But in the past thirty years this movement seems to have got stuck, except for one trend: the 'new' labour aristocracy of white-collar technical and professional workers has become unionised, and the students and intellectuals – from whom it is largely recruited – have also been radicalised to a greater extent than before.

[...] how far does the development of class consciousness of the British working class reflect these trends? Let us take the most elementary index of it, trade unionism. This undoubtedly increased pretty steadily from a century ago, though we haven't any comparable figures before the 1890s: say from 13 per cent of the labour force in 1900 to 45 per cent just after world war two (1948). But thereafter it remained stagnant for quite a bit, or even dropped a little, and though it grew in the 1960s and 1970s, it is now only a little higher (as a percentage) than in 1948 – 46 per cent. And – a point we don't often note – it is much lower than in Denmark, Sweden and Belgium, where it is around 70 per cent and actually a little lower than Italy. Now of course the composition of trade unionism has changed – there are a lot more women and white-collar workers – but the point I wish to note regretfully is that 35 per cent of the employed are not in any trade union, and that this percentage has not declined for thirty years. And also, that Britain, the home of mass trade unionism, has clearly fallen behind some other countries.

Declining vote
If we look at the political expression of class consciousness, which means in practice, support for the Labour Party, the picture is even more troubling … if we are to take the active membership of all socialist organisations as a very rough criterion – as distinct from trade union activism – then I also suspect that from some time after the early 1950s there is a decline, perhaps broken in the late 1960s. However, a very high proportion of the new socialist activists inside and outside the CP and other Marxist groups, in this most recent period, have probably been not manual workers, and especially not younger manual workers, but students and white-collar or professional workers.

The crisis – not inevitable
[…] it simply won't do to say that this crisis of the working class and the socialist movement was 'inevitable', i.e. that nothing could have been done about it. We have already seen that the halt in the forward march began even before the dramatic changes of the past twenty years; that even at the peak of the 'affluent society' and the great capitalist boom, in the middle 1960s, there were signs of a real recovery of impetus and dynamism: the resumed growth of trade unions, not to mention the great labour struggles, the sharp rise in the Labour vote in 1966, the radicalisation of students, intellectuals and others in the late 1960s. If we are to explain the stagnation or crisis, we have to look at the Labour Party and the labour movement itself.

The workers, and growing strata outside the manual workers, were looking to it for a lead and a policy. They didn't get it. They got the Wilson years – and many of them lost faith and hope in the mass party of the working people.

Economist militancy
At the same time the trade union movement became more militant. And yet this was, with the exception of the great struggles of 1970–4, an almost

entirely economist militancy; and a movement is not necessarily less economist and narrow-minded because it is militant, or even led by the left. The periods of maximum strike activity since 1960 – 1970–2 and 1974 – have been the ones when the percentage of pure wage strikes have been much the highest – over 90 per cent in 1971–2.

And, as I have tried to suggest earlier, straightforward economist trade union consciousness may at times actually set workers against each other rather than establish wider patterns of solidarity.

So my conclusion is that the development of the working class in the past generation has been such as to raise a number of very serious questions about its future and the future of its movement.

What makes this all the more tragic is that we are today in a period of world crisis for capitalism, and, more specifically, of the crisis – one might almost say the breakdown – of the British capitalist society; i.e. at a moment when the working class and its movement should be in a position to provide a clear alternative and to lead the British peoples towards it.

Forward march faltered

We cannot rely on a simple form of historical determinism to restore the forward march of British labour which began to falter thirty years ago. There is no evidence that it will do so automatically.

On the other hand, as I have already stressed, there is no reason for automatic pessimism.

Men, as Marx said (the German word means men and women), make their history in the circumstances that history has provided for them and within its limits – but it is they who make their history. But if the labour and socialist movement is to recover its soul, its dynamism, and its historical initiative, we, as Marxists, must do what Marx would certainly have done: to recognise the novel situation in which we find ourselves, to analyse it realistically and concretely, to analyse the reasons, historical and otherwise, for the failures as well as the successes of the labour movement, and to formulate not only what we would want to do, but what can be done. We should have done this even while we were waiting for British capitalism to enter its period of dramatic crisis. We cannot afford not to do it now that it has.

Eric Hobsbawm, 'The Forward March of Labour Halted?' *Marxism Today* (September 1978; the 1978 Marx Memorial Lecture), pp. 279–86.

12.4 Eurocommunism

The hesitant official criticisms of the Communist regimes associated with John Gollan's leadership were a thing of the past in
the 1980s. The Communist's theoretical journal was by now far
more searching in its analysis of 'actually existing socialism'. As the
article below indicates the appearance of 'Eurocommunism' in Italy
assisted this process of frankly acknowledging the democratic deficit
in the Communist tradition.

[...] The two major attempts to carry through thoroughgoing democratisation, in Czechoslovakia in 1968 and in Poland in 1980–81, have been
brutally crushed. The first by direct outside military intervention by Soviet
and other Warsaw Pact armies; the second by internal armed forces enjoying
outside backing from the same quarters.

Earlier assumptions that the example of socialist democracy and
economic prosperity predicted in the socialist countries would strengthen
the appeal of socialism in the West have proved totally untenable. The
overall effect of these countries has been rather the reverse, notwithstanding
their many positive features compared with capitalism.

Moreover the problem is now posed with particular force: what chances
do these countries have for democratic socialist renewal? Is it inevitable
that all attempts at this will end as tragically as they did in Czechoslovakia
and Poland? The conviction that the Soviet leaders, directly or indirectly,
will make sure that this is so is very widespread in Eastern Europe now, and
can only serve to discourage such attempts in the future. Yet the absence of
democratic structures can only conflict with the needs of socialist development and contribute to the accumulation and aggravation of problems and
dissatisfactions in all these countries – including the Soviet Union itself. It
must inevitably bring the recurrence in one form or another of the dramatic
crises that we have seen in so many socialist countries.

If, following the Russian Revolution of October 1917, the main revolutionary influence came from the East, that is no longer the position in the
world today. As Enrico Berlinguer, general secretary of the Italian Communist Party has argued, for 'a new period of democratic renewal and development' in Eastern Europe, 'two conditions are necessary: the reduction
of international tension and the emergence in the West of a new socialism
founded on the principles of freedom and democracy'.

Urging the immediate release of all detained trade unionists in Poland
along with the restoration of democratic rights and civilian rule, the Executive Committee of the Communist Party of Great Britain has emphasised the

need for the combination of socialism and democracy, seen as a universal principle. The Polish experience creates the need for a deeper analysis of the causes of the violations and limitations of this principle to be sought not in conjunctural phenomena but in the structures of power prevailing in most socialist countries in the world.

Monty Johnstone, 'Poland's Military Crackdown', *Marxism Today* (February 1982), pp. 13–17.

12.5 Post-industrial trade unionism

At the same time that *Marxism Today* was annoying traditional supporters of the Soviet Union within the CPGB it was antagonising defenders of its customary stance within the unions by suggesting that sweeping social changes were in process and the unions were not equipped to deal with them. Indeed, the demise of heavy industries in the economic slump of 1979–81 had diminished the base of the CPGB and of many of the unions Communists had sought to lead. By the mid-1980s the CPGBs influence at the annual TUC was nil. Within the party, however, the *Morning Star*, in defiance of the new thinking, continued to uphold the party's traditional stance in industry and to back the Alternative Economic Strategy, even after the consolidation of Thatcherism in 1983. After a special congress in May 1985 such people were purged from the party, including its former industrial organiser Bert Ramelson and leading industrial militants such as Derek Robinson and Ken Gill.

[...] Much has changed since ... the mid-70s. The dock industry, an important exemplar, organising centre and training ground for activists has been all but wiped out in Liverpool, Hull and London's East End; the heavy engineering industry has been battered in Manchester, Coventry, Tyneside and Clydeside; the steel industry has been decimated in Sheffield and South Wales; the West Midlands foundry, car and car components industries have suffered huge job losses. These were the highly organised industries with long traditions of struggle [...]

[...] Plainly *all* is not lost in the cities. Nevertheless, the fact of the dispersion of industry around and well beyond city boundaries must mean that the old pattern of leaders and laggards in ratchet relation will be transformed [...]

[...] From the trade unionist's point of view the multi-plant firm raises a host of not readily resolvable problems. The wide dispersion of plants over considerable distances, with location in areas differing in their labour movement traditions, means that within the divisional structure of any one firm uneven development of trade union practice as between plants is the norm. Attempts at forming combine committees always fall foul of this problem – and doubly so where combine committees organise on an inter-divisional or inter-company basis. If there are difficulties of involving the activists in such schemes, imagine the problems of interesting the rank and file.

[...] By no means all of the unions' problems can be attributed to changes in the industrial environment. In one form or another there is plenty of evidence to suggest that trade unionism in general is not nearly as popular with its own members as a healthy movement ought to be [...]

[...] In the early 1960s George Woodcock, whom recent history has incredibly forgotten, exhorted the movement in a memorable speech at the TUC to make up its mind about its purpose: it had to decide whether it wanted to be the collective entrepreneur of labour, adopt the jungle ethics of the market and practise business unionism, or whether it wanted to play a significant part in the creation of a new society constructed on a morality of equity instead of greed. The unions failed to make up their minds then and have continued in that failure subsequently. This central ambiguity confuses people. On the one hand the unions proclaim their commitment to equity and draw widely on a moral vocabulary. On the other hand there are many instances where it is clear enough that sectional interest has prevailed and little attempt is made to hide the fact.

[...] In looking back over the entire span of the 20th century thus far it is obvious, if we ignore the Second World War, that the trade unions reached their peak of influence sometime in the mid-1970s: they had defeated the Tories' Industrial Relations Act and sold the social contract to an ungrateful and uncomprehending Labour government.

Since then it has all been downhill. Morale now is at such a low ebb that grave legal threats to the very existence of the unions are inadequately resisted [...]

[...] Some years ago, when but recently retired from the general secretaryship of the National Union of Mineworkers, Will Paynter expressed reservations about the shift of power within the trade union movement toward shop stewards. Paynter's anxieties had nothing to do with an erosion of 'bureaucratic centralism' or with a personal loss of power. What concerned him was that such developments might give full rein to activity narrowly based on localised sectional interest. Looking at the problem as a *socialist*, Paynter was pondering the classic dilemma: while short run economic gains might be made through vigorous bargaining at plant level, gains made there would make it increasingly difficult for unions operating across a range of industries to devise national policies [...].

Tony Lane, 'The Unions: Caught on the Ebb Tide', *Marxism Today* (September 1982), pp. 6–13.

12.6 Trade union problems in the 1980s

In June 1983 the Thatcher government was returned to power with an increased majority of 144 seats. The Labour vote fell by over 3 million and the party's electoral performance was in some ways its worst since 1918. Labour had offered the electorate its most left-wing manifesto ever. The Conservative government of 1979–83 had made a major contribution to the return of levels of unemployment not seen since the 1930s. Yet Labour had been rejected by most of the voters, millions of whom had turned to the Liberal–Social Democratic Alliance, formed with the crucial assistance of defectors from Labour who would not tolerate the dominance of the left within the Labour Party, which they perceived in 1979–81. This second consecutive defeat for Labour reinforced the convictions of the Communist revisionists that the left as a whole needed to rethink fundamentals.

Pete Carter succeeded Bert Ramelson as the party's National Industrial Organiser. His contributions to the discussion below illustrate the prevailing sense of the left's weakness and the extent to which this was seen as a legacy of past failures as well as the consequence of the initiatives taken by Conservative governments.

Pete Carter [...] The last two decades have produced some incredible trade union activities and struggles. We've seen the development of left policies within trade unions and the TUC. There's also been quite a shift in a lot of unions in terms of their leaderships. After the Heath defeat, however, the Tories worked out a complete new strategy to change all that. The Government has been very clever ... First, they have sought to change the climate of opinion – on unemployment, the welfare state, the power of the unions and so on. And when they have moved, they have done so where the trade unions are most vulnerable in the present climate: for example the election of trade union officials to governing bodies and the political activities of trade unions and ballots before strikes. To argue on the factory floor against the things that [Norman] Tebbit is saying is going to be one almighty job, because they have conditioned the working class in their favour, and they've timed this piece of legislation based on that conditioning [...]

[...] This separation of the unions from politics is the nub of the problem. In the period since 1945 ... there has been a growth in the trade union movement and, with the exception of 1966, a steady decline in Labour's share of the vote with an all-time low this year. It's not just a question of Labour in power, it's also the question of Labour in opposition. This was demonstrated clearly during the election. Labour presented, just three weeks before the election, the most left manifesto that we have seen since the war. And to think you can reverse the decline of political thinking over that period amongst trade unionists in three weeks with a manifesto that is not fought for really is an underestimation by the leadership of the labour movement of the deep political crisis that faces the working class.

[...] I've just got a whole list of TUC education material. You look through it – and this has been going on for years and years – and all the classes are based on how to be a good shop steward, how to be a good representative health and safety wise, how to conduct negotiations and so on.

This expertise is absolutely essential for trade unionists in today's complex world of bargaining, but what is lacking is any vision, any socialist ideas, we're our own worst enemies [...]

[...] I agree very much with the need to politicise the unions, but the two immediate things that come to mind are the question of the leadership of the Labour Party and the political levy. Now if we want to defend certain things, we must be honest and open about existing problems. Now I'm not happy about the question of the political levy and the way it frequently operates now. I've signed hundreds of workers into the building union and when they've asked me the contribution I've told them it's 75p or whatever it was, but I have never, ever told them – now I may be unique but I would think that many trade union officials operate like that – that 5p of their contribution was going to Labour. Now that kind of approach has stopped the debate about the relationship between the unions and the Labour Party. I asked someone in the AUEW the other day about people in his branch opting out. He said, 'No problem. We make it that difficult for them. When they turn up at the branch the form's not there and they aren't going to come back to opt out'. Now if this is the level of argumentation or the strategy for winning the conviction from people to vote or commit themselves to the Labour Party through their union, then we're on a suicidal course. Tebbit's going to win on that issue and we have to recognise that fact. On the question of leadership, I believe that every member who pays the political levy should have the right to a say who that leader should be, be it by a postal, branch or factory ballot. Now if we take these two issues on board and confront them, then it's going to force us to develop argumentation that is going to enrich the whole movement [...]

'For Whom the Block Votes? A Roundtable Discussion', *Marxism Today* (September 1983), pp. 18–25.

268

12.7 Labour's lost millions

Marxism Today was now a vehicle for attacking virtually all the received thinking and established practices on the left. In fact it specialised in such critique and had plenty of targets at a time when rival Marxists – such as the Militant Tendency and other elements of the left in the Labour Party – were conspicuous advocates of confrontation with the Conservative government.

[... During the election campaign] it also became more and more evident that the main question at issue on the Left was not: what government? But: what Labour Party? To put it brutally, for many, a Thatcher government was preferable to a reformist Labour government.

Since very few, even on the wilder fringes of the Left, genuinely believe that Denis Healey is actually worse than Norman Tebbit, various theories were invented to delude ourselves. The old-style Labour Party could not win. A proper socialist Labour Party could win, because somewhere out there, millions of radical left-wing voters were abstaining, waiting only to flock to candidates and programmes of the Left. The election was lost anyway, so it didn't much matter that potential Labour voters were puzzled and demoralised by the sight of party leaders and activists tearing each others' guts out in public for years on issues difficult to see the point of. And so on. However, the basic fact cannot be denied, that a large body of the Left acted as though another Labour government like the ones we have had before from time to time since 1945, was not just unsatisfactory, but *worse than no Labour government*. And this means that it would be worse than the only alternative government on offer, which was Mrs Thatcher's.

The new Toryism
This attitude raises grave problems of political judgment. Not only did it (as is now totally obvious) grossly misread the attitude of the voters to the Labour Party, but it also, and more dangerously, underestimates the historical novelty of Thatcherism and the seriousness of the threat it represents. Past Tory governments were based on the principle of avoiding class confrontation in order to prevent a radicalisation of the working class, which represented the substantial majority of the British people [...]

[...] Thatcherism is committed to a radical and reactionary change in British capitalism, and indeed in the British political system. It is pushing ahead with this new, militant, and formidable policy of class struggle from above, and the dismantling of the past reformist consensus with all the more confidence, because it has discovered that the weakening of and divisions

269

within the working class and the self-ruination of the Labour Party make it apparently much less risky than the old Toryism had supposed.

Thatcherism aims to transform Britain irreversibly in its own way, not just to keep the system on an even keel. To defeat it ... is the condition of survival for a decent Britain, and of such chances as exist of advancing to a better society [...]

[...] like it or not, Labour will either have to win back those who switched from Labour to the Alliance, those who stayed at home, and a lot of those who are increasingly opting out of politics. Or alternately, it will have to learn how to lead a broad front of other parties or their supporters into backing Labour's policy. This is not impossible. But it means, first of all, understanding why the people who left us or stayed away did not wish to vote Labour, and if we are to lead them forward we have to get them to vote or support Labour for reasons which seem good to *them*, even if we do not like their reasons. That, by the way, is how socialists once built the Labour Party and eventually got it committed to a socialist objective, starting with a working class and others who were Liberals, Conservatives or something else and who did not vote for Labour because no more than a small minority were attracted by socialism or knew what it was. They learned as they struggled – but the socialists were with them to help the learning. Rebuilding Labour, or building a broad front around Labour, will once again be like that. We think the masses need Labour, but if we ask them to come to us on our terms, they won't. Not any more. Then the chances are they will never find out what Labour could do for them.

And neither will we.

Eric Hobsbawm, 'Labour's Lost Millions', *Marxism Today* (October 1983), pp. 7–13.

12.8 Debating defeat

Many socialists perceived the 1980s as a continuation of the crisis of capitalism announced in the previous decade but *Marxism Today* moved increasingly towards the view, especially after 1983, that the crisis of the labour and socialist movements was the real issue confronting them.

The participants in the round table were: Dave Cook, member of the Communist Party's National Executive Committee and Communist parliamentary candidate for Vauxhall, London; John Hoffman, member of the

Communist Party East Midlands District Committee and *Marxism Today* Editorial Board; Lou Lewis, member of the Communist Party National Executive Committee and a regional organiser for UCATT; Jane Woddis, active feminist and chairwoman of the Communist Party Birmingham City Committee.

We've seen a very severe setback for the labour movement since 1979. What is the nature of this crisis, how profound is it, and what do you think the Communist Party has to offer the labour movement in the way of over-coming it.

Jane It is not just a crisis of the labour movement. It is important to emphasise this, particularly as the CP has a conception of other social forces besides the labour movement, for the same crisis is affecting what we would broadly call the other democratic movements, the other social forces [...]

John It's important that we don't overstate the problems, although you are absolutely right that we have suffered a setback in the labour move-ment. We must always remember that the real crisis in our society isn't a crisis of the labour movement, or of the working class, or of Marxism, it is fundamentally a crisis of capitalism. It is crucial to see mass unemployment, a move to authoritarianism of a dangerously populist kind, a climate of fear and intimidation as the backcloth to understanding why the labour move-ment has suffered this defeat and how we can move out of it [...]

Lou I agree with John that the main crisis is the capitalist crisis, and the crisis of the labour movement is how to deal with the crisis itself and its effects, which include major structural changes in the working class ... We have to reflect back to the militancy of the 60s and 70s where there were considerable gains in the short term, but the militancy lacked a political perspective. We had the defeat of Heath, the return of a Labour govern-ment, but no perspective of what we wanted from that Labour government. So we had the chapter of disasters which led to 1979 and the return of the Tories [...]

Dave It is the depth of the capitalist crisis which throws into sharp relief the failure of the labour movement. At a time of mass unemployment and all the other problems of the crisis, you might have expected the Left to be in a much stronger position. The fact that it is not is evidence of its failure to capitalise on the disaffection which exists on a wide scale. The Left has failed to face up to the extent of the labour movement's long term decline, which is undeniable if you look at the share of the Labour vote and the impact of socialist ideas amongst large sections of the working class. There has been a tendency to attribute the recent problems of the Labour Party, and indeed the CP, to short term factors. The responsibility of the CP in this situation is to refuse to acquiesce in these glib explanations and to help the movement face up to those deep long term reasons for its difficult situation, to try and suggest ideas and initiatives, based on its own activity, its Marxist tradition and strategy, to point the way forward.

Jane I agree with Dave that it isn't enough to say it is all due to the crisis of capitalism. We have to put a lot of responsibility at the door of the labour and democratic movements themselves including the party. It is not just the failure to give a long term perspective, we have also failed to link that perspective with very immediate things [...]

'A Roundtable Discussion, Chaired by Martin Jacques: The Long and Winding Road, Britain's Communists in 1983', *Marxism Today* (November 1983), pp. 26–30.

12.9 Failures of socialism

Monty Johnstone was one of those Communists who decided to stay in the party in 1956 while realising that there were fundamental defects in Soviet and Communist history which were not explained by Khrushchev or any of the official pronouncements that followed him. This article, written just before Gorbachev succeeded Konstantin Chernenko as General Secretary of the CPSU, focuses on the failure of an economy whose earlier dynamism had previously been invoked to silence critics like Johnstone. All attempts to reform the Communist command economies had failed, he concluded, because they had left its bureaucratic authoritarianism untouched.

A quarter of a century ago the socialist countries were making an impact on the world with their impressive rates of economic and social progress. Extrapolating from them the 22nd Congress of the Soviet Communist Party in 1961 adopted a new programme which stated that by 1970 the USSR would surpass the USA in production per head of population. By 1980 Soviet labour productivity would exceed that of the USA by roughly 100%, there would be 'an abundance of material and cultural values for the whole population' and 'a communist society will in the main be built in the USSR'.

Since then, the socialist countries, in most cases preserving full employment in contrast to the capitalist countries, have continued on the whole to advance more rapidly than the latter and to expand rather than cut their social services and education.

However there has been a pronounced decline in rates of growth in the European socialist countries from 10% in the 1950s to 7% in the 1960s, 5% in the 1970s, down to a planned rate for 1981–85 of around 3.5% annually. The share of the socialist countries in world industrial production, which rose from 20% in 1950 to 36% in 1960, has since then only risen to its present level of 40%. Soviet industrial production has only risen since 1970 from 65% to 67% of the US level. Labour productivity in Soviet industry has since 1976 been officially listed each year as 'more than 55%' and in agriculture as 'about 20–25%' of the US level. The heady targets of the 60s have long since been consigned to oblivion.

[…] Unfulfilled expectations and the contrast between promise and performance in the USSR and other socialist countries have led, internally, to growing signs of apathy, malaise and dissatisfaction, which have from time to time in different countries assumed critical proportions. Externally, they have invalidated the conception of the socialist countries exerting 'an ever increasing influence on the struggles of the peoples in the capitalist countries' and 'by the force of example … revolutionising (their) thinking'. Paradoxically, after a decade of world capitalism's worst economic crisis for half a century, the attractive power of the socialist countries has diminished.

Every socialist in Britain who is not completely isolated or blinkered knows this from his or her own experience.

In the case of France statistical confirmation has come in a survey which shows that in the last decade the proportion of the population holding a negative opinion about the functioning of the socialist system in the Soviet Union and Eastern Europe has risen from 43% to 69%, whilst those expressing a positive one has declined from 28 to 11%. Among young people the negative view is even higher.

A variety of factors have contributed to this worsened image. They include the detention of dissidents in prisons and psychiatric hospitals, the invasions of Czechoslovakia and Afghanistan, the Sino-Soviet conflict, and martial law and the suppression of trade union freedoms in Poland, along with growing economic problems. These things were not created by anti-communist propagandists, although they certainly play into their hands. They are structural rather than conjunctural and arise from an authoritarian and bureaucratic form of socialism, whose roots lie in the Stalin period […]

Monty Johnstone, 'Back in the USSR: The Past Catches Up', *Marxism Today* (March 1985), pp. 12–17.

12.10 A party divided

Though he'd left the Communist Party in 1956, historian Raphael Samuel was deeply troubled by what he saw as the sectarianism of CPGB modernisers and their journal, *Marxism Today*.

Once upon a time the Communist Party stood – or believed it stood – for unity. It played down differences within the Left, or at any rate those within the left wing of the Labour Party and the trade union movement. It made common cause with people of different persuasions when there was a campaign that it was anxious to forward [...].

Today however, the party, or at any rate those in the editorial direction of *Marxism Today* who publish in its name, seems to be setting up in business as professional splitters, and though extending an apparently limitless tolerance to people on the Right, it attempts to build a Chinese Wall on the Left, both in the CPGB itself, where supporters of the *Morning Star* are consigned to outer space [...]; and within the labour movement, where the Left is scythed into two opposing camps. [...]

Marxism Today's article on [National Union of Mineworkers' vice-president] Mick McGahey (September 1986) exemplifies what is in one aspect a deeply sectarian project: the discovery of enemies on the Left, and the undermining of traditional loyalties. [...] McGahey is a towering figure in the CPGB but also, for those out of sympathy with the party's tradition of industrial work, an uncomfortable one [...].

If there is to be a free and wide-ranging discussion on the Left – and if *Marxism Today* is to be a forum for it – then the Communist Party cannot claim a privileged immunity from the critical scrutiny which it – or *Marxism Today* – extends to others. [...]

Criticism and self-criticism would be particularly in order in relation to the aftermath of the [1984–85 miners'] strike when the CPGB seemed to be far more concerned to settle accounts with the 'hard-line' followers of the *Morning Star* than with building on the enormous public sympathy which then existed for the miners' cause. [...]

The CPGB may no longer have the power to act as a unifier, but, as can be seen from the schisms in its own ranks, it has a formidable capacity to divide and to act as a symbolic focus of doubt. In the last 18 months it has been visiting on others the discomfort which it feels with itself. Its schisms and expulsions, in the immediate aftermath of the miners' strike, seem to have been paradigmatic of those which are making a graveyard of the Labour Left [...].

The spectacle of recantation and confession is seldom an edifying one [...], and in the present instance it is not clear why it should be of help to the miners' cause. One of the great strengths of the 1984–5 strike was the miners' pride – pride in the NUM, pride in the leadership (a displaced expression of *collective* self-regard), pride in each other, pride in the family, pride in the bedrock of national life.

Part of that pride was a belief that the miners were setting an example to others, and that their strike – sustained against the entire might of the state – could serve as a symbolic focus for the defence of jobs and employment. Those who belittle the strike may succeed in sowing doubt, but they will rob the miners of their greatest strength. As a historian of socialist convictions but conservative loyalties, I do not believe you can make a new politics by doing dirt on the past.

Raphael Samuel, 'Reopening Old Wounds', *Marxism Today* (October 1986), pp. 60–1.

12.11 Gorbachev to the rescue?

Just a month after the publication of document 12.9, with its pessimistic analysis of Soviet economic problems, the same author raised hopes with *Marxism Today*'s first piece on Mikhail Gorbachev.[14] It was a time when *Marxism Today* editorials were preoccupied by domestic issues and showed very little interest in the Soviet Union. The piece was nevertheless criticised as an expression of the journal's 'anti-Soviet' views by CPSU member Alexey Pkozlov, who called it a 'malicious falsification' and typical of 'your journal's generally unfriendly attitude to our Party and to Soviet society'.[15] Following the 27th Congress of the CPSU in February–March 1986 *Marxism Today* became much more interested in the Gorbachev reforms, which had now extended to foreign relations and promised to overthrow the Cold War system. Throughout 1987, however, the journal's focus was on glasnost in accordance with its conviction that democratisation was the precondition for real economic changes.

[…] On Gorbachev's initiative the USSR has been resuming a process of renewal, which it began very unevenly and inconsistently under Khrushchev after Stalin's death in 1953. The present reforms are taking place when the Soviet Union is at a much higher level of economic and cultural development than at that time. But, as in that period, the requirements of the Soviet Union's socialist development are seen to be increasingly incompatible with existing structures and practices. The crying contradiction between communist words and highly un-communist deeds was contributing to a crisis of confidence and a degree of alienation which more perceptive and committed Soviet leaders could not ignore. Due to the paralysis of the independent initiative of the working people brought about by Stalinism, the ushering in of change could only come from above. As in Czechoslovakia in 1968, but unlike Poland in 1980, this was to come from the Communist Party, and was spearheaded by a newly-elected general secretary.

It is now recognised in the SovietUnion that the earlier attempts at democratisation were brought to an end under Brezhnev.

In that period, and above all from the mid-70s, stagnation grew along with the 'immobilism' associated with an increasingly gerontocratic leadership [...]

[...] The changed social atmosphere created by democratisation, self-management at work, and the more direct material interest in increasing production under the new Soviet enterprise law, should contribute to tangible benefits in the subsequent period in terms of economic advance and higher living standards. The growth of individual and co-operative services under another new law now passed should also help. With progress towards both a pluralist socialist democracy – valuable in its own right – and a transformed and expanding modernised economy giving higher priority to consumer satisfaction and social welfare, the possibility of the process of reform being halted and turned back, as under Brezhnev, will diminish. An educated population, having developed self-confidence and political experience through running its own affairs (which it did not have a chance to do under Khrushchev), would not easily allow itself to be deprived of such democratic gains. But nobody should underestimate the obstacles and struggles ahead in the drive for *perestroika*.

As Gorbachev recently indicated, the USSR is now 'entering a decisive phase'.

Monty Johnstone, 'The Gorbachev Era: Glasnost and After', *Marxism Today* (November 1987), pp. 14–19.

12.12 New times

Meanwhile, the British Conservative Party won its third consecutive general election in June 1987. Communists now argued that class politics could only disadvantage the Labour Party – by alienating the majority of voters, including a section of the working class.[16] Labour needed electoral allies to oust the Conservatives. The party's programme was updated as 'Facing Up to the Future' in September 1988. The emphasis throughout was on the 'fundamental restructuring of the economy and social life' involving the breakdown of the 'Fordist era'. The sense that capitalism had renewed itself and undermined the old social blocs of the labour movement was central to this analysis.

[...] Throughout the 80s, the Left has been on the defensive, bewildered by an adversary, Thatcherism, whose confidence has grown by the year, and whose capacity to move and innovate has steadily expanded.

But why? It's had something to with the decay of the Labourist tradition in the post-war period. It's had much to do with Thatcherism's powerful critique of that experience and its espousal of a clear alternative. But increasingly, at the heart of Thatcherism, has been its sense of New Times, of living in a new era. While the Left remains profoundly wedded to the past, to 1945, to the old social democratic order, to the priorities of Keynes and Beveridge, the Right has glimpsed the future and run with it. As a result, it is the Right which now appears modern, radical, innovative, and brimming with confidence and ideas about the future. It is the Left which seems backward-looking, conservative, bereft of ideas and out of time. In short, the Right has appropriated New Times.

[...] At the heart of New Times is the shift from the old mass-production Fordist economy to a new, more flexible, post-Fordist order based on computers, information technology and robotics. But New Times are about much more than economic change. Our world is being remade. Mass production, the mass consumer, the big city, big-brother state, the sprawling housing estate, and the nation-state are in decline: flexibility, diversity, differentiation, mobility, communication, decentralisation and internationalisation are in the ascendant. In the process our own identities, our sense of self, our own subjectivities are being transformed. We are in transition to a new era.

In the 1980s *Marxism Today* pioneered the analysis of Thatcherism and the state of the labour movement. It was the era of critique. Now to reconstruction. We present New Times.

Editorial, *Marxism Today* (October 1988), p. 3.

12.13 Disagreements among the reformers

The reconstruction promised by *Marxism Today* never materialised. Critics within the party, including some who well understood the need for reform, saw that the documents that promised reconstruction were devoid of any real sense of a socialist alternative to capitalism.

Although we were members of the group appointed to prepare the 'Facing Up to the Future' discussion document ... We wish to make it clear that we have substantial disagreements with some major aspects of its analysis [...]

Whilst agreeing on the importance both of current technological changes and of social, moral, sexual and ethnic struggles, we are critical of the document's failure to recognise the centrality of class struggle in capitalist Britain today [...]

[...] Moreover the democratic, pluralistic and self-managing socialism, for which we need to win conviction as a viable and desirable alternative to capitalism, is treated in only two brief paragraphs.

Nowhere is it defined as a society based on social ownership and control of the major sectors of the economy [...]

Marian Darke, Bill Innes and Monty Johnstone, letter to *Marxism Today* (October 1988), p. 40.

12.14 Out with the old, out with the Communist Party

The collapse of Communist systems across Eastern Europe beginning in October 1989, after popular uprisings, prepared the way for most of the remaining members of the CPGB to conclude in favour of self-dissolution.

Nina Temple [...] What is needed is the political imagination to take the values of equality, co-operation and solidarity, and fuse them inseparably with the touchstone of individual liberty. To grasp hold of and develop convincing visions for the great issues of our time: human survival and protection of the environment, underdevelopment and debt, overpopulation, citizenship, the nature of work, and the future of the family.

And to see how these issues will fit in a new settlement of power away from the nation-state towards European, global and more local institutions.

The Manifesto For New Times, initiated in articles in *Marxism Today* and developed into a strategic intervention by the Communist Party, embraces this vision but the party itself is a totally inadequate vessel for this politics.

Although rooted in the British socialist tradition, the party bore a heavy Soviet stamp which it progressively broke from in the postwar years. The party was able to educate and organise an earlier generation of working class activists, but was slow to respond to the changing nature of class and the challenges of anti-racism, feminism and cultural politics.

The party structures were cast in the mould of the Bolshevik Party of 1917 and did not move on. They are still top-down stifling and unresponsive. They restrict rather than facilitate people getting together and taking initiatives.

As a result, the party has been declining relentlessly for decades and would on present trends cease to exist in 1994.

This year it has been involved in a no-holds-barred discussion about itself and its future. Seeking new forms to facilitate its politics [...]

Monty Johnstone [...] what has failed, in my view, is not the Communist project of a socialist society based on social ownership and democratic control, but a bureaucratic and oppressive Stalinist caricature of it, long criticised by British Communists.

The Communist Party was formed to offer Marxism analysis and leadership in struggle against capitalism here. Events in eastern Europe have done nothing to lessen the case for this. Enormous power remains concentrated in the hands of huge, increasingly international, companies which subordinate human beings and the environment to the drive for profit.

[Neil] Kinnock has secured the removal of more and more socialist elements from Labour's programme. There is a need for a Communist Party uniting with others on the left to oppose Labour's drift to the right. The election of a Labour government, for which Communists should be working, will make this even more necessary.

The Left can benefit from a renewed Communist Party, actively participating in day-to-day political, industrial and social struggles, able to project its strategic analysis and socialist perspectives into the broader Labour and trade union movement. The party's decline means that it can at present only do this on a modest scale (foregoing parliamentary contests) with no guarantee of success. But the effort is worth making.

There are others in and around the Labour and trade union left and organisations like the Socialist Society and the Socialist Movement with whom Communists share many fundamental ideas. They should be discussing common perspectives together, seeking to build the basis ultimately for the creation of a larger socialist party based on nondogmatic Marxism with feminist and green dimensions, into which the Communist Party should, I believe, be willing to merge. It would thereby give up its separate Communist name and identity. I can see no advantage in doing so before the realisation of such socialist unity.

Nor do I consider there to be any basis for the proposal put forward by the majority of the Communist Party's executive committee to involve the party in helping launch in early 1991 a new, vaguely conceived, broader formation to exist alongside itself. There are any number of broad formations already existing, from trades unions to new social movements, in which Communists should be working, without suddenly trying to initiate another one.

Even less do I agree with the proposal of a minority of the party's executive to dissolve the Communist Party and form an ill-defined political association without any single comprehensive viewpoint, and I strongly reject the minority's assertion that 'the existing assets of the Communist Party would be transferred to a Trust Fund' not controlled by the membership of the new association.

I believe that the Communist congress this month should and will decide in favour of retaining the Communist Party and transforming along more drastic lines.

Bea Campbell [...] The Communist Party – as communist rather that a radical party was both energised and yet exhausted by intelligent despair after 1968 and the invasion of Czechoslovakia, and again after 1979 and Thatcherism, and certainly after the splits and realignments of the 1980s. The raison d'etre was Communists' critique of their own orthodoxies, albeit constrained by the fact the party still shared the same international address as communisms' culprits. 1989 ended all that. It was all over. A party cannot live by critique alone, critique isn't a politics [...]

Nina Temple, Monty Johnstone and Beatrix Campbell, 'The Moment of Truth', *Marxism Today* (December 1990), pp. 32–3.

12.15 Gorbachev's failure

The failed attempt to overthrow Gorbachev in August 1991 further destabilised the Soviet Union and precipitated the dissolution of the CPSU. The falling apart of the USSR itself took place in the course of September and October, and it was officially terminated on 25 December. But it was already clear that the attempt to rescue something for socialism from the reforms of Gorbachev had failed.

[...] The coup failed because the Party had lost its central authority. The army was not united enough to take over. Even the KGB appears to have been divided. In short, the coup had no support, whether from democrats or from nationalists or from any one else who believed the Emergency Committee would know what to do about the hyper-inflation, for instance, which is virtually certain. Nothing in the past six years suggests that anyone in power in the USSR does. For this is the tragedy of Mikhail Gorbachev, the long foretold victim: the last hope of communists, a great historical figure, who wanted the best and achieved some of it. He rightly became one of the most universally admired statesmen of the century abroad, while his countrymen saw only a man who destroyed a clumsy but operational economy and replaced it by a void, where there is no longer bread. Perestroika did not fail: it did not happen.

Perhaps the only way to restructure the economy was from the top. But the catch-22 was that the command system, the only way of getting things done in the USSR, was also the main obstacle to changing the ways of doing them. So Gorbachev chose glasnost in order to force perestroika; it should have been the other way round. And neither Marxism nor western economists had either experience or theory that helped. So Gorbachev the reconstructor became Gorbachev the politician, and increasingly the symbol and figurehead. That is what he will still be.

Eric Hobsbawm, 'The Centre Cannot Hold', *Marxism Today* (September 1991), pp. 2–3.

Notes

1 Geoff Andrews, *Endgames and New Times: The Final Years of British Communism 1964–1991* (London: Lawrence & Wishart, 2004), pp. 219–20; Francis Beckett, *Enemy Within: The Rise and Fall of the British Communist Party* (1995: London: Merlin, 1998), p. 2.

2 Beckett, *Enemy*, p. 8.

3 Martin Jacques, 'The Last Word', *Marxism Today* (December 1991), pp. 28–9.

4 Martin Jacques, 'Goodbye, and Thanks', *Marxism Today* (December 1991), p. 3.

5 An archive of *Marxism Today* from 1980 and 1991 can now be accessed online at http://www.amielandmelburn.org.uk/.

6 See Raphael Samuel, 'Reopening Old Wounds', *Marxism Today* (October 1976), pp. 60–1.

7 A special 'New Times' issue of *Marxism Today* was published in October 1988, a theme which ran through the magazine for the next year. *A Manifesto for New Times* was published in 1989, and originally conceived as the replacement for *The British Road to Socialism*.

8 J. Kelly, *Trade Unions and Socialist Politics* (London, Verso, 1988), p. 101.

9 An account of these factional disputes written by an insider (on the *Marxism Today* wing of the party) can be found in D. Cook, 'No Private Drama', *Marxism Today* (February 1985), pp. 25–9.

10 See J. Callaghan, *Socialism in Britain Since 1884* (Oxford: Blackwell, 1990), pp. 214–41.

11 See D. S. Bell (ed.), *Western European Communists and the Collapse of Communism* (Oxford: Berg, 1993), especially pp. 121–39.

12 The CPGB modernisers admitted this in their *Manifesto for New Times: A Strategy for the 1990s* (London: Communist Party, 1990), pp. 58–9.

13 For further detail, see M. Waller and M. Fennema (eds), *Communist Parties in Western Europe: Decline or Adaptation?* (Oxford: Blackwell, 1988), pp. 224–44.

14 M. Johnstone, 'Gorbachev Ushers in a New Period', *Marxism Today* (April 1985).

15 A. Pkozlov, 'Viewpoint', *Marxism Today* (May 1985).

16 E. Hobsbawm, 'Out of the Wilderness', *Marxism Today* (October 1987).

Biographical notes

Aaronovitch, Sam: Served as the party's National Cultural Secretary from 1947–55; prominent figure in the St Pancras Rent Strike of 1956.

Adhikari, Gangadhar: Best known for advocating a multinational analysis of India during the Second World War and supporting the creation of Pakistan. He joined the Communist Party in Berlin, where he acquired a PhD in chemistry, before returning to India in 1928. He was one of the accused in the Meerut Conspiracy Case. He was a member of the CPI politburo at the time of the nationalities controversy.

Arnot, Robin Page: Founder member of the Communist Party and former conscientious objector. One of the twelve Communists imprisoned in 1925. Historian of the British miners. Member of the CP Central Committee 1927–37.

Benes, Edvard: A leader of the Czechoslovak independence movement. President of the Czechoslovak Republic in 1945. Resigned in June 1948 after the Communist seizure of power of 25 February.

Bernal, John Desmond: A pioneer of X-ray crystallography and Professor of Physics at Birkbeck College, University of London. Member of the CPGB from 1923. Awarded the Stalin Peace Prize in 1953.

Bloomfield, Jon: Modernising CP intellectual, prominent in student work before becoming Birmingham City Secretary in 1976. Served on CPGB Executive Committee and the editorial board of *Marxism Today* in the 1980s.

Bond, Ralph: Film-enthusiast and documentary film-maker. Bond was a CPGB member from the late 1920s and a founder member of the London Workers' Film Society. Later worked at John Grierson's General Post Office Film Unit and was a key figure in the ACTT union.

Bose, Subhas Chandra: Indian nationalist and leader of the Indian National Army, formed to overthrow British rule in India, from 1943.

Bowman, Dave: Activist in the National Union of Railwaymen who became president of the union 1975–77. Member of the CPGB from the 1930s.

Bradley, Ben: CPGB member who was sent to India in 1927 and helped to build trade unions among railway and cotton workers in Bombay.

Bramley, Ted: Joined the party's London District Committee in 1932, before serving as London District Secretary from 1937–47 and as an elected councillor in Stepney (1945–46 and 1948–49).

Branson, Noreen: Lifelong Communist and historian of the CPGB, Labour Research Department worker from 1938 until her death in 2003. Daughter of Lord Alfred Browne, married artist Clive Branson.

Bridgeman, Reginald: Former diplomat and Communist sympathiser who became secretary of the League Against Imperialism and was active in various international causes including friendship with the Soviet Union.

Bridges, George: From a London Communist Party family, Bridges was prominent in the YCL in the 1960s and became a party moderniser in the 1970s.

Bukharin, Nikolai: Bolshevik, member of the Politburo of the Communist Party of the Soviet Union, 1924–29, chairman of the Communist International, 1926–29. Tried as a traitor and executed in March 1938.

Burns, Emile: Communist Party intellectual close to Harry Pollitt. A significant figure behind CP cultural policy in the 1930s, Burns became chair of the National Cultural Committee on its formation in 1947. Edited a number of party journals including *Modern Quarterly* and *Marxist Quarterly*.

Bush, Alan: Composer who joined the party in 1935. A co-founder of the Workers' Music Association, for which Bush served as president between 1941 and 1995. Composer of four symphonies and many operatic works, including *Wat Tyler* (1948–50), co-written with his wife, Nancy, and the music for several mass pageants of the 1930s.

Campbell, Beatrix: Journalist and feminist who played a public role in the CPGB from the 1970s as a leading proponent of reform.

Campbell, John Ross: Founder member of the Communist Party, elected to the Executive in 1923, editor of *Workers' Weekly*, 1924–25, and close ally of Harry Pollitt with whom he shared a better understanding of the British trade unions than many of his colleagues in the party leadership.

Carrit, Gabriel: 'Bill' Carrit was the Oxford University friend of the poets W. H. Auden and Stephen Spender. He joined the CP in the USA, campaigning in the Southern states to recruit black Americans, and showed similar courage in Spain and Nazi Germany in the mid-1930s. He also fought in Burma with the Welch Fusiliers and led the London squatters' campaign of 1946.

Carter, Pete: National Organiser of the YCL in the mid-1960s and, succeeding Mick Costello, National Industrial Organiser from 1983, from which position he gave support to the 'Gramscian' reformers who rejected the traditional policy of wage militancy.

Caudwell, Christopher: Born Christopher St John Sprigg, Caudwell worked as a journalist and writer of thrillers and books on aviation before joining the Poplar Branch of the CPGB in 1935. He joined the International Brigades in December 1936 and was killed in action at Jarama on 12 February 1937. His posthumously published theoretical and critical writings include the influential *Illusion and Reality: A Study of the Sources of Poetry* (1937).

Collard, Dudley: Communist sympathiser and King's Counsel who affirmed the integrity of the Moscow Trials of 1936–38.

Daly, Lawrence: Fife miner born into a Communist family. Active in the CPGB from 1940, he left the party in 1956. Formed the Fife Socialist League in 1957 and was regarded as a leading figure in the New Left. In 1968 he was elected General Secretary of the National Union of Mineworkers.

Dash, Jack: Leading shop steward among the London dockers and Communist since 1936.

Day Lewis, Cecil: Poet and critic who joined the party in 1936 and left two years later. Though only briefly a party member, Day Lewis made a significant contribution to Communist cultural life and debate in the late 1930s, notably as editor of the symposium *The Mind in Chains: Socialism and the Cultural Revolution* (1938).

Dimitrov, Georgi: Bulgarian hero of the Leipzig Trial, Dimitrov became a Soviet citizen in 1934. He served as General Secretary of the Comintern from 1934 to 1943. After the war he became premier of his native Bulgaria. Died in 1949.

Dobb, Maurice: Cambridge University economist and member of the CPGB from 1920.

Duranty, Walter: Moscow correspondent of the *New York Times*, winner of the Pulitzer Prize in 1932, and now regarded as an apologist for Stalinism.

Dutt, Rajani Palme: Founder member of the CPGB, one of its experts on India and the British Empire, leading theorist of Marxism-Leninism within the party and an unswerving supporter of the Soviet leadership.

Eisenstein, Sergei: Supporter of the Bolsheviks and pioneer of innovative film-making who directed *Strike* (1925), *Battleship Potemkin* (1925), *October* (1927) and *The General Line* (1929). Was invited to work for Paramount Studios in 1930 but departed before the end of the year by 'mutual consent'.

Etheridge, Dick: Communist shop steward at Austin Longbridge near Birmingham. Member of the Executive Committee of the party from 1961 to 1973.

Ewer, William Norman: Chief foreign correspondent of the *Daily Herald*. Left the Communist Party in 1929. Actively anti-Communist thereafter.

Fagan, Hymie: Joined the party in 1925 and attended the Lenin School, Moscow, in the 1930s. His books include *Nine Days that Shook England: An Account of the English People's Uprising in 1381* (1938) and *England For All* (1940).

French, Sid: French joined the YCL aged fourteen in 1934, and became a full-time party official in 1946. Increasingly critical of what he saw as revisionist and anti-Soviet positions of the CPGB leadership through the

1960s and 1970s, French formed the breakaway New Communist Party in 1977.

Friell, James ('Gabriel'): Joined the staff of the *Daily Worker* in 1933 and became the paper's cartoonist as 'Gabriel' in 1936. Broke with the party and the paper in 1956.

Fryer, Peter: Joined the CPGB in 1945 and the staff of the *Daily Worker* in 1948. Reported on the show trial of Rajk in 1949, and the Hungarian uprising in 1956. Broke with the CP over Soviet suppression of the Hungarian uprising. Went on to write books including *Staying Power: The History of Black People in Britain* (1984).

Gallacher, Willie: Engineering worker, member of the Social Democratic Federation and founding member of the CPGB. Chair of the Clyde Workers' Committee in 1915. Elected Communist MP for West Fife in 1935. Chairman and President of the Communist Party and long-serving member of its Executive.

Gill, Ken: General Secretary of the Tass and MSF unions, Gill was expelled from the Communist Party in 1985 for his opposition to the party leadership's revisionism.

Glading, Percy: Founding member of the party and an early envoy to India on its behalf in 1925.

Gollan, John: Succeeded Harry Pollitt as General Secretary of the CPGB in 1956.

Gollancz, Victor: Publisher, writer and one of the founding editors of the Left Book Club. Close to the Communist Party in the mid- and late 1930s, but never a member.

Haldane, J. B. S.: Geneticist and evolutionary biologist. Regular contributor to the *Daily Worker* on science. Allowed his membership of the party to lapse after the Stalin regime interfered with Soviet biology to support the (erroneous) theories of Trofim Lysenko and persecute those who opposed him such as Nikolai Vavilov.

Hill, Christopher: Joined the CPGB in the late 1930s and became a distinguished historian, specialising in the seventeenth century and particularly the English Revolution. Based for much of his career at Balliol College, Oxford. Hill left the CP in 1957.

Hobsbawm, Eric: Distinguished historian and member of the CPGB since the 1930s.

Hogarth, Paul: Artist and illustrator who joined the CPGB while at Manchester School of Art in the Popular Front years. Left in the wake of 1956.

Horner, Arthur: Founder member of the CPGB who was General Secretary of the National Union of Mineworkers from 1944 to 1959.

Horrabin, Frank: Prolific illustrator and short-lived member of the Communist Party. Elected Labour MP for Peterborough in 1929.

Jackson, T. A.: Former member of the Social Democratic Federation and the

Socialist Party of Great Britain, Jackson was a founding member of the CPGB but was removed from the leadership in 1929, remaining a paid journalist for the party.

Jacques, Martin: Editor of *Marxism Today* 1977–91 and a leading theorist of the party's retreat from Marxism-Leninism.

Jinnah, Mohammed Ali: Leader of the Muslim League and first Governor-General of Pakistan in August 1947.

Johnstone, Monty: A long-standing critic of aspects of the theory and practice of Soviet socialism who remained convinced of the validity of the Communist movement until his death in 2007.

Joshi, Puran Chand: General Secretary of the Communist Party of India from 1935–47. Joshi was removed from the leadership for advocating unity with the Indian National Congress at a time when the leadership moved towards an insurrectionary policy.

Kartun, Derek: Joined the Communist Party during the war having been raised in France in an upper-middle class family with Polish and Russian connections. Foreign editor of the *Daily Worker* and contributor to *The Week*. He dropped out of Communist politics after 1956 and returned to the world of business. Wrote a series of spy novels in the 1980s.

Kane, Jock: Scottish miner victimised after the General Strike. Moved to Yorkshire. Communist from the age of fifteen. Secretary of the Sheffield Communist Party from 1935. In 1963 was the first Communist to be elected to a full-time position in the Yorkshire NUM. In 1969 elected to the NUM National Executive.

Kettle, Arnold: Literary critic and party member who served on the Executive Committee. Kettle taught at the University of Leeds and the Open University, and wrote books including *An Introduction to the English Novel*, 2 vols (1962).

Kettle, Margot: Member of the party, active in the students' movement during the Second World War. Married to the literary critic and CPGB executive member, Professor Arnold Kettle.

Khrushchev, Nikita: First Secretary of the Communist Party of the Soviet Union between 1953 and 1964. At the 20th Party Congress in February 1956 he denounced and exposed aspects of the dictatorial terror policies of Joseph Stalin.

Klugmann, James: Norman John Klugmann was a graduate of Gresham's School and Trinity College Cambridge. He joined the CPGB in 1933 while still a student. Long suspected of espionage links, Klugmann was openly Communist. He edited *Marxism Today* from its inception and wrote the first two volumes of the official history of the CPGB. He worked for Special Operations Executive during the Second World War in the Yugoslav section. He devoted his life to full-time party work.

Kostov, Traicho: General Secretary of the Bulgarian Communist Party executed after a show trial in December 1949 for treason in alliance with Tito.

Lehmann, John: Educated at Eton and Trinity College Cambridge. English poet and man of letters, founder of the periodical *New Writing* in 1936. Close friend of Tom Wintringham. Managing director of Hogarth Press, 1938–46.

Levy, Hyman: Professor of Mathematics at Imperial College, London, from the early 1920s, Levy joined the CPGB in 1931. Increasingly critical of the Soviet Union and the party leadership from 1956, Levy was expelled in 1958.

Lewis, John: Former Unitarian Minister who built a network of Left Book Club discussion groups in the 1930s. He was married to full-time party worker Betty Reid.

Lindsay, Jack: Australian born novelist, poet, dramatist and critic who formally joined the party in 1941, but who was a loyal supporter from 1936. Though Lindsay was regarded with suspicion by members in the party leadership on account of his bohemian past and unorthodox views on cultural matters, he remained a member after 1956.

Lloyd, A. L. (Albert Lancaster): Born in 1908, Lloyd joined the CPGB in the 1930s and never left. Keenly attuned to international literary currents, Lloyd translated the works of Kafka and Lorca into English. He later became best known as a folklorist, singer and broadcaster. His book *Folk Song in England* (1967) remains a standard work on the subject.

MacColl, Ewan: born James Miller, MacColl joined the YCL in Salford in 1929 and remained a party member until the early 1960s, when he was drawn to Maoism. MacColl was a founder member of Theatre Workshop, a playwright, folksinger, songwriter and broadcaster.

MacDiarmid, Hugh: Distinguished Scottish poet and Communist whose enduring commitment to Scottish nationalism frequently brought him into conflict with the party leadership. CPGB member 1934–38 and again from 1957–78.

MacDonald, Ramsay: First Labour Prime Minister and revered leader of the party who was held to have betrayed his colleagues by heading the National Government which emerged from the collapse of the second Labour Government in 1931.

MacEwen, Malcolm: Member of the party's Executive Committee 1941–43 and *Daily Worker* journalist 1944–56. Broke with party over Hungary and was formally expelled in 1958.

McGahey, Mick: Scottish miner. Joined the YCL at the age of fourteen. The son of a founder member of the party, elected to the NUM Executive in 1966. NUM Scottish Area President from 1967 and Vice-President of the NUM from 1973. Member of the TUC General Council 1982–86.

Machen, Alwin: Elected president of the National Union of Mineworkers in 1960.

MacManus, Arthur: A member of the Socialist Labour Party and leader of the Clyde Workers' Committee during the First World War. Founder member and first Chairman of the CPGB, he also served as its Colonial Secretary. He died in Moscow in 1927.

Mahon, John: A member of the CPGB from 1920 and an organiser of the National Minority Movement, working closely with Harry Pollitt. His biography of Pollitt was published in 1976.

Matthews, George: Joined the CPGB in 1938 and was elected onto the Central Committee in 1943. A leading figure from then until 1979, Matthews was a delegate to the 20th Congress in 1956 and edited the *Daily Worker/Morning Star* between 1959 and 1974.

Moffat, Abe: Worked as a miner on the Fife coalfield from 1910. Communist councillor. Elected president of the Scottish miners in 1942. Member of the CPGB Executive for 30 years.

Montagu, Ivor: Member of the party from the early 1920s. A man of many talents, Montagu was an early devotee of the great Soviet film-maker Eisenstein.

Morton, A. L. (Arthur Leslie): Communist historian whose works include *A People's History of England* (1938) and *Language of Men* (1945).

Murphy, J. T.: Manchester born, Jack Murphy was a trade union activist, member of the Socialist Labour Party and leading figure in the Shop Stewards' Movement during and immediately after the First World War in Sheffield. He was a founder member of the CPGB and a member of its Central Committee. He resigned from the party in 1932.

Narain, J. P.: Jayaprakesh Narayan formed the Congress Socialist Party in 1934.

Niven, Barbara: Manchester-based artist who, with her husband Ern Brooks, was prominent in the Artists' International Association. A friend of Hugh MacDiarmid, Niven designed sets for the Manchester Popular Front period theatre troupe, Theatre Union. From 1950 Niven turned from painting to become National Organiser for the *Daily Worker/Morning Star*.

Nehru, Jawaharlal: First Prime Minister of independent India and a leader of the national struggle against British rule.

Orwell, George: Committed socialist and critic of socialist totalitarianism who published best-selling works such as *Animal Farm* (1945) and *Nineteen Eighty-Four* (1949).

Papworth, A. F.: Bert Papworth was a London bus workers leader who rose to the Executive of the Transport and General Workers' Union and became the first Communist to be elected to the General Council of the TUC in 1944. He lost these positions when the union voted to deny Communists the right to serve as officials from 1 January 1950.

Paynter, Will: Thomas William Paynter was a Rhondda coalminer who joined the CPGB in 1929. He served the party in Nazi Germany and Spain as well as in the South Wales miners' union, rising to become General Secretary of the National Union of Mineworkers from 1959 to 1968.

Pepper, John: John Pepper was an alias of the Hungarian Communist Jozsef Schwartz (aka Jozsef Pogány) who served as a full-time worker of the Communist International in Germany, the USA and Britain.

Piratin, Phil: Joined the party in 1934 and became prominent in London anti-fascist activity. Piratin served as the Communist Party MP for the Mile End constituency, 1945–50.

Pollitt, Harry: Manchester boilermaker and leading figure in the shop stewards' movement and Hands Off Russia campaign of 1919. A founding member of the CPGB and its most talented leader. He was General Secretary of the party from 1929–1939 and 1941–1956.

Postgate, Raymond: Founding member of the Communist Party who resigned in 1922. Best known as a socialist journalist and author of numerous histories and biographies.

Purdy, Dave: A critic of the party's wage militancy strategy in the 1970s who was then employed in the economics department of Manchester University.

Rajk, Laszlo: Hungarian Communist leader executed in 1949 as a Titoist spy.

Rakovsky, Christian: Bolshevik and close associate of Trotsky who was persecuted by Stalin and finally executed during the Second World War.

Ramelson, Bert: Baruch Ramilevich Mendelson settled in Britain in 1939, having fought in the Spanish Civil War with the Canadian battalion of the International Brigade. He was a tank commander in the Second World War, who was captured at Tobruk in 1941 and organised a successful mass breakout from the prisoner of war camp in which he was detained. He worked full-time for the CPGB after the war and rose to be National Industrial Organiser in 1965.

Ranadive, B. T.: Bhalchandra Trimbak Ranadive succeeded Joshi as leader of the Communist Party of India in 1948 and led it on an insurrectionist path until he was himself deposed in 1950.

Rechnitz, Erik: An activist in the Transport and General Workers' Union who was awarded its gold medal in the 1980s, its highest award, for services to the union.

Reid, Jimmy: Joined the YCL in 1948 and rose to national prominence as one of the leaders of the occupation of Upper Clyde Shipbuilders in February 1972 for the right to work. He resigned from the party in 1976.

Rickword, Edgell: Poet, critic and editor who founded the influential literary journal *Calendar of Modern Letters* (1925–27). Joined the CPGB in 1934 and served as editor of *Left Review* (1936–37) and *Our Time* (1944–47). A key figure in cultural Communism in the 1930s and 1940s, Rickword left the party in 1956.

Robinson, Derek: Longbridge car worker who joined the party in the 1940s and rose to national prominence as 'Red Robbo' in the 1970s during numerous pay disputes and in the unsuccessful fight against mass redundancies. When Robinson himself was sacked in November 1979 the protest of his colleagues was minimal. The tide had turned against militant shop stewards.

Rothstein, Andrew: Foundation member of the CPGB who lived long enough to see its demise. A staunch opponent of the revisionist tendencies in the party that gathered strength from the 1970s.

Rust, William (Bill): Joined the party in 1920 and was the youngest of the twelve party leaders arrested for 'seditious conspiracy' in 1925. Rust worked for the Comintern in Moscow in the late 1920s, and was editor of the *Daily Worker* between 1930–32 and 1939–49. Died suddenly of a heart attack in 1949, aged forty-five.

Saklatvala, Shapurji: Joined the CPGB just after its creation. He was elected Labour MP for Battersea North in 1922, at a time when it was still possible for individuals to belong to both parties. He was re-elected for the same seat as a Communist in December 1923 and held it until 1929.

Samuel, Raphael: Gifted historian and a leading figure in the New Left that developed after 1956.

Saville, John: Professor of Economic History at the University of Hull. Resigned from the Communist Party in 1956 after establishing *The Reasoner* with Edward Thompson in an effort to reform the party in the light of the Khrushchev revelations about Stalin. Thereafter associated with the first New Left in Britain.

Scargill, Arthur: Joined the YCL in 1956 but dropped out of the CPGB in 1963. Rose to prominence as the Marxist leader of the NUM in the strike of 1984–85.

Sinfield, George: Sinfield became secretary of his local branch of the British Workers' Sports Federation in 1923 and a party member in 1927. A key figure behind the party winning control of the BWSF, Sinfield joined the staff of the *Daily Worker* in 1935, where he spent a long career as sportswriter and industrial correspondent.

Slansky, Rudolf: Czech Communist leader executed in November 1952 after a show trial in which he was accused of Titoism.

Sloan, Pat: Economist and nephew of the great economist Alfred Marshall, resident in the Soviet Union for most of the period 1931–37 and thus taken as an authority on its political and economic health about which he published numerous books in the 1930s.

Spender, Stephen: Poet, novelist and critic who joined the party in 1937, but left shortly afterwards.

Spratt, Philip: Cambridge graduate who was sent to India in 1926 at the age of twenty-four to help organise the nascent Communist Party of India and its legal cover, the Workers' and Peasants' Parties. A defendant in the Meerut Conspiracy Trial, who was sentenced to twelve years' imprisonment, he was released from prison two years later and remained active in radical politics in India, though outside the Communist Party.

Stanley, Frank: Joined the YCL in 1937 and was active in the Amalgamated Engineering Union after the Second World War.

Strachey, John: Supported the Communist Party for most of the 1930s without open membership. Influential publicist of Marxist analysis. Broke with the party in 1940.

Sweet, Colin: Communist activist in the peace campaigns of the 1950s and 1960s. Honorary Secretary of the British Peace Council.

Swingler, Randall: Distinguished poet, editor and man of letters who joined the party in the mid-1930s and left in 1956. Served as editor of *Left Review*, *Our Time* and of the *Daily Worker*'s book page.

Taylor, Sammy: Yorkshire miner. Communist candidate in the Barnsley local elections of 1945. In 1959 became the first Communist to be elected to the NUM National Executive from the Yorkshire coalfield.

Temple, Nina: Born into a Communist family, Nina Temple became General Secretary of the YCL in the late 1970s and was prominent on the Euro-communist wing of the party. She became the last leader of the party in January 1990 and advocated its dissolution in November of the following year. She helped to found the Democratic Left as its successor.

Thompson, E. P.: Distinguished historian who joined the CPGB as a student but resigned in 1956 after the Soviet invasion of Hungary. Founding figure of the British New Left.

Thomson, George: Marxist classicist who joined the party in 1936 and produced works including *Aeschylus and Athens* (1941) and *Marxism and Poetry* (1945). Served on both the National Executive Committee and the National Cultural Committee, but was sceptical of *The British Road to Socialism* (1951). Later became a Maoist.

Tito, Josip Broz: Leader of the Yugoslav Communist Party and founder of Communist Yugoslavia in 1945. He defied Stalin's attempts to determine Yugoslav policies and was excommunicated from the Communist bloc in 1948. This signalled the beginning of the hunt for like-minded Titoists throughout Eastern Europe as Stalin sought to destroy national Communists who might develop independent policies.

Tocher, John: Trade union activist in aerospace, prominent in the Roberts Arundel strike of 1968 and in the campaign against the Conservative government's Industrial Relations Act of 1971.

Torr, Dona: Founder member of the CPGB, journalist, historian, editor, translator. A key, if sometimes overlooked, figure in the CPGB historians' group. Author of works including *Tom Mann and His Times* (1957).

Warner, Sylvia Townsend: Novelist, poet and authority on early music, Warner joined the CPGB in 1935. Most prominent during the Popular Front years, she nevertheless remained a party member beyond 1956. Arguably the finest novelist to have belonged to the party, she produced major works including *Summer Will Show* (1936) and *After the Death of Don Juan* (1938).

Warren, Bill: A critic of the party's economic and industrial policies of the 1960s who broke with the organisation and was prominent as an independent Marxist writer in the 1970s until his early death in 1978.

Watters, Frank: A Communist from his teenage years as a miner in Lanarkshire, Watters worked full-time for the party from 1953 and helped to build its influence in the Yorkshire NUM.

Webb, Sidney and Beatrice: Prominent Fabian intellectuals who famously turned to the Soviet Union for socialist inspiration after the fall of the second Labour Government in 1931.

Whelan, Joe: Nottinghamshire miner and member of the CPGB from 1949. Elected NUM Area Agent in 1965. Elected to the National Executive of the NUM in 1971. Nottinghamshire Area General Secretary from 1977.

Williams, Emlyn: Welsh miner elected to the South Wales Executive in 1955 rising to President of the South Wales Miners in 1974.

Wilkinson, Ellen: Manchester suffragette, trade union official, campaigner for the Non-Conscription Fellowship, member of the Independent Labour Party from 1916, foundation member of the Communist Party, Manchester councillor, Labour MP, novelist, champion of the Jarrow Hunger March, and Minister for Education in 1945.

Wintringham, T. H.: Tom Wintringham achieved lasting significance as specialist in military affairs. He joined the CPGB in 1923, served in Spain and helped to create the Home Guard and promote guerrilla warfare training in Britain.

Woddis, Jack: Secretary of the party's International Department in the 1960s and 1970s and the author of several books on imperialism.

Select bibliography

Adi, Hakim, 'West Africans and the Communist Party in the 1950s', in Andrews, Fishman and Morgan, *Opening the Books*, pp. 160–76.

Andrew, Christopher, *Defence of the Realm: The Authorized History of MI5*. London: Allen Lane, 2009.

Andrews, Geoff, *Endgames and New Times: The Final Years of British Communism 1964–1991*. London: Lawrence & Wishart, 2004.

Andrews, Geoff, Nina Fishman and Kevin Morgan (eds), *Opening the Books: Essays on the Social and Cultural History of the British Communist Party*. London: Pluto, 1995.

Archer, R. A. (trans.), *Second Congress of the Communist International, Minutes of the Proceedings*. London: New Park, 1977.

Beckett, Francis, *Enemy Within: The Rise and Fall of the British Communist Party*, 2nd edn. Merlin: London, 1998.

Bell, David. S. (ed.), *Western European Communists and the Collapse of Communism*. Oxford: Berg, 1993.

Branson, Noreen, *History of the Communist Party of Great Britain 1941–1951*. London: Lawrence & Wishart, 1997.

Bruley, Sue, 'Women Against War and Fascism: Communism, Feminism and the People's Front' in Jim Fyrth (ed.), *Britain, Fascism and the Popular Front*. London: Lawrence & Wishart, 1985, pp. 131–57.

Bruley, Sue, 'Women and Communism: A Case Study of the Lancashire Weavers in the Depression', in Andrews, Fishman and Morgan, *Opening the Books*, pp. 44–64.

Burnham, Paul, 'The Squatters of 1946: A Local Study in a National Context', *Socialist History*, 25 (2004), pp. 20–46.

Bush, Nancy, *Alan Bush: Music, Politics and Life*. London: Thames, 2000.

Callaghan, John, 'The British Left and the Unfinished Revolution: Perceptions of the Soviet Union in the 1950s', *Contemporary British History*, 15, 3 (autumn 2001), pp. 63–83.

— *Cold War, Crisis and Conflict: The CPGB 1951–68*. London: Lawrence & Wishart, 2003.

— 'The Communists and the Colonies', in Andrews, Fishman and Morgan (eds), *Opening the Books*, pp. 4–23.

— *The Far Left in British Politics*. Oxford: Blackwell, 1987.
— 'Industrial Militancy, 1948–79: The Failure of the British Road to Socialism?', *Twentieth Century British History*, 15, 4 (2004), pp. 388–410.
— 'The Plan to Capture the Labour Party and its Paradoxical Results', *Journal of Contemporary History*, 40, 4 (October 2005), pp. 707–27.
— *Rajani Palme Dutt: A Study in British Stalinism*. London: Lawrence & Wishart, 1993.
— *Socialism in Britain Since 1884*. Oxford: Blackwell, 1990.
Campbell, A., B. McLoughlin and J. Halstead, 'The International Lenin School: A Response to Cohen and Morgan', *Twentieth Century British History*, 15 (2004), pp. 51–76.
Carter, Trevor, *Shattering Illusions*. London: Lawrence & Wishart, 1986.
Challinor, Raymond, *The Origins of British Bolshevism*. London: Croom Helm, 1977.
Chambers, Colin, *The Story of Unity Theatre*. London: Lawrence & Wishart, 1989.
Cohen, Gidon and Kevin Morgan, 'Stalin's Sausage Machine: British Students at the International Lenin School, 1926–1937', *Twentieth Century British History*, 13 (2002), pp. 327–55.
Cohen, Phil (ed.), *Children of the Revolution*. London: Lawrence & Wishart, 1997.
Cope, Dave, Introduction to online version of the CPGB Bibliography, www.amielandmelburn.org.uk/cpgb-biblio/maintextt.htm.
CPGB, *The British Road to Socialism*. London: CPGB, 1951.
— *Manifesto for New Times: A Strategy for the 1990s*, London: Communist Party, 1990.
— *For Soviet Britain*. London: Marston, 1935.
Croft, Andy, *Comrade Heart: A Life of Randall Swingler*. Manchester and New York: Manchester University Press, 2003.
— *Red Letter Days: British Fiction in the 1930s*. London: Lawrence & Wishart, 1990.
— (ed.), *A Weapon in the Struggle: The Cultural History of the Communist Party*. London: Pluto, 1998.
— 'Writers, the Communist Party and the Battle of Ideas, 1945–50', *Socialist History*, 5 (1994), pp. 20–5.
Crossman, R. H. S. (ed.), *New Fabian Essays*. London: New Turnstile Press, 1952.
Davidson, Basil, *The Black Man's Burden: Africa and the Curse of the Nation-State*. London: Times Books, 1992.
Day Lewis, Cecil (ed.), *The Mind in Chains: Socialism and the Cultural Revolution*. London: Muller, 1937.
Degras, Jane (ed.), *The Communist International 1919–43; Volume One 1919–22*. London, Frank Cass, 1971.

Dimitrov, Georgi, *The Diary of Georgi Dimitrov, 1933–1949*, introduced and edited by Ivo Banac. New Haven: Yale University Press, 2003.

— *The Working Class Against Fascism*. London: Martin Lawrence, 1935.

Dromey, Jack and G. Taylor, *Grunwick: The Workers' Story*. London: Lawrence & Wishart, 1978.

Durham, Martin, 'The Origins and Early Years of British Communism, 1914–24'. Unpublished PhD thesis, University of Birmingham, 1982.

Dutt, Rajani Palme, 'Intellectuals and Communism', *Communist Review* (September 1932).

— *World Politics 1918–1936*. London: Gollancz, 1936.

Dworkin, Dennis, *Class Struggles*. Edinburgh: Pearson, 2007.

Edwards, Ruth Dudley, *Victor Gollancz: A Biography*. London: Gollancz, 1987.

Fishman, Nina, 'CPGB History at the Centre of Contemporary British History', *Labour History Review*, 69, 3 (2004), pp. 381–3.

Forgacs, David, 'Gramsci and Marxism in Britain', *New Left Review*, 176 (July–August 1989), pp. 70–88.

Fried, Albert (ed.), *Communism in America: A History in Documents*. New York: Columbia University Press, 1997.

Fyrth, Jim (ed.), *Britain, Fascism and the Popular Front*. London: Lawrence & Wishart, 1985.

Gramsci, Antonio, *Selections from Prison Notebooks*, edited and translated by Quintin Hoare and Geoffrey Nowell Smith. London: Lawrence & Wishart, 1971.

Harker, Ben, *Class Act: The Cultural and Political life of Ewan MacColl*. London: Pluto, 2007.

— 'Mediating the 1930s: Documentary and Politics in Theatre Union's *Last Edition* (1940)' in Alison Forsyth and Chris Megson (eds), *Get Real: Documentary Theatre Past and Present*, London: Palgrave, 2009, pp. 24–38.

Hilliard, Christopher, 'Producers by Hand and Brain: Working-Class Writers and Left-Wing Publishers in 1930s Britain', *Journal of Modern History* 78 (March 2006), pp. 37–64.

Hinton, James, 'Self-Help and Socialism: The Squatters' Movement of 1946', *History Workshop Journal*, 25 (spring 1988), pp. 100–27.

Hinton James and Richard Hyman, *Trade Unions and Revolution: the Industrial Politics of the Early British Communist Party*. London: Pluto Press, 1975.

Hobsbawm, Eric, *Revolutionaries*. London: Weidenfeld and Nicolson, 1973.

Hogarth, Paul, *Drawing on Life* [1997]. London: Royal Academy of Arts, 2002.

Hogenkamp, Bert, *Deadly Parallels: Film and the Left in Britain 1929–39*. London: Lawrence & Wishart, 1986.

Howkins, Alun, 'Class Against Class: The Political Culture of the Communist Party of Great Britain, 1930–35' in Frank Gloversmith (ed.), *Class, Culture and Social Change: A New View of the 1930s*. Brighton: Harvester, 1980.

Isserman, Maurice, *Which Side Were You On? The American Communist Party During the Second World War*. Middleton: Wesleyan University Press, 1982.

Jones, Jean, *Ben Bradley: Fighter for India's Freedom*, Occasional Papers Series No. 1. London: Socialist History Society, nd.

— *The League Against Imperialism*, Occasional Papers Series No. 4. London: Socialist History Society, 1996.

Kaye, Harvey J., *The British Marxist Historians*. Oxford: Blackwell, 1984.

Kelly, John. *Trade Unions and Socialist Politics*. London: Verso, 1988.

King, Francis and George Matthews (eds), *About Turn: The Communist Party and the Outbreak of the Second World War*. London: Lawrence & Wishart, 1990.

Klehr, Harvey, *Communist Cadre: The Social Background of the American Communist Party Elite*. Stanford CA: Hoover Institution Press, 1976.

— *The Heyday of American Communism: The Depression Decade*. New York: Basic Books, 1984.

Kozlov, Nicholas N. and Eric D. Weitz, 'Reflections on the Origin of the Third Period', *Journal of Contemporary History*, 24, 3 (July 1989), pp. 387–410.

Kriegel, Annie, *The French Communists: Profile of a People*. Chicago: University of Chicago, 1972.

Lessing, Doris, *Walking in the Shade*. London: Harper Collins, 1997.

Lewis, John, *The Left Book Club: An Historical Record*. London: Victor Gollancz, 1970.

Lindsay, Jack, *British Achievement in Art and Music*. London: Pilot, 1945.

Linehan, Thomas, *Communism in Britain, 1920–39: From the Cradle to the Grave*. Manchester: Manchester University Press, 2007.

MacEwen, Malcolm, *The Greening of a Red*. London: Pluto, 1991.

Macleod, Alison, *The Death of Uncle Joe*. London: Merlin, 1997.

Macpherson, Don (ed.), *British Cinema: Traditions of Independence*. London: British Film Institute, 1980.

Madeira, Victor, 'Moscow's Interwar Infiltration of British Intelligence, 1919–29', *The Historical Journal*, 46, 4 (2003), pp. 915–35.

— 'The Open Conspiracy of the Communist Party and the Case of W. N. Ewer, Communist and Anti-Communist', *The Historical Journal*, 49, 2 (2006), pp. 1–16.

Mann, Michael, *Consciousness and Action Among the Western Working Class*. London: Macmillan, 1973.

Margolies, David (ed.), *Writing the Revolution: Cultural Criticism from Left Review*. London and Chicago: Pluto, 1998.

Select bibliography

Martinov, Alexander, 'Lessons of the Elections in England', *Communist International*, 8 (1924).

Mates, Lewis, *The Spanish Civil War and the British Left: Political Activism and the Popular Front*. London and New York: I. B. Tauris, 2007.

Matthews, George, 'Stalin's British Road', *Changes*, 23 (September 1991), pp. 1–3.

McIlroy, John, 'The Establishment of Intellectual Orthodoxy and the Stalinization of British Communism 1928–33', *Past & Present*, 192 (August 2006), pp. 187–226.

McIlroy, J. and A. Campbell, 'For a Revolutionary Workers' Government: The Communist International, the Communist Party of Great Britain and Revisionist Interpretations of the Third Period, 1927–35', *European History Quarterly*, 32 (2002), pp. 535–69.

— 'Histories of the British Communist Party: A User's Guide', *Labour History Review*, 68, 1 (2003), pp. 33–59.

McIlroy, J., B. McLoughlin, A. Campbell and J. Halstead, 'Forging the Faithful: the British at the International Lenin School', *Labour History Review*, 68 (2003), pp. 99–128.

McShane, Harry. *No Mean Fighter*. London: Pluto, 1978.

Morgan, Kevin, *Against Fascism and War: Ruptures and Continuities in British Communist Politics, 1935–41*. Manchester: Manchester University Press, 1989.

— 'The Communist Party and the *Daily Worker*' in Andrews, Fishman and Morgan, *Opening the Books*, pp. 142–60.

— *Harry Pollitt*. Manchester: Manchester University Press, 1993.

— 'Labour with Knobs On: The Recent Historiography of the British Communist Party', in S. Berger (ed.), 'Labour and Social History in Great Britain: Historiographical Reviews and Agendas', *Mitteilungsblatt des Instituts fur soziale Bewegungen*, 27 (2002).

Morgan, Kevin, Gidon Cohen and Andrew Flinn, *Communists and British Society, 1920–1991*. London: Rivers Oram Press, 2007.

Morris, Lynda and Robert Radford, *The Artists International Association 1933–1953*. Oxford: Museum of Modern Art, 1983.

Morton, A. L., *A People's History of England*. London: Gollancz, 1938.

Naison, Mark, *Communists in Harlem During the Depression*. Urbana: University of Illinois Press, 1983.

Orwell, George, *The Road to Wigan Pier*. London: Gollancz, 1937.

Pollitt, Harry, *Looking Ahead*. London: CPGB, 1947.

— *Serving My Time* [1940]. London: Lawrence & Wishart, 1941.

Pooke, Grant, *Francis Klingender 1907–1955: A Marxist Art Historian Out of Time*. London: Marx Memorial Library, 2008.

Rettie, John, 'How Khrushchev Leaked His Secret Speech to the World', *History Workshop Journal 62*, 1 (2006), pp. 187–93.

Roy, M. N., *The Future of Indian Politics*. London: Bishop, 1926.

Select bibliography

Russell, Bertrand, *The Theory and Practice of Bolshevism*. London: Allen and Unwin, 1920.

Samuel, Raphael, *The Lost World of British Communism*. London: Verso, 2006.

Spratt, Philip, *Blowing-Up India: Reminiscences and Reflections of a Former Comintern Emissary*. Calcutta: Prachi Prakashan, 1955.

Stourac, Richard and Kathleen McCreery, *Theatre as a Weapon: Workers' Theatre in the Soviet Union, Germany and Britain, 1917–1934*. London and New York: Routledge & Kegan Paul, 1986.

Thompson, Willie, *The Good Old Cause: British Communism 1920–1991*. London: Pluto, 1992.

Thorpe, Andrew, *The British Communist Party and Moscow, 1920–43*. Manchester: Manchester University Press, 2000.

— 'Comintern "control" of the Communist Party of Great Britain, 1920–43', *English Historical Review*, 113 (June 1998), pp. 637–62.

Waite, Mike, 'The Young Communist League and Youth Culture', *Socialist History*, 6 (1994), pp. 3–16.

— 'Sex 'n' Drugs 'n' Rock 'n' Roll (and Communism)' in Andrews, Fishman and Morgan, *Opening the Books*, pp. 195–210.

Waller, M. and Fennema, M. (eds), *Communist Parties in Western Europe: Decline or Adaptation?* Oxford: Blackwell, 1988.

Warren, Bill and Mike Prior, *Advanced Capitalism and Backward Socialism*. Leicester: Spokesman, 1975.

Weitz, Eric, *Creating German Communism, 1890–1990*. Princeton: Princeton University Press, 1997.

Workers' Music Association, *A Policy for Music in Post War Britain*. London: WMA, 1945.

Worley, Matthew, 'The Communist International, the Communist Party of Great Britain and the Third Period, 1928–32', *European History Quarterly*, 30 (April 2000), pp. 353–78.

— *Class Against Class: The Communist Party in Britain Between the Wars*. London and New York: I. B. Tauris, 2002.

Zhadanov, A. A., *On Literature, Music and Philosophy*. London: Lawrence & Wishart, 1950.

Index

Index